Global Statesman

Global Statesman

How Gordon Brown Took New Labour to the World

David M. Webber

EDINBURGH
University Press

Edinburgh University Press is one of the leading university presses in the UK. We publish academic books and journals in our selected subject areas across the humanities and social sciences, combining cutting-edge scholarship with high editorial and production values to produce academic works of lasting importance. For more information visit our website: edinburghuniversitypress.com

© David M. Webber, 2017, 2019

Edinburgh University Press Ltd
The Tun – Holyrood Road,
12(2f) Jackson's Entry,
Edinburgh EH8 8PJ

First published in hardback by Edinburgh University Press 2017

Typeset in 11/13 Adobe Sabon by
IDSUK (Dataconnection) Ltd, and
printed and bound by CPI Group (UK) Ltd, Croydon CR0 4YY

A CIP record for this book is available from the British Library

ISBN 978 1 4744 2356 4 (hardback)
ISBN 978 1 4744 4574 0 (paperback)
ISBN 978 1 4744 2357 1 (webready PDF)
ISBN 978 1 4744 2358 8 (epub)

Contents

List of Figures, Tables and Boxes

Acknowledgements

This book initially emerged as a PhD dissertation written in the main part as the Labour Party struggled to establish its post-Blair–Brown identity in the wake of its General Election defeat two years previously. The main themes of this dissertation appear here and, as such, this book would not have been possible without the guidance provided by my supervisors, Matthew Watson and Ben Clift. Mat deserves a particular mention since it was his enthusiasm and confidence in the original project that persuaded me to join him at Warwick in the Department of Politics and International Studies.

However, had it not been for the mentorship of Christopher Moran, also in PAIS, the PhD would, I am sure, have remained on the shelf. It was Chris who persuaded me to convert my thesis into a monograph and kindly helped me to put together a viable proposal that I am delighted that Edinburgh University Press accepted so warmly. As well as being a talented scholar in his own right, Chris is also a generous colleague and friend, continuing to provide me with advice and guidance, coffee, beer and the occasional Oasis bootleg.

At EUP I have been fortunate to work with a small team of individuals who have demonstrated enormous confidence in the viability of this book. I am particularly grateful to Jenny Daly, Ersev Ersoy, Joannah Duncan, David Lonergan and Rebecca Mackenzie for their advice, patience and professionalism throughout the publishing process. I am grateful too, to my copy-editor, Eliza Wright, and indexer, Lisa Scholey, for their diligence and meticulous attention to detail in their respective roles. It has been a pleasure working with each of them, and I look forward to doing so again soon.

Having spent nearly a decade in PAIS, I am grateful to all those colleagues, past and present, who have at some stage or another, provided much-valued advice and support to me during my time in the Department. As a lecturer of Politics in the UK, Politics of Developing Areas, and Gender and Development over the course of several years at PAIS, I have been extremely fortunate to have taught some exceptionally talented individuals. I hope my teaching has been as helpful as their intellectual contributions have been to me, sharpening my thinking, and strengthening the arguments contained in this book.

Finally, I would like to dedicate this book to my family, but in particular, Hannah, whose unwavering patience, grace and love, often through some intensely difficult times, means the world to me. I am blessed to be your best friend, soul mate and your husband. I would also like to dedicate this book to our son, Daniel, whose laughter and love of life has brought us so much joy and happiness. I thank God for you both, and love you very much.

David Webber

Warwick, January 2017

List of Abbreviations

ABPI	Association of the British Pharmaceutical Industry
AIDS	acquired immune deficiency syndrome
BOAG	British Overseas Aid Group
BOND	British Overseas NGOs for Development
CBI	Confederation of British Industry
CDC	Commonwealth Development Corporation
CFGP	Concessional Finance and Global Partnerships
CSM	Christian Socialist Movement
CTF	Child Trust Fund
DAC	Development Assistance Committee
DFID	Department for International Development
ERM	Exchange Rate Mechanism
EU	European Union
G7/G8	Group of 7/Group of 8 countries
GAVI	Global Alliance for Vaccines and Immunisation
GDP	gross domestic product
HIPC	heavily indebted poor country
HIV	human immunodeficiency virus
IBRD	International Bank for Reconstruction and Development
IDA	International Development Association
IDTF	International Development Trust Fund
IFF	International Finance Facility
IFFIm	International Finance Facility for Immunisation
IFI	International Financial Institution
IGFAM	Industry Government Forum on Access to Medicines
IMF	International Monetary Fund
IMFC	International Monetary and Financial Committee
IP	intellectual property
MDGs	Millennium Development Goals
MDRI	Multilateral Debt Relief Initiative

MP	Member of Parliament
MPC	Monetary Policy Committee
NGO	non-governmental organisation
NHS	National Health Service
ODA	overseas development aid
OECD	Organisation for Economic Co-operation and Development
PFI	Private Finance Initiative
PICTF	Pharmaceutical Industry Competiveness Taskforce
PPP	Public-Private Partnership
PRSP	Poverty Reduction Strategy Paper
R&D	research and development
SAP	Structural Adjustment Programme
TRIPS	trade-related aspects of intellectual property rights
UN	United Nations
WTO	World Trade Organization

1 A Son of the Manse with a Missionary Zeal

For more than a decade, New Labour was Britain's defining political and economic project. Borrowing many of its cues from Thatcherism, New Labour took the Britain that Thatcher herself had created, and reoriented its place in the world in the party's redesigned image. As befitting a government in office at the start of a new millennium, New Labour drew upon the past to deliver a political vision for its future. At the heart of this vision, Gordon Brown was the centrifugal force. Tony Blair and New Labour are, of course, inextricably linked but it was Brown who remained central in the renewal, redemption and ultimately rejection of the party by the British people. As the New Labour story unfolded across almost two decades, virtually all of its main actors, including Blair himself, entered and departed the stage before the curtain finally fell on the ever-present Brown. Labour's last man standing, Brown saw his influence steadily increase within the party, across Whitehall and, as we shall see in this book, stretch out into the world. By the time Brown finally left office in May 2010, no other Labour politician had enjoyed such prolonged prominence and power in equal measure.

Global Statesman tells the story of how Gordon Brown reached the apex of political power in Britain – even prior to becoming prime minister – and how as Chancellor of the Exchequer, he leveraged his position to pursue a personal crusade against poverty both at home and abroad. Borrowing extensively from the model of political economy that he himself had crafted for Britain, Brown went on to become the chief architect behind the New Labour government's much vaunted commitment to 'eliminate global poverty' overseas. As Chancellor, Brown was aided to this end by his close political rival, Tony Blair. Yet certainly insofar as Brown was concerned, poverty was far more than just another sphere of policy. Poverty animated his political, economic, philosophical and theological vision, and addressing it was central to Brown's commitment to realising a more socially just and egalitarian world.

If Tony Blair's own desire to, as his biographer, Anthony Seldon describes, 'improve the lot of Africa' saw the prime minister at his most 'spiritually inspired', Blair's religion was undoubtedly interlaced with self-interest.[1] Blair was of course, a conviction politician – particularly concerning matters of poverty and conflict – but these underpinned his personal quest for a legacy, and what his premiership would ultimately be remembered for. In this sense, the difference between the two men was stark. For Gordon Brown, his commitment to addressing global poverty was borne out of a childhood spent growing up in his father's manse in Kirkcaldy and driven by a deep compassion for the most vulnerable in society. Brown's childhood experiences as a Presbyterian 'son of the manse' imprinted upon him the virtues of Christian socialism and instilled in the future Chancellor, prime minister and leader of the Labour Party a burning desire for social justice.

Brown's father, the Reverend John Brown, ministered to a dwindling and increasingly impoverished congregation. A poor relation to the elegance and splendour of Edinburgh that lay just across the Firth of Forth, Kirkcaldy in the 1950s was emblematic of the gross inequality that Brown would write later, 'had disfigured Scottish social life'.[2] In a town racked by the decline of its local coalmines and factories, Brown grew up witnessing at first hand the rise in joblessness and destitution this caused in his immediate community. As the numbers of those seeking help from the Browns increased, John and his wife, Jessie, responded in kind, opening their doors to those in need: feeding the hungry, giving money to the poor, and tending the sick. As Gordon himself joined in his parents' local mission, Brown quickly learnt about matters of life and death, and the true meaning of poverty, injustice and unemployment.[3]

As well as these deeply practical issues, life in the shadow of St Brycedale also imbued Gordon Brown with both a deep theological understanding of the Bible and the writings of a whole host of philosophers, politicians and poets whose observations of the world his father wove into his weekly sermons. As this book will show, Brown the younger would later imitate this style of preaching; fleshing out his personal crusade against global poverty with a philosophical and spiritual creed of his own. A mark of the deep admiration that Brown had for his father, it was an approach that stood Brown the politician apart from the rest of the New Labour machine. For a party frequently accused of spin and soundbite, Brown presented his own political economy with an intellectual weight and gravitas to anchor and justify his own carefully measured approach to international development.

Yet, as Gordon Brown's own career unfolded, there were clear political and economic limits to the non-conformist tradition in which Brown was raised. Despite appearing to follow his fellow Scot, William McIlvanney, in claiming that 'the economy and the market should serve the people', Brown's own approach to development was predicated upon strengthening the grip of those institutions that promoted the existing market orthodoxy of Anglo-liberal capitalism.[4] Placing increased emphasis upon 'competition, supervision and the right conditions for growth',[5] Brown knelt at the altar of the market as the only means through which poverty and underdevelopment might be addressed. Under Brown's close watch, many of New Labour's international development policies adopted precisely the self-same neoliberal doctrine preached by the 'post-Washington Consensus'. This revised orthodoxy, still based upon the principles of free trade and private investment that lay at the heart of the original Washington Consensus, now required national governments to put in place a much more robust and transparent regulatory framework.

This ostensibly new set of political and economic reforms would promote both stability – so as to reduce the exposure of countries to the financial crises that had, since the start of the 1970s, punctured the global economy – and growth. If investors could be made to feel more confident that their capital would be 'safe' in a particular country, they would be more likely to scale up their investment and contribute more towards the economic growth of that country and, concomitantly, its development. Crucially, insofar as Gordon Brown was concerned, although an anti-poverty agenda provided the pretext for his appeal for a 'new economic architecture' (as discussed in Chapters 4 and 5), it was, in reality, his own general growth theory that informed this framework.[6] Here the calls made by Brown for international reform acted in tandem with his own pursuit of 'stability', 'prudence' and 'cautionary discretion' in the setting of monetary and fiscal policy – and it was these that were prioritised over the altogether more urgent imperatives of tackling poverty and inequality.

Even in an area such as debt relief (Chapter 5) where there was a clear mandate for debt forgiveness alongside institutional reform, Gordon Brown and other New Labour colleagues remained reluctant to cede to these demands. Ministers chose instead to frame their response firmly within the neoliberal paradigm espoused by the World Bank and IMF.[7] Any calls to redesign the existing architecture of the global economic system remained wedded to the understanding that only by following a broadly neoliberal strategy of development – one that promoted free markets, the virtues of the private sector and 'good' (i.e. market-friendly) governance – could New Labour deliver its own goals of poverty reduction. However, by continuing to embed his response to matters of global poverty within the same set of institutions and ideas that had distorted and disrupted the development of many countries in the first place, Brown's mission to resolve these issues remained ultimately limited.

The conformism of Gordon Brown, and the zeal with which he pursued it ended up reinforcing a post-colonial mindset in which the former Chancellor and prime minister believed he, and he alone, had the answers to the problems that confronted the global South. His was a model of political economy that could not only orientate Britain towards the global economy and the opportunities that globalisation offered, but which could also be exported to meet the challenges faced by some of the poorest countries in the world. There was certainly the view amongst Western bankers and finance ministers, noted elsewhere by Robert Wade, that Anglo-American or liberal capitalism was the 'normal' or 'proper' type of capitalism,[8] and Brown certainly believed this. Despite his social democratic credentials, by demanding that these countries follow suit and reorder their political and economic priorities to meet the demands of his model and the liberal capitalism that it espoused, Brown undermined the autonomy and the agency of those he sought to 'save'.

To this end, Gordon Brown embedded his approach to international development within a constellation of Western economic actors, and chose to engage only with audiences that would continue to afford his own political economy the 'credibility' that he and Treasury colleagues deemed necessary. While it is true that

Brown frequently spoke the language that activists, NGOs and the development community wanted to hear, it was almost always the interests of economic actors that were prioritised. Time and time again, the demands of those actors deemed to be driving globalisation inexorably forward – the aforementioned World Bank, the IMF, as well as pharmaceutical corporations and market investors – were all afforded a place at Brown's top table. Those living in poverty were left with the crumbs and the benevolence of Western political and economic elites. By failing to orientate New Labour's anti-poverty strategy towards the immediate needs of those living in poverty, Brown's model of development was one that reinforced rather than challenged the self-same systemic failings of these elites, and which kept poor countries locked in a cycle of chronic underdevelopment.

New Labour and the politics of international development

Few, if any, British governments have commanded the level of interest shown in New Labour. Indeed, despite some seven years passing since the party was last in office (at the time of writing), this particular period of British politics continues to attract considerable attention from scholars and commentators alike. It is not the place of this book to consider the reasons why this might be the case, but given this volume of analysis, it was perhaps inevitable that an extensive canon of scholarship would appear in its own right assessing New Labour's Department for International Development (DFID) and the policies that it was responsible for.[9] It is to this literature that this book now briefly turns its attention, not least because it provides a sense of where the contribution that this book makes might be situated.

Alongside the Treasury, DFID was, under the Blair and Brown governments, an intriguing department. For many, it represented all that was positive about New Labour in office – taking seriously the issue of global poverty and making a real difference to the lives of millions across the world. Institutionally however, right from its creation in 1997, there was within the department all manner of fascinating sub-plots at play, not least between Clare Short – the department's first secretary of state – and the Treasury, and Number

10 itself. Short was a popular figure within the wider party but her appointment was surprising since she was by no means an ally of Blair.[10] Indeed, Short was a vocal critic of Blair – especially concerning matters of international development – long before she eventually resigned in 2003 over the government's decision to go to war with Iraq. 'He hadn't taken a blind bit of notice of Africa in his first term', she would later tell Anthony Seldon, 'he was questing for a legacy . . . "what about me? What am I going to be known for?"'[11]

Clare Short herself certainly appeared committed to Africa and addressing global poverty. Her department was prolific, publishing not one but two White Papers within its first term in office, each one offering bold statements of intent as to the largely economic ambitions of the new department.[12] These were followed up with a further two White Papers, one in 2006 that focused upon the issue of governance in development, and the other published in 2009 that provided more or less a stocktake of its achievements in office.[13] For the first time then, international development had more or less received real government recognition, certainly at cabinet level. The dynamics of this, combined with the policy initiatives that followed and the broader level of public interest in global poverty, certainly gave scholars and practitioners alike plenty to consider.

The existing literature surrounding New Labour's international development policies falls broadly into two camps. The first provides more or less a descriptive narrative or review of New Labour's policies in this area.[14] This 'output'-orientated literature is useful in providing an overview of both New Labour's successes and shortcomings concerning international development, and in doing so is able to offer some explanation for the outcomes that emerged within this area of policy. The literature found in the second camp, however, moves beyond these performance-based assessments to offer a far more structural analysis of its policies.[15] These more critical accounts – alluded to already – focus upon the 'inputs' of New Labour policy by interrogating the material and ideational factors that came to shape the formation and subsequent outcomes of government policy. As I have already suggested, the literature located in this second camp provides what is arguably a far more detailed explanation of New Labour's specific international development policies, and it is within this particular body of literature that this book should be read.

Many scholars, however, tended to be less critical, preferring to give the initial forays that the Blair government made into international development the benefit of the doubt. While Conservative governments had been broadly dismissive of matters concerning global poverty and overseas aid, the remit of this new department differed considerably from even previous incarnations attempted by Labour governments in the past. This reflected in part New Labour's own period of modernisation post-1992, but also the changes that had occurred within the international community since Labour was last in office. Reviewing DFID's first White Paper, Peter Burnell was fulsome in his praise of the promises New Labour offered, identifying strong continuities from Labour's past work in this area and suggesting ways in which DFID could breathe new life into development debates both within the UK and abroad.[16] Katy Gardner and David Lewis echoed these sentiments. Welcoming the creation of the new department, they noted its purposefulness and the lessons it offered to other development agencies.[17]

Other accounts shared certainly some of this optimism but acknowledged that questions still remained concerning the longer-term impact of New Labour's work in this area. For this reason, at this early stage of New Labour's time in office a number of scholars decided to adopt a 'wait-and-see' approach before reaching any definitive conclusions. While it was still a fledgling Whitehall institution, Ralph Young noted how DFID's autonomy and newly acquired independence from the Foreign Office could be used to chart a distinctive course for Britain's aid agenda.[18] Despite expressing concerns over the lack of policy instruments at Clare Short's disposal, Paul Mosely nevertheless also applauded DFID's honesty and pragmatism in confronting the central dilemma of 'making globalisation work for the poor'.[19]

Concerns were raised, however, over the specific implementation of DFID policies. For Adrian Hewitt and Tony Killick, although DFID's 1997 White Paper was certainly much broader and more sophisticated in its outlook than the 1975 White Paper, it nevertheless lacked the strategy and policy specifics of its predecessor.[20] White agreed. Although DFID's White Paper was strong on broad ambitious statements of intent, it lacked the necessary detail as to how to deliver on these promises effectually.[21] Although New Labour's commitments to refocus aid towards poverty reduction, replace one-sided conditionalities with 'partnerships', and increase policy coherence were all welcomed, all three authors pointed to a clear gap in the delivery of DFID policy. This, they each suggested, would make it extremely difficult for New Labour to meet the challenges set out in its own White Paper.

In a relatively short space of time DFID quickly established itself as a key Whitehall department. It became an important focal point for the rising public interest in matters of global poverty, and went on to play a critical role in the 'Blair–Brown' nexus as the so-called 'John and Paul of global development' sought to press the case both at home and abroad to confront the challenges faced by Africa and other developing areas.[22] Praising the efforts of Blair and Brown at the 2004 party conference, the singer-turned-poverty-activist, Bono, urged New Labour's Lennon and McCartney to come together and 'change the world' when it was Britain's turn to take up the presidency of the G8 the following year.

It transpired that 2005 was a momentous year in the fight against global poverty. Within the space of twelve months, the Commission for Africa (featuring the British triumvirate of Blair, Brown and recently appointed secretary of state, Hilary Benn) published its findings; the United Nations (UN) World Summit in New York met to discuss progress on the Millennium Development Goals (MDGs); and the Hong Kong Ministerial Conference took place as part of the ongoing Doha Development Round of the World Trade Organization (WTO). This coincided with an unprecedented push amongst non-governmental organisations (NGOs) to raise public awareness about international poverty through the Make Poverty History campaign. This campaign was made visible by white wristbands worn by members of the public, politicians and celebrities alike, a rally that took place in Edinburgh as political leaders of the G8 met at their summit in Gleneagles, and the global *Live8* concerts.[23]

This heightened interest in the issues of international development prompted further scholarship to emerge as a means of evaluating New Labour's policy outputs, performance and achievements in this field. Again, however, opinion over New Labour's success was divided. On the positive side, Adrian Wood, Oliver Morrissey and Alan Webster were among the authors who fully endorsed the approbation that New Labour was receiving over its development record.[24] In altogether critical terms, however, Paul Cammack and Paul Williams both noted the persistence of New Labour officials to embed their response to global poverty within the neoliberal paradigm,[25] while Tom Porteous, Ian Taylor and Anthony Payne each contended that conflicts with other strategic objectives and a misreading of the complex issues faced by the global South left the government's efforts as being rather more problematic than its admirers would admit.[26] Taken together, the tensions and problems identified by these authors raised more questions than solutions, thereby limiting the success that New Labour might have otherwise claimed.

The conclusion of Blair's premiership in 2007 triggered a further reappraisal of New Labour's international development policies, and a number of scholars contributed to what were broadly healthy assessments of New Labour's policy record in this area.[27] For these authors, in spite of the tensions that may have existed in DFID's policies, the increases in aid, debt relief, and largely successful efforts to combat HIV and AIDS within the developing world left Tony Blair with a broadly positive legacy in this particular aspect of foreign affairs. Despite his extensive contribution to New Labour's international development policies, however, Gordon Brown's own achievements were overshadowed by his brief and largely unsuccessful premiership, and a time that, due to the financial crisis, coincided with a period of deep recession for the British economy.

Gordon Brown, however, was *the* central figure in the political economy of New Labour and the design of its international development policies. As Chancellor of the Exchequer, Brown afforded himself the role of bringing about stability and prosperity in an era of globalisation. While globalisation presented challenges to national governments, the Chancellor frequently argued, it could, if managed correctly, also present tremendous opportunities for citizens and countries alike. Brown therefore set about creating a set of economic and political arrangements that would in the first instance enable Britain to successfully navigate the global economy but which crucially could also be exported abroad to improve the lives of millions across the globe.

Yet this very same model of political economy upon which Brown built Britain's economic foundations, and which he believed could eliminate world poverty, would be ruthlessly exposed at home by the financial crisis. The 'boom and bust' that the Chancellor had once claimed to have consigned to history returned with a vengeance. Despite his best efforts, his own premiership was fatally undermined and the job that he had craved for so long was no longer his. More importantly, the question must therefore be asked as to whether the model promoted by Brown at home was in fact suitable to be exported abroad to address the chronic instability and poverty already experienced by countries in the global South. As this book will argue, despite Brown's promise of a 'new economic architecture' and 'global compact' with the poor, Britain's global statesman remained wedded to the crisis-ridden orthodoxy of those institutions of international finance that had caused much of this vulnerability in the first place. Unwilling to move beyond this conventional wisdom and offer a genuinely radical alternative, Brown was unable to deliver the truly reformist, social democratic 'global New Deal' that he had pledged.

Methodology and structure of the book

Despite its focus upon the hand of Gordon Brown in the design and setting of New Labour's international development policies, *Global Statesman* is not a biographical account of Brown's political career. Given his unparalleled position in modern British politics, it is hardly surprising that a number of books are already in print concerning his life and his politics. There are four main dimensions to the literature that focuses upon the life and political career of Gordon Brown. Firstly, the biographical;[28] secondly, his domestic policies as Chancellor;[29] thirdly, what a Brown premiership might look like;[30] and fourthly, his brief tenure as prime minister, focusing specifically upon his management of the global financial crisis,[31] including his own assessment of it, and the personal role that he played in dealing with the 'first crisis of globalisation'.[32] Each of these accounts – perhaps with the notable exception of William Keegan's text, and Brown's own book – focuses upon the sphere of domestic policymaking; paying little attention to Brown's concern for global poverty, and the role that he carved out for himself in the institutions of international finance to address this.

Despite Brown's obvious concern for poverty both at home and abroad, international development in these accounts is treated as an 'extra-curricular' activity, receiving little more than a chapter or in some instances just a few pages of coverage. This, of course, reflects to a certain degree the relatively minor importance afforded to international development in British politics more generally, and the extent to which other events, particularly during Brown's premiership, overtook this area of policy. However, to neglect the issues of global poverty when discussing the personality and politics of one of the most powerful and influential figures in the modern era is to ignore an integral part of Brown's political economy, and one of the very reasons he pursued a career in politics.

Unlike other accounts of Gordon Brown, this book does not draw upon clandestine interviews or off-the-record briefings but rather the very *public* pronouncements of policy made by Brown and his colleagues. While this might diminish the sensationalism and subterfuge that appears in other accounts, it does enable the book to make a more factual, detailed and balanced assessment of the actual policies designed and implemented by Brown during his time as shadow Chancellor, Chancellor and finally prime minister. In the preparation of this manuscript, thousands of speeches and statements made by senior New Labour officials either in Parliament itself or at other events elsewhere in Britain and across the world were read or listened to. Of all of these speeches, it was Brown who, by some distance, delivered the majority. Not only does this reveal the seriousness that he, more than any other senior New Labour figure, afforded matters concerning poverty and development, it also demonstrates just how influential Brown was in designing and implementing this and other areas of government policy. These statements were subsequently scrutinised for both context and content before being woven together to form a narrative of development that could be examined in the light of Brown's own vision of development. It is this book that, based upon this discourse analysis, provides the critical assessment of the political economy of Brown's vision to deliver a more socially and economically just world.

In pursuing this line of inquiry, this book proceeds by mapping out the strategic terrain that Gordon Brown and New Labour were faced with during the final stages of the party's modernisation and ascent towards government. Chapter 2 considers the significance of globalisation in New Labour's break from 'old' Labour, and the various ways in which the perceived realities of 'globalisation' were internalised and articulated by various government officials. The place of Gordon Brown is crucial in this. His role as architect-in-chief of the New Labour project both at home and abroad reveals an interesting paradox at the heart of its policy thinking. For while colleagues frequently viewed 'globalisation' as an inevitable constraint or brake upon the politically possible, Brown actually saw it as representing a golden opportunity for both Britain and, as I show later in the book, those countries he sought to offer development assistance to. The rhetoric, if not the actual realities of globalisation, would shape Brown's redesign of Britain's macroeconomic architecture, New Labour's claim as the 'new party of business', and its welfare strategy. Crucially, these areas of policy would all feed into the development policies that Brown would oversee, and that the latter chapters of this book explore in greater detail. The Chancellor's hand in both domestic and foreign policymaking would enable there to be a clear transmission of policy from one spatial scale of governance to another.

Chapter 3 offers analysis of three key areas of domestic policy that Gordon Brown would transpose to the realm of international development: (1) macroeconomic policy, (2) business, and (3) welfare. The focus of this chapter is the design of these policies by Brown, and the themes that would again reappear in New Labour's flagship international development policies. Having configured New Labour's political economy in the light of the strategic context of globalisation mapped out in Chapter 2, Brown believed in the need to demonstrate a commitment to open, long-term economic policymaking predicated upon a set of clearly defined rules and codes. Here, the Chancellor worked alongside his longstanding political ally and economic adviser, Ed Balls, to promote the importance of market credibility. This, the pair argued, was crucial to deliver growth and continued investment in Britain's economy. Although existing accounts of New Labour rarely afford Balls any great significance in the setting of its economic policy, this book reveals just how pivotal Balls was in the design and implementation of New Labour's political economy both at home and, as Chapter 5 demonstrates, abroad as well. Balls's own influence was writ large upon the key policy decisions taken by the Chancellor, and through Balls, Brown was able to reach out to and convince the City of London and other key financial actors as to the probity of his policies.

Alongside the City of London, New Labour sought to develop a fruitful relationship with what it called the 'jewel in the crown' of Britain's 'knowledge economy': the pharmaceutical industry. Foregrounding this relationship, however, is New Labour's claim as the 'party of business'. Partly to distance itself from 'old' Labour and partly, again, to orientate itself as a party fit for office in an era of globalisation, officials talked up New Labour's business credentials so as to secure the credibility that Brown deemed crucial, not simply for New Labour's continued electability, but crucially, for Brown himself to achieve all that he sought to do in office. This second section, however, reveals just how much ground New Labour and in particular Gordon Brown ceded to business in terms of its own political programme. Although Brown frequently spoke of a Britain built upon economic strength and social justice, it was frequently the former that was prioritised over the latter. Any provision of fairness and/or social justice was contingent upon a clear and unambiguous commitment to markets, competition and enterprise. Despite the tensions between the two, Brown and other New Labour officials maintained that these imperatives were in fact commensurate with one another. This view will be assessed in the light of the government's response to the unfolding AIDS epidemic and the unique role that it afforded to the pharmaceutical industry in the delivery of lifesaving antiretroviral drugs.

The third and final area of policy considered in this chapter is that of welfare, and specifically Gordon Brown's (new) 'New Deal'. Revisiting and claiming the spirit, if not quite the politics and policies of Roosevelt's own programme of the same name launched in the United States during the 1930s, Brown's 'New Deal' was a deliberate attempt to position himself amongst the pantheon of liberal, progressive thinkers. The Chancellor's own policy programme, however, was predicated upon a clear and contractual commitment to 'rights and responsibilities', and an increased emphasis upon social and economic inclusion by 'making work pay'. This provided the framework for a welfare strategy that was no longer simply concerned with putting in place a safety net that might catch those whom market capitalism had failed, but rather one that disciplined the individual into becoming an active participant in the global economy. As the narratives of globalisation articulated in Chapter 2 suggest, globalisation precluded individuals from relying upon the state. Gordon Brown's redesign of the welfare state placed the onus squarely upon the individual to work with the grain of globalisation and the state to act 'virtuously' in enabling the self-same individual to take up the opportunities afforded by globalisation. This thinking would underpin and become evident in Brown's own 'global New Deal', the centrepiece of which would be his flagship development policy, the International Finance Facility (IFF).

Having established in Chapter 3 the domestic policies that were identified by Gordon Brown to be transmitted into the realm of international development, the focus of Chapter 4 is the institutional arrangements that Brown, alongside Ed Balls, put in place to make the Treasury the pilot agency of New Labour's political economy. Insofar as the newly established Department for International Development was concerned, this approach would ensure that it was the Chancellor, rather than the secretary of state for international development, who designed New Labour's international development policy. This meant that although Tony Blair had granted the newly established DFID formal independence from the Foreign and Commonwealth Office, the Treasury restrained its autonomy. It was therefore, as the following chapters go on to show, the imprint of the Treasury, and Gordon Brown in particular, that was writ large over New Labour's policy interventions in the global South.

The role that the Treasury played in 'internationalising' New Labour's domestic political economy went beyond the conquest of other Whitehall departments, and Gordon Brown was instrumental in taking the macroeconomic blueprint that he had mapped out at home to a number of key international financial actors abroad. This blueprint would create a 'new Jerusalem', a biblical phrase that the Chancellor, invoking his intimate knowledge of the Scriptures, used to describe the vision that he had of a world free from poverty. This 'new Jerusalem' represented a 'new world', one free from poverty, debt and disease. Constructed of the same 'building blocks of prosperity' that the Chancellor had put in place in Britain, these blocks of stability and 'sound' policies would, according to Brown, enable developed and developing nations alike to realise the opportunities of globalisation and deliver global prosperity for all. Embedding his vision into the orthodoxy of the 'post-Washington Consensus', Brown took his blueprint to a constellation of international institutions of economic governance abroad. This would ensure that there was not only a clear transmission of policy but also a distinct institutional transmission from the domestic to international spheres of economic governance. This policy and institutional transmission between the domestic and international levels would be crucial for it would lock in the Chancellor's 'new economic architecture' and provide the basis for the policies explored in the following three chapters.

The first of these case studies in Chapter 5 draws parallels between the economic architecture that was drawn up by Treasury officials at home and the 'new international economic architecture' that Gordon Brown was keen to pursue abroad. Both sets of frameworks were predicated upon the same ideas of macroeconomic stability, 'open rules for an open economy', and credibility through transparency and clear standards and codes. These principles were deemed to be essential for 'inclusion' – a key discourse of New Labour – in the global economy where 'opportunities' (another core New Labour theme) for wealth creation and increased prosperity lay. Eligibility for debt relief for the poorest countries under the Heavily Indebted Poor Countries (HIPC) Initiative and latterly, the Multilateral Debt Relief Initiative (MDRI) would be conditional upon recipient countries meeting their obligations towards the 'good economic governance' supported by the 'post-Washington Consensus'. Embedded firmly within this 'new economic architecture' by the international financial institutions (IFIs), these policy initiatives emphasised the new economic orthodoxy as a means of achieving the economic growth understood to be necessary for development.

This approach to policy, however, would bring Brown in particular into conflict with those members of civil society who viewed debt relief in 'moral' rather than simply 'economic' terms, and as an issue of social justice and economic redemption. Under a series of high-profile anti-poverty campaigns, some Labour backbenchers joined with trade unions, church groups and celebrities in urging the New Labour government, other creditor countries and lenders to cancel developing world debt on more normative grounds of morality and social justice. This left New Labour in a further difficult position: whether to focus upon increasing the urgently needed funds for global development (as it would do through initiatives such as the International Financial Facility explored in Chapter 7) and in doing so answer the calls of justice demanded by civil society, or impose, as the IFIs themselves had done in the past, a new form of 'conditionality' – a specific form of economic governance upon developing countries designed to discipline these states into meeting the challenges presented by globalisation.

The second case study, explored in Chapter 6, addresses New Labour's commitment to increase the availability of antiretroviral drugs needed to combat HIV and AIDS in the developing world. The main theme of this chapter is New Labour's claim to be the 'party of business' explored in Chapter 3, and its special relationship with the British pharmaceutical industry. This chapter reveals a clear tension between the priority that New Labour afforded to the pharmaceutical industry, and the commitment that Brown and other government officials made concerning the delivery of antiretroviral medicines. Despite the scale of the emergency, and the urgent need to roll out these drugs to stem the tide of AIDS-related deaths in the global South, New Labour's policies – again designed principally by Brown – were dominated by a series of demand- and supply-side policies designed to accommodate the preferences of the pharmaceutical industry and its shareholders in the global North. Whilst Gordon Brown was amongst a number of government officials who agreed that the price of these drugs remained prohibitively high, he was also instrumental in introducing a number of market-based measures to incentivise rather than regulate the industry into meeting its wider obligations towards HIV and AIDS.

This relationship with the pharmaceutical industry was central to the realisation of New Labour's ambitions both at home and abroad. Whereas at home, as Chapter 3 demonstrates, government ministers had talked at length about placing Britain and its pharmaceutical industry right at the heart of the 'knowledge economy', it was in this particular area of international development abroad that these firms had a crucial role to play. So political was this relationship, however, that questions remained over what space was left for other 'non-market' actors to voice their concern over the lack of provision of lifesaving drugs. Although Gordon Brown too expressed his alarm at the critical shortfall in the amount of antiretrovirals that were available in the developing world, he nevertheless shied away from pressing the pharmaceutical industry into taking more urgent action. Instead, Brown set about creating an economic and regulatory framework conducive to retaining and attracting further domestic investment from the pharmaceutical industry. Consequently, the framework mapped out by the

Treasury appeared to prioritise the economic competitiveness of the UK-based pharmaceutical firms over more moral concerns relating to public health.

The final case study chapter picks up the theme of financing for development explored in Chapter 5. However, whereas this first case study chapter considers the macroeconomic context within which debt relief would be delivered, Chapter 7 examines the welfare reforms, and specifically Gordon Brown's 'New Deal' programme that, as Chancellor, Brown had introduced at home, and the 'global New Deal' that he sought to promote abroad. Focusing in particular upon the centrepiece of this 'global New Deal', the International Finance Facility (or latterly the International Finance Facility for Immunisation), this chapter explores this mechanism as a means by which finance could be raised upon international bond markets for immediate investment and repaid at a later date. The chapter draws clear linkages between Gordon Brown's approach to government spending at home, and in particular his 'golden rule' to 'borrow only to invest', and his enthusiasm to use private capital to fund public goods, as he had at home through the rolling out of several Private Finance Initiatives (PFIs) and Public-Private Partnerships (PPPs).

Alongside these spending proposals, Brown's 'New Deal' was internationalised as a means of encouraging greater inclusion in the global economy. At home, the 'New Deal' was designed to lift people out of unemployment and include them in the world of work; this 'global New Deal' worked on the same principles of 'rights and responsibilities' as a means of including developing countries in the global economy so that they might enjoy its benefits. Like the discourse of globalisation that underpinned New Labour's approach to debt relief, the discourse here was one of negotiable constraint through disciplined opportunity. If 'properly managed' – that is, if developing countries opened up their economies and pursued pro-trade policies – then globalisation would be more likely to work in their favour.

The role of aid in this was similar to that of welfare: not an end in itself but a springboard for inclusion in the global economy; and for poor countries, development and growth. In this interim period, however, like Britain's own welfare claimants who were compelled to undertake training and voluntary work under New Labour, recipients of this aid had to meet a set of obligations, orientated towards full participation in the global economy, in order to become eligible for this finance. Having already explored the macroeconomic implications of this in Chapter 5, it is argued here that by casting aid as a form of 'global welfare', Brown and his colleagues were presented with a similar dilemma to the one they faced when attempting to negotiate the issue of debt relief. Ascribing aid with the same contractual obligations of 'rights and responsibilities' served only to obscure the structural causes of inequality, while imposing a new form of 'conditionality' only restricted the already-limited economic autonomy of those countries in need of this financial assistance.

Drawing this book to a close, the concluding chapter returns to the core theoretical and empirical claims made here in this opening chapter, and throughout the book. Both as Chancellor of the Exchequer and as prime minister, Gordon Brown was clearly passionate about matters of global poverty, and indeed, even out of office, remains so. Yet in his zeal to deliver lasting change in some of the world's poorest areas, Brown contrived to embed his antipoverty strategy within the strictures of neoliberal orthodoxy.

This book therefore concludes by critiquing the attempt made by Gordon Brown to address global poverty by explicitly working with and indeed enhancing the self-same structures of market capitalism that had reinforced and produced the levels of inequality and underdevelopment experienced across the global South in the first place. His mission to save the developing world did not simply assimilate 'market' actors in the development process but more often than not, *prioritised* these actors over the delivery of a more socially and economically equitable set of outcomes. Brown's approach then, coupled with a failure to understand and address the structural causes of underdevelopment in the global South, limited the scope for any genuine success in this field and, ultimately, undermined his and New Labour's otherwise laudable desire to address the poverty experienced by billions of people across the world.

Notes

1. Seldon, *Blair*, 2005, p. 529.
2. Brown, 'The socialist challenge', 1975, p. 9.
3. Bower, *Gordon Brown*, 2007, p. 2.

4. Brown, 'Rediscovering Public Purpose in the Global Economy', 1998.
5. Ibid.
6. Coates and Hay, 'The internal and external face of New Labour's political economy', 2001, p. 456.
7. Dixon and Williams, 'Tough on debt, tough on the causes of debt', 2001.
8. Wade, 'A new global financial architecture?', 2007, p. 126.
9. Hewitt and Killick, 'The 1975 and 1997 White Papers compared', 1998; Young, 'New Labour and international development', 2000; Dixon and Williams, 'Tough on debt, tough on the causes of debt', 2001; Williams, *British Foreign Policy under New Labour, 1997–2005*, 2005; Manning, 'Development', 2007; Webster, 'New Labour, new aid?', 2008; Gallagher, 'Healing the scar?', 2009.
10. Short, *An Honourable Deception?*, 2005.
11. Seldon, *Blair*, 2005, p. 529.
12. DFID, *A Challenge for the 21st Century*, 1997; DFID, *Making Globalisation Work for the Poor*, 2000.
13. DFID, *Making Governance Work for the Poor*, 2006; DFID, *Building Our Common Future*, 2009.
14. White, 'British aid and the White Paper on international development', 1998; Webster, 'New Labour, new aid?', 2008.
15. Abrahamsen and Williams, 'Ethics and foreign policy', 2001; Cammack, 'Global governance, state agency and competitiveness', 2006.
16. Burnell, 'Britain's new government, new White Paper, new aid?', 1998.
17. Gardner and Lewis, 'Dominant paradigms overturned or "business as usual"?', 2000.
18. Young, 'New Labour and international development', 2000, p. 265.
19. Mosley, 'Making globalisation work for the poor?', 2001.
20. Hewitt and Killick, 'The 1975 and 1997 White Papers compared', 1998.
21. White, 'British aid and the White Paper on international development', 1998.
22. Bono, speech delivered at the annual Labour Party conference, 2004.
23. Commission for Africa, *Our Common Interest*, 2005; Lockwood, 'Will a Marshall Plan for Africa make poverty history?', 2005; Bond, 'Global governance campaigning and MDGs', 2006; Ware, 'Reassessing Labour's relationship with sub-Saharan Africa', 2006; Biccum, 'Marketing development', 2007; Brainard and Chollet, *Global Development 2.0*, 2008; Harrison, 'The Africanization of poverty', 2010; van Heerde and Hudson, '"The righteous considereth the cause of the poor"?', 2010.

24. Wood, 'Making globalization work for the poor', 2004; Morrissey, 'British aid policy in the "Short–Blair" years', 2005; Webster, 'New Labour, new aid?', 2008.

25. Cammack, 'Global governance, state agency and competitiveness', 2006; Williams, 'Who's making UK foreign policy?', 2004; Williams, *British Foreign Policy under New Labour, 1997–2005*, 2005; Williams, 'Blair's Commission for Africa', 2005; Curtis, 'Africa's false friends', 2005.

26. Porteous, 'British government policy in sub-Saharan Africa under New Labour', 2005; Taylor, '"Advice is judged by results, not by intentions"', 2005; Payne, 'Blair, Brown and the Gleneagles agenda', 2006.

27. Morrissey, 'Aid and international development', 2009; Brown, 'Debating the year of Africa', 2007; Manning, 'Development', 2007.

28. Routledge, *Gordon Brown*, 1998; Beckett, *Gordon Brown*, 2007.

29. Pym and Kochan, *Gordon Brown*, 1998; Rawnsley, *Servants of the People*, 2001; Keegan, *The Prudence of Mr Gordon Brown*, 2004; Peston, *Brown's Britain*, 2005; Lee, *Best For Britain?*, 2007; Lee, *Boom and Bust*, 2009; Richards, *Whatever It Takes*, 2010.

30. Bower, *Gordon Brown*, 2007; Giddens, *Over to You, Mr Brown*, 2007.

31. Harvie, *Broonland*, 2010; Hughes, *What Went Wrong, Gordon Brown?*, 2010; Rawnsley, *The End of the Party*, 2010; Richards, *Whatever It Takes*, 2010; Seldon and Lodge, *Brown at 10*, 2011; Keegan, *Saving the World?*, 2012; McBride, *Power Trip*, 2014.

32. Brown, *Beyond the Crash*, 2011.

2 A World of Challenge and Opportunity

In attempting to establish itself as the defining political project of late British capitalism, New Labour anchored its own novelty and necessity in what Hall and Jacques termed the 'new times' that Britain faced as it approached the twenty-first century.[1] Prior to New Labour's emergence, the end of the Cold War and the concomitant triumph of liberalism had all but sealed the neoliberal hegemony established in Britain by Margaret Thatcher's Conservative Party. Between 1979 and 1990, Thatcher presided over a social and economic revolution that altered, almost beyond recognition, the country's industrial landscape and the traditional class cleavages that had sustained 'old' Labour.

The transition from the Fordism that had defined the experience of modernity in the first two-thirds of the twentieth century, to 'post-Fordism' saw Britain's own manufacturing sector hollowed out and its historic commitment to banking and the City restated and renewed. Cutting adrift many of Labour's traditional heartlands, this process of deindustrialisation tipped the balance of the British economy firmly in favour of an increasingly global financial services sector. The wealth that it created fuelled the expansion of a new, salaried, home-owning middle class, one concentrated in London and the surrounding South East of England but one which was also appearing in the suburban provinces of Britain's towns and cities.

The 'new times' that Britain inhabited and New Labour inherited are crucial to our understanding of the terms upon which Gordon Brown and Tony Blair would begin their own renewal of both the Labour Party and the country as a whole. Central to these 'new times', however, and what, by extension, was fundamental to the political economy designed by Gordon Brown, was globalisation. A key driver behind the financialisation of the British state, globalisation quickly became accepted as the *leitmotif* amongst Brown and his colleagues. It provided New Labour with not only an understanding of contemporary economic and social life, but also the lens through which its officials were able to survey the qualitatively new terrain upon which they found themselves.[2] It would lead to Brown, Blair and many other New Labour ministers displaying an unprecedented degree of sensitivity and awareness as to the global pressures now faced by national governments.

Of course, in many respects, these pressures were not anything particularly new. Britain – whether as 'the workshop of the world', colonial superpower, or centre of global finance – had always been at the heart of the world economy. While the speed, scale and intensity of these pressures may have altered, the politics and the policies of the governments of this tiny island have always been inflected to at least some degree by forces similar to those experienced in this putatively 'new' age of globalisation.[3] Yet this New Labour government was the first that operated in a post-Cold War, post-Keynesian era – one where international borders and relations were more open than and complex than in any preceding period.[4] According to officials, policy now had to be conceived and applied in the context of the globalisation of financial markets, while fundamental reconfigurations of international economic power and a transformed macroeconomic environment made interest rates, inflation and public sector borrowing far more difficult to manage.[5] Globalisation therefore posed major problems, not just for Keynesian social democracy but, more generally, for the national economic policy autonomy of medium-sized nations such as Britain.[6]

If globalisation appeared to pose a headache for British policy-makers, at the start of the 1990s, Labour was hardly coming to the issue from a position of strength. The party's own record in managing the British economy, certainly insofar as voters were concerned, left much to be desired. Still haunted by images from the so-called 'Winter of Discontent' of 1978/9, Labour had spent over a decade in opposition to an otherwise deeply unpopular government, fruitlessly trying to convince the electorate that it could be trusted to manage the British economy. Following his election as

Labour leader in July 1994, Tony Blair jettisoned the gradualism of Labour's post-1983 renewal and replaced it with an altogether more fundamental break with the party's past. Formalised with the creation of a 'New Labour' later that year, Blair's rebranding of the party enabled New Labour to speak far more authoritatively and authentically of the material realities that it believed Britain now faced in this new global economy.

Mapping out the 'radical' changes that were taking place in the new global economy,[7] Tony Blair's message was unequivocal: the 'globalisation of the world economy is a reality'.[8] 'We are all internationalists now', he argued, 'whether we like it or not',[9] because 'we have one economy, all of which is affected profoundly by developments in both technology and global markets'.[10] There was no other alternative for countries to be successful; globalisation had to be 'accepted'.[11] It was 'transforming the world economy'[12] and, quite simply, 'a fact of life'.[13]

This stark message also featured heavily in the speeches and policy announcements of other senior cabinet members. For Clare Short, New Labour's first secretary of state for international development, the fixed realities of globalisation meant that 'it is not a question of whether people are for or against it', globalisation was for 'real', as 'part of history, just as industrialisation was [and] as big a historical change as the industrial revolution'.[14] Not only was globalisation an undisputed reality, it was, according to the late Robin Cook, also as inevitable as the sunrise. During his time as foreign secretary, Cook remarked, 'it is a good thing that the sun rises every day, but I also know there is nothing I can do to stop it even if I wanted to'.[15]

During his first stint at the Treasury as its chief secretary, Alistair Darling offered a similarly fatalistic assessment of the strategic environment that now faced New Labour and Britain. 'We live in a global economy', Darling noted, one in which 'we are moving towards a single global economy'.[16] Indeed, many New Labour figures shared this sense of inevitability towards globalisation. As the Labour peer, Lord McIntosh, remarked, 'I just take the view that it is a fact which we can do nothing about; we will not turn it back.'[17] The defence secretary, Geoff Hoon, agreed. He, like both Blair and Brown, viewed globalisation as 'a fact of life'.[18]

Echoing these remarks, the leader of the House of Commons, Peter Hain, stated that globalisation was indeed 'a fact of life' and that 'we, in Britain, are part of a global economy'.[19] This 'fact' could not, according to the home secretary, Charles Clarke, 'be un-invented'; it was simply 'the realities with which we have to live',[20] which meant for the science and innovation minister, Malcolm Wicks, that it was 'here to stay'.[21] New Labour's last international development secretary, Douglas Alexander, summed up his government's unshakeable belief in the very real existence of globalisation: 'In our age, shaped as it is by the twin forces of globalisation and interconnectedness, to talk of one world is no longer to utter an abstract thought but to describe a concrete reality.'[22] Having themselves adapted to the 'new times' with which they were faced, '"New" Labour' not only understood globalisation, they could now also prepare 'New Britain' for the demands that this new global economy was placing upon it.

Although very much rooted in the social democratic traditions of 'old' Labour from which Blair was keen to distance his party, Gordon Brown was nevertheless at the heart of New Labour's invocation of globalisation. A disciple of the gospel of globalisation preached by New Labour, Brown, like his ministerial colleagues, also spoke repeatedly of the inevitable challenges presented by globalisation and the global economy. Brown too argued that 'globalisation has happened', and the challenges that had arisen from it had done so 'from our ever greater interdependence in an integrated global economy'.[23] 'With its ever more rapid waves of innovation and its fast-moving and often destabilising capital markets', Brown warned of the uncertainty that globalisation now brought to economic policymaking.[24] At a social level, Brown remarked how changes in the global economy had created a worldwide culture: global communications and travel, global brand names, global music, films and entertainments and global media outlets.[25] These changes meant that governments were 'of course subject not just to national pressures, *but to global pressures too*'.[26] That New Labour felt compelled to yield to these global pressures is striking as it illustrates the extent to which officials felt constrained to internalise a clear 'logic of no alternative' and treat globalisation as an inevitable outcome.[27]

Yet as closely as this logic was pursued, it did not cause Gordon Brown or New Labour to restrict but rather *modify*, often as they saw fit, the parameters of the politically possible. For Brown, in presenting a challenge to national governments, globalisation also represented an *opportunity*: an opportunity not only to increase prosperity, but also to bring about justice and peace. Brown frequently argued that globalisation was not simply an economic process – it also placed a series of moral obligations upon all of us. 'We are part of both one global economy and one moral universe', Brown argued.[28] This rendered economic and social justice as indivisible, with each element essential to the success of the whole.[29] Seizing upon the mutuality of these two elements, Brown set about designing a model of political economy fit for this global age.

Gordon Brown's own open reading of globalisation made it possible for there to be a far clearer line of transmission to exist between the previously distinct boundaries that had demarcated domestic and foreign policymaking in the past. Indeed, for Brown's Treasury, globalisation provided the opportunity to apply the principles of economic reform and social justice at home to its work abroad.[30] Since globalisation had rendered the lines between 'the domestic' and 'the foreign' indistinguishable, policies designed for consumption at home could be adapted to meet the perceived realities and challenges of this new global economy abroad. As shadow Chancellor, Chancellor of the Exchequer and then prime minister himself, globalisation was woven into the blueprint of Brown's own macroeconomic architecture at home and later abroad; it would underpin New Labour's claim as the 'new party of (global) business', and inform the demands that its welfare strategy would place upon both individuals and developing countries alike. Crucially, therefore, globalisation actually gave Brown considerable latitude to fulfil his personal mission to take New Labour to the world.

Of course, Brown was not alone in viewing globalisation as both a challenge *and* as an opportunity. His successor in the Treasury, Alistair Darling; the minister for the armed forces, Bob Ainsworth; the economic secretary to the Treasury, Ed Balls; and his predecessor, Ivan Lewis all implored their respective audiences to 'embrace' and 'respond' to both 'the challenges *and* opportunities presented by globalisation'.[31] It was Brown, however, who frequently used 'globalisation' as a rhetorical device to frame expectations amongst the electorate and the wider polity concerning what was (or indeed, what was not) politically

25

or economically feasible. As this chapter will show, for Brown, globalisation represented a 'constraint' upon government policy – but it also represented an opportunity to deliver 'social justice on a global scale'.[32]

This ambiguity would suggest that there was a certain amount of what Bob Jessop has termed 'strategic selectivity' on the part of Gordon Brown as he sought to frame certain policy decisions and appeal to a range of very different audiences.[33] Borrowing from Nicos Poulantzas's account of the state as a social relation, Jessop uses this concept throughout his work to describe the ways in which the state, over a given period of time, pursues its interests by deploying different strategies relative to the specific strategies pursued by other actors over that same period of time. Insofar as New Labour's political economy was concerned, Brown's own strategic selectivity created a series of tensions between these different policy actors that was frequently heightened by this inconsistent logic of globalisation internalised and articulated by New Labour officials, most notably by Brown himself. This tension would appear in each of the three areas of domestic policymaking and the three international development policies in which Brown was instrumental.

Not only did this suggest a great deal of contingency in the realities and rhetoric of globalisation in New Labour policy, it also meant that this particular Labour government prioritised and worked far more closely with 'pro-market' audiences than any of its successors had, in order to fulfil its policy objectives. Within the field of international development, however, since many of those self-same market actors and institutions had themselves been responsible for deepening this poverty experienced in the global South (see Chapter 4), this was particularly problematic. Any radicalism that Brown might have claimed in respect of his policies that he argued could eliminate global poverty was therefore blunted by his own strategic selectivity in the market mechanisms that he chose to deliver his personal crusade.

The chapters that follow consider the terms upon which Gordon Brown operationalised his own strategically selective rhetoric concerning globalisation, and later on in this particular chapter, I explore in very broad terms the relationship between New Labour's rhetoric of globalisation and that of international development as a key area of government policy. Before discussing this, however, I take as my point of departure the different ways in which 'globalisation' was understood and articulated by various New Labour officials. Drawing upon an extensive array of speeches and policy announcements made by government ministers throughout New Labour's time in office, I argue that these statements concerning globalisation can be arranged into three distinct but also inter-linked sets of discursive claims.

The first discourse, quite simply, treats globalisation as some-thing that was inevitable and able to impose a clear constraint upon the setting of policy. The second accepts the claims of the first discourse, by emphasising the constraint upon policy imposed by globalisation. Crucially, however, this second discourse sug-gests that globalisation could be successfully negotiated *if* – and only if – the 'correct' (i.e. market-appeasing) strategy was selected. The third discourse represents what appears at first to be a clear and contradictory break from the previous two discourses, empha-sising as it does the possibility that globalisation also presented an opportunity for policymakers rather than simply a constraint. This opportunity, however, is squared with the condition that indi-viduals (and in the context of international development, national governments) fulfil a pre-determined set of market-orientated obligations. The difference between this third discourse and the previous two is significant for whereas the first and second dis-courses meant policymakers simply accepting the constraints that globalisation was assumed to bear as a *fait accompli*, this third discourse enabled governments to shift the burden of this con-straint onto those of the individual citizen. Invoking the 'threat' of globalisation and the external challenges present in the global economy, globalisation was viewed as an opportunity that may be negotiated but only if certain (again, largely market-appeasing) constraints were internalised by and accepted by the electorate.

New Labour's construction of globalisation as a series of over-lapping discourses is essential to our understanding of its political economy. Not only did globalisation alter the *a priori* ideas and perceptions that officials had of the world that surrounded them,[34] as we shall see over the coming chapters, it became instructive in the design and mobilisation of a set of strategies and tactics to deliver policy objectives both at home and abroad. It is to these discourses that I now turn my attention before considering the terms upon which New Labour understood international development in an era of globalisation.

Discourse 1: The inevitability of globalisation

This particular discourse was derived from arguably the dominant understanding of globalisation, certainly within the more mainstream literature. This 'business school' literature, labelled by Watson and Hay for its influence in expounding the conventional wisdom of globalisation amongst the business and media elites, was 'the public face' of globalisation in Britain during the mid to late 1990s.[35] According to these accounts, globalisation was understood as being a constellation of dynamics all mediating and interacting with one another. Increasing flows of capital, production and other resources across borders and continents – all mobilised by advances in technology and communication – placed severe and inexorable pressures upon the political economies of national governments. Governments were effectively helpless in the face of this tidal wave of change, unable to postpone or prevent this transformation.[36]

New Labour officials were far from slow in detecting these trends, and indeed, one of the leading lights of New Labour, Peter Mandelson, remarked during his time as the secretary of state for trade and industry how 'the growth of electronic mail and the internet, changing customer demands and greater liberalisation of markets [were] the key drivers of change worldwide'.[37] For Tony Blair, these changes meant that Britain was situated 'in a completely new world', with the increased liberalisation of financial markets making it possible for trillions of dollars to move across the foreign exchanges in a single day.[38] However, the 'completely new world' that Blair envisaged was rapidly transferring power from the state to the market. In his now famous 'Doctrine of the International Community' speech, Blair warned his audience in Chicago that 'any government that thinks it can go it alone is wrong. If the markets don't like your policies, they will punish you.'[39]

Never one to miss an opportunity to stress his own business credentials, Blair mapped out to industry leaders his understanding of the global environment that British firms now faced. 'What is happening today is not complex but simple', Blair remarked. 'There is huge restructuring, here and elsewhere in the industrialised world.'[40] Taking place 'across continents', Gordon Brown added, this restructuring was driving forward the 'mobility of capital and openness to competition'.[41] The key problem then that now confronted policymakers was not merely economic downturn but these 'very large and profound global structural changes'.[42] Hollowing out the political imperative behind deindustrialisation, Brown argued that it was these structural changes that were responsible for 'shifting many industries and services to the industrialising world' and challenged 'us in the industrialised world to respond and adjust more quickly and more flexibly'.[43]

Understood in these terms, globalisation was for New Labour an inevitable part of contemporary life. The pace at which globalisation was taking place was, according to Blair, leading to people being displaced, industries being made obsolete, communities reshaped, and even torn apart.[44] 'The premium is on a country's ability to adapt', the prime minister argued; 'adapt quickly and you prosper. Fail to do so and you decline.'[45] The chief secretary to the Treasury, Des Browne, invoked this specific 'business school' understanding of globalisation to make a similar point to Blair. Drawing upon the analysis of the latest proponent of this conventional wisdom, Thomas Friedman,[46] Browne noted how the world is now 'flatter', and that globalisation had made outsourcing, teleworking and other modern ways of working even more necessary. Browne, like Friedman and Blair, stated the importance of facing up to this challenge or risk being left behind.[47]

These stark warnings left no doubt as to the significance of globalisation. Yet it posed a clear dilemma to policymakers; namely, the type of role governments now had in the midst of these inevitable global pressures. By assuming the near perfect mobility of capital and factors of production, New Labour officials were left, by implication, to pursue a set of policies centred upon national competitiveness, cost reductions, a low corporate tax regime, welfare retrenchment and greater labour market flexibility: in effect, policies that ceded power to the markets.

These policies, however, left big question marks over any remaining commitment to social democracy that New Labour might have claimed. In order to retain investment, maintain economic prosperity and secure re-election, Stephen Driver and Luke

Martell conceded that it was necessary for New Labour to priori-tise the demands of global capital over some of its most cherished social democratic beliefs.[48] Quite simply, if New Labour wanted to deliver social democracy, it could only do so by accepting and, as we shall see shortly, playing by the rules dictated by globalisation.

Although clearly well intentioned, this attempt to reformu-late social democracy merely served to restrict what Colin Hay termed 'the limits of the possible, the feasible and the desirable to that imaginable within the ascendant neoliberal worldview'.[49] For Alan Finlayson, this simple assessment of globalisation not only allowed neoliberal theories of the market to remain domi-nant, but enabled New Labour itself to 'take the easy way out' and merely adjust Britain to a post-Thatcherite settlement.[50] This is crucial since it quickly dissipate any radicalism or novelty that New Labour might have been keen to claim. By simply accepting the shift in the balance of power from the state to the market, their policies became self-fulfilling prophecies merely reinforcing this transfer of power by accommodating and conforming to the expectations of market actors.

The explanation offered by the Chancellor, Alistair Darling, concerning the Treasury's approach to corporation tax provides a useful illustration of this point:

> A few years ago, one of our airlines used to say 'we never forget you have a choice'. Today, governments should remember that. Business does have a choice. Business is increasingly mobile. Tax rates have to be globally competitive. I am determined that British business will not be the fiscal fall guy. Business is the lynchpin of the British economy. Business creates jobs, wealth and generates growth. And government must ensure the right framework within which business can prosper. And tax is an essential part of that framework . . . We need to ensure that the tax system is competitive and predictable, as well as ensur-ing that the business environment is attractive to increasingly mobile businesses.[51]

There is a clear and somewhat disarmingly simple logic in Dar-ling's statement here. In a global economy, businesses are footloose and can relocate with ease. In the light of this context, if the New Labour government wished to retain the investment of these firms (thereby safeguarding jobs and prosperity), then it would be nec-essary to make the British tax system globally competitive. The underlying message here is that while businesses have a choice, governments do not. Irrespective of whether Darling was correct in his assessment, his statement demonstrates how this particular discourse of globalisation might result in two very real material outcomes. Firstly, the discourse embedded the Treasury's tax framework within the perceived demands made by market actors for a more competitive and less burdensome tax regime. By doing this, however – and this is the second outcome – Darling himself actually imposed constraint upon the government's own corporate fiscal policy, thereby reinforcing the shift in power from the state to the market.

As the next discourse will reveal, despite its clear concession to the market, this was not New Labour's only understanding of globalisation. It was, however, an understanding that would prove convenient for government officials as they sought to discipline the expectations of the politically possible. In the midst of these profound structural changes in the wider global economy, ministers and other Party officials frequently treated globalisation as a constraint upon policy. If this then was the material reality with which New Labour was faced, what role did it now envisage for itself in government? It is to the second discourse that this chapter now turns, and how an altogether more contingent view of globalisation enabled New Labour to exercise more in the way of 'discretionary constraint' in the way policy was set within the domestic sphere.

Discourse 2: Discretionary constraint

The second discourse of globalisation invoked by New Labour gave policymakers slightly more latitude in setting policy. Like the first discourse, it took as its point of departure the inexorability of globalisation. However, this second discourse possessed what Hay and Rosamond have termed a 'fragile and contingent quality'.[52] If managed correctly through the prescription of the right policy mix, New Labour could ensure that globalisation was less a threat but more an opportunity that could stand to benefit the British economy. Here, the transforming context of the new global economy compelled policymakers to act with 'discretionary constraint'. Borrowed from the then chief economist and future deputy governor of the Bank of England, Mervyn King, this particular term appeared in the post-monetarist policy framework of the Treasury. It underpinned the 'key principles for policymaking in an open economy' advocated by its chief economic adviser, Ed Balls, and supported Gordon Brown's New Labour's commitment to credibility during first term in office.[53]

For King, and latterly Balls, 'credibility is the elusive elixir of modern macroeconomics'.[54] According to Balls, the rapid globalisation of the world economy had made achieving credibility *more* important than ever – particularly for an incoming left-of-centre government that had been out of power for two decades.[55] The importance of credibility in this particular discourse of globalisation can be traced back to the 'conventional wisdom' coined and conceptualised by John Kenneth Galbraith. For Galbraith, relationships between events and the ideas that interpret them are crucial in our understanding of economic and social life.[56] Yet of these, it is only those ideas that are most familiar to audiences that in turn become acceptable, and the hallmark of any conventional wisdom is acceptability.[57]

This was a theme later taken up by Paul Krugman when he remarked that 'one's agreement with that conventional wisdom becomes almost the litmus test of one's suitability to be taken seriously'.[58] For Gordon Brown and New Labour, policy was framed in a manner that the government's core economic audiences, at home and abroad, would find both 'familiar' and 'acceptable'. Certainly insofar as Brown himself was concerned, the credibility of his own economic policies required external, and indeed international, validation.[59] If his policies were 'familiar' to – that is to say, if they internalised the same logic as – international markets concerning the increased mobility of global capital, then it would be far more likely that these policies would be accepted as being authoritative and credible by these self-same constituencies.

Gordon Brown was instrumental in hard-wiring the conventional wisdom concerning globalisation into the political economy of New Labour and, with it, the type of constraint he believed that it was necessary to impose upon his government. Brown recognised that national governments were, *in theory*, free to run the economy as they saw fit, and to exercise unfettered discretion.[60] Indeed, even in an era of globalisation, national governments could implement any type of policies that they wished. However, almost in the same breath, Brown also warned that such was the structural power of global capital, *in reality*, should a government exercise 'unfettered discretion', then this would result in market distrust and the likelihood of rapid disinvestment, unemployment and a loss of confidence in the government itself.[61] In order to secure the trust of the markets, it was therefore vitally important for national governments to put in place policies that supported a long-term, predictable macroeconomic framework. For Brown, this meant sending the UK down a 'post-monetarist path to stability', and locking into place 'the discipline of a long-term institutional framework' through a series of binding fiscal rules.[62] Despite the political constraints that it would invoke – particularly for a party traditionally committed to high levels of public spending and redistribution – this approach to policymaking was deemed crucial to secure the economic acceptability and credibility of New Labour's political economy.

Gordon Brown for one was fearful of the lack of credibility from which his approach to policy might suffer. 'Governments which lack credibility, or who are pursuing policies which are not seen to be sustainable', Brown warned, 'are punished not only more swiftly than in the past but more severely and at a greater cost to their future credibility.'[63] It was almost as if Brown and his New Labour colleagues felt compelled to reassure markets that the party had learnt the painful lessons of its own past, and in office it would promote a policy framework which prioritised the expectations of an increasingly transnational class of investors. To this end, Ed Balls offered four symbiotic principles to consolidate the Treasury's commitment to the broadly neoliberal, 'conventional wisdom' of globalisation and maintain its own credibility with international investors: (1) stability through constrained discretion; (2) credibility through sound, long-term policies; (3) credibility through maximum transparency; and (4) credibility through pre-commitment.[64]

The Treasury's pursuit of credibility, particularly amongst its core market constituencies, demonstrated not only the extent to which New Labour accepted the inexorability of globalisation, but also the degree to which it was deemed vital to respond to it through a series of constrained policy decisions. This discourse of globalisation enabled Gordon Brown in particular to re-envisage globalisation not simply as a threat, but as a 'discretionary constraint' upon policy – essentially a self-imposed means of 'changing the rules' by which the game of economic governance must now be played. However, only by playing by these new rules could Britain grasp the opportunities presented by globalisation. It is to these opportunities that this chapter now turns its attention.

Discourse 3: Disciplined opportunity

Given the analysis offered thus far, it may be tempting to view New Labour's invocation of globalisation as simply having, to a greater or lesser degree, a constraining effect upon policy formation and the activity of state actors. While there was little, if any, evidence of antipathy amongst New Labour officials towards globalisation, the discourses assessed so far present globalisation to have seriously restricted the manoeuvrability that government ministers had when it came to setting policy. As widespread and as pervasive as these two discourses were, however, even they do not fully reflect New Labour's invocation of globalisation. A wider reading of policy pronouncements and speeches made by government officials actually reveals globalisation to have presented a series of opportunities for Britain, adding a further layer of complexity to New Labour's political economy.

Amidst the constraints that globalisation was understood to now impose upon national governments, a number of New Labour officials were in fact hugely enthusiastic about the opportunities that these increased levels of global integration offered to Britain. Unsurprisingly perhaps, no more clearly was this evident than in New Labour's trade policy. Indeed, the secretary of state for trade and industry, Stephen Byers, viewed globalisation 'as a bringer of opportunity, not of threat'.[65] Another trade minister, Mike O'Brien, would later argue that globalisation offered 'great opportunities and benefits'.[66] As Chancellor, Alistair Darling believed that the possibilities that had arisen from opening new markets and sharing new ideas were in fact 'endless'.[67] For Darling, far from being the constraint he had argued previously, globalisation actually appeared to offer instead infinite possibilities. For these and other government ministers, it was vital that Britain seized these opportunities. Yet in the light of this particular discourse, an important question immediately arises: what happened to the overarching narrative of 'constraint' that was evident elsewhere? It was, as this section demonstrates, still present, but in a far more subtle way. The burden of constraint would be shifted away from the state and onto the individual.

This shift was especially evident in New Labour's welfare strategy, and specifically those policies concerning its education, skills, training and employment programmes. The chapter that follows elaborates upon the content and the significance of these policies in the context of New Labour's broader political economy, but here it is crucial to note the significance of globalisation in the way in which the Blair and Brown governments operationalised their respective welfare strategies. It was in this policy domain in particular that the self-imposed constraint of globalisation was articulated through a discourse of 'rights and responsibilities'. In practice, this meant that it was obligatory for recipients of welfare to increase their skills and training in order to improve their job prospects and employability in an increasingly globalised labour market. Should claimants of welfare be unwilling to meet these 'responsibilities', they would be denied the 'rights' afforded to them under previous welfare regimes.

New Labour maintained that for the opportunities of globalisation to be realised, individuals needed to take far greater responsibility for their physical and financial well-being, their employment prospects and role within society. Gordon Brown, for one, was quite clear on this: 'This old and misguided view of the state, irrelevant for a global economy, was accompanied by a failure to place sufficient emphasis on personal responsibility.'[68] Situating New Labour's welfare strategy within this new strategic context of globalisation, Brown believed that for its benefits to be realised, this should be done 'by asserting the responsibility of the individual'.[69] This meant that although the Blair government remained committed to giving 'people the chance to get off benefit and into work',[70] a 'new social contract' was necessary; one based upon 'the citizen sharing responsibility with the state'.[71] 'The government can't do it for the people', Blair argued, 'we have to do it together.'[72]

The imperative of 'competitiveness' was also integral to New Labour's welfare strategies and this particular discourse of globalisation. For Britain to remain competitive within the global economy, it was vitally important that labour markets were made more flexible; that individuals acquired the right skills, and public services reflected the demands of this global economy. In his role as the minister of state for employment and welfare reform, Stephen Timms remarked that 'developing Britain's skills base [was] key for competing in the global economy'.[73] To this end, New Labour's welfare strategy was primed to 'make work pay', and to equip individuals with the skills required to participate and to compete in an increasingly competitive, global labour market. Under New Labour, welfare was to act not as a 'hammock' but rather as a 'springboard' into this labour market. It was therefore up to the individual to respond to the challenges and seize the opportunities presented by globalisation.

It is at this point that New Labour's three discourses of globalisation merge and link up with one another. While the first two discourses emphasised the inevitability of globalisation, and the need for the government – in the light of these inexorable pressures – to design and implement policies that accommodated the demands of global capitalism, the third discourse compelled the *individual* to take responsibility for his or her integration into the global economy. Although the underlying message of constraint remained the same throughout, the nuance of each of these discourses reflected the complex and the contingent strategic selectivity with which these discourses were articulated.

Despite the handbrake of constraint that globalisation was understood to place upon government policy, strikingly, not one official viewed globalisation as 'a bad thing'. Of course, it may be argued that given the extent to which globalisation was viewed as being an irreversible and inevitable 'fact of life', any such antagonism would have been understood to be futile anyway. Perhaps the most surprising aspect of New Labour's understanding of globalisation, however – even more so in the light of the observations made in this chapter – was the sense of *opportunity* that it offered, but only *if the right policies were adopted*. Given the centrality of globalisation to New Labour's political economy, this created a clear split in the policy thinking of senior Party officials. Policies designed for domestic consumption and loaded with this discourse of 'constraint' were recycled for use overseas and framed using a discourse of 'opportunity'. No more clearly did this contradiction appear than in New Labour's international development policies. It is to the relationship between this particular discourse of globalisation and these policies that this chapter now turns its attention.

Framing international development in an age of globalisation

The new global politics of international development, upon which Gordon Brown embarked with such relish, appeared to stand in stark contrast with the language of 'constraint' and 'discipline' that he and other colleagues had invoked at home. Brown's personal mission to address and eliminate global poverty was predicated upon the opportunities and benefits of globalisation; a means to generate the wealth needed to eliminate want, squalor and disease in the developing world.

Yet these two different positions raise a paradox in our assessment of New Labour. Where do these two contrasting narratives of globalisation leave the transmission or 'internationalisation' of policy that both this book and indeed officials claimed was evident in New Labour's political economy? A detached reading of this paradox would appear to reveal an almost fatal flaw in the core argument put forward by this book of 'policy transmission'. If this claim *were* correct, then one would surely expect New Labour to have claimed that the pressures brought about by globalisation would be just as great, if not greater within the realm of international development. Indeed, British policymakers could quite plausibly have argued that the different structural factors understood to be at the root of global poverty were well beyond their control. Given the structural constraints inherent within the processes of international development, one would expect any internationalisation of policy to be framed within the language of 'constraint' rather than that of 'opportunity', and the subsequent formation of international development policies to be severely limited. That they were not is surely striking, and warrants further investigation as to why this was, or certainly appeared to be the case.

It is to the great credit of Gordon Brown and his ministerial colleagues that they chose not to shrink from the challenge of international development, but rather set about addressing matters of global poverty. However, this does raise three crucial questions, most notably concerning the transmission of these domestic policies overseas.

Firstly, where did the discourse of constraint that was so evident in New Labour's policy discourse at home disappear to when these same policies from the same model of political economy were exported abroad? Secondly, why, given the 'inevitable' constraints that it placed upon government and individual autonomy, did Brown and other New Labour officials view globalisation as an opportunity to eliminate world poverty? Thirdly, did New Labour *over*-emphasise the constraints that its senior figures spoke about at home? In order to answer these questions, I begin by exploring two areas. The first of these examines the discourse of globalisation that was present in New Labour's international development policies. Secondly, and perhaps more importantly, as in my analysis of the domestic context, I assess the *terms* upon which ministers appealed to the 'opportunity' that globalisation offered as a means of fulfilling New Labour's stated aim of eliminating world poverty.

As I have already remarked, the very public commitment of both the Blair and the Brown governments to eradicating global poverty was made clear by the succession of White Papers published by DFID between 1997 and 2009. Up until 1997, only two White Papers concerning overseas development – one in 1964 and another in 1975 – had been published, both by Labour governments. Under New Labour, four White Papers were published by DFID; each one committed to and set out under the banner of 'Eliminating World Poverty'. The first of these noted 'the increasing globalisation of the world economy in terms of trade and finance' and the challenge of creating 'a global society in which people everywhere are entitled to live in peace and security with their families and neighbours, and enjoy in full their civil and political rights'.[74] This was certainly a high-minded and ambitious aim. Yet in the light of the other assessments made by New Labour concerning the challenges presented by globalisation at home, it would suggest that, if they were truly committed to creating this global society, officials believed they had more by way of latitude in the international sphere than they did at home. The only challenge to New Labour in this respect was not globalisation itself, but how to make the most of the 'massive new wealth' that it was creating so as to extend DFID's commitment to social justice abroad.[75]

New Labour's secretary of state for international development, Clare Short, argued that 'the challenge before our generation is to ensure that wealth is used to lift up that fifth of humanity by establishing basic, decent standards for all. The wealth gives us an opportunity.'[76] The fastest rates of poverty reduction were to be found in East Asia where for the past thirty years there had been rapid economic growth. According to Short, this growth had occurred because inward investment had been attracted from multinational capital, which had brought with it knowledge and technology. Therefore, for Short the answer lay in harnessing that capital and technology and attracting investment to create opportunities to export and trade that would grow economies rapidly.[77]

DFID's first White Paper was supplemented three years later with the publication of its second, *Eliminating World Poverty: Making Globalisation Work for the Poor*. As well as reaffirming New Labour's commitment to the elimination of poverty and the achievement of the recently launched Millennium Development Goals, it laid out clearly New Labour's belief that:

> Managed wisely, the new wealth created by globalisation creates the opportunity to lift millions of the world's poorest people out of their poverty. Managed badly and it could lead to their further marginalisation and impoverishment. Neither outcome is pre-determined; it depends on the policy choices adopted by governments, international institutions, the private sector and civil society.[78]

Invoking the sentiment of New Labour's first discourse of globalisation, Gordon Brown was clear that there would be no 'retreat from globalisation'.[79] Crucially, however, government policy would not, as it appeared to be at home, be pre-determined by globalisation. Globalisation could, and indeed should instead be *managed*. As Clare Short would later argue, the purpose of this second White Paper was to:

> set out an agenda for managing globalisation, increased trade, investment and the new technologies in a way that could ensure that the abundance of wealth currently being generated brings benefits to the one in five of humanity who live in extreme poverty.[80]

Rejecting the fatalism that was a feature of New Labour's globalisation discourse at home, Short added: 'the future is not pre-determined; it is a matter of will and choice'.[81] Therefore although globalisation was viewed to be inevitable, its outcomes were not and New Labour's international development policy would be concerned principally with 'managing globalisation to ensure that poor people are able to share in its benefits'.[82] Clare Short argued that:

> properly managed, globalisation opens up possibilities we have never had before . . . creating conditions that make it possible for us to overcome deep-seated historical inequalities . . . in a way that can begin to heal the divisions inherited from colonialism and uneven development.[83]

This message of 'managing' globalisation was repeated across Whitehall and beyond. In the Treasury, Gordon Brown recognised that:

> globalisation can be for the people or against the people. Poorly managed, globalisation can create a vicious circle of poverty, widening inequality and increasing resentment. Managed wisely it can lift millions out of deprivation and become the high road to a more just and inclusive global economy.[84]

For the Chancellor, 'proper management' of globalisation required 'greater global co-operation not less, and . . . stronger, not weaker, international institutions'.[85] This assessment squared with Brown's proposals for a new global financial architecture (explored in Chapter 4); an international framework designed to deliver economic and social justice to those living in the developing world. Elsewhere, the secretary of state for trade and industry, Patricia Hewitt, stressed the importance of 'maximising the benefits of globalisation to deliver greater opportunity and prosperity for all'.[86] Again, it was understood that globalisation offered opportunity rather than constraint; a point elaborated upon by Peter Hain, the minister of state in the Foreign Office. He cited an address made to a Special Session of the United Nations by the minister for employment, welfare to work and equal opportunities, Tessa Jowell, in which she had emphasised 'the government's determination to ensure that the wealth and opportunities created by globalisation are used to reduce global poverty'.[87]

It is perhaps not surprising that having been instrumental in orientating the Labour Party towards the global economy, Tony Blair was similarly keen to extol the opportunities presented by globalisation. What is perhaps surprising, however, was the prime minister's view that the process of globalisation within the sphere of international development was – unlike at home – *not* inevitable. For Blair, the very *failure* of globalisation to reach much of the developing world had contributed to underdevelopment and continued poverty. In a series of speeches in the Far East, Blair expressed the view that there were no 'losers' or 'victims of globalisation', merely people who 'are not participating in globalisation'.[88] Offering two reasons for this lack of participation, Blair suggested that 'sometimes it is through their own choice. Sometimes, to our collective shame, it is through our own imposition.'[89] Blair repeated this claim a few days later: 'Those who are usually suggested to be losers in this are not actually the victims of globalisation. Their problem, on proper analysis, is that they are not participating in globalisation.'[90]

These assessments are striking since they emphasise a clear understanding amongst officials of the need to manage globalisation in the correct or 'proper' way. Although the actual benefits of globalisation were taken as a given, it was nevertheless crucial that policymakers adopted the 'right' policies. Both required carefully made decisions on the part of policymakers to ensure that the wealth and extension of social justice that globalisation promised were in fact realised. Blair's assessment in particular is interesting in this respect since it reinforces the self-fulfilment of the globalisation 'prophecy' that was present in New Labour's domestic discourses – particularly concerning the provision of welfare and, as Chapter 7 reveals, overseas aid as well. The opportunities promised by globalisation to both individuals and states could only be realised through the active participation of these self-same actors.

This brings us to a critical point made earlier in the chapter. What is at stake is not the material reality of globalisation but rather its *discourse*. Indeed, for Colin Hay and Matthew Watson, it is precisely this that drove political change within Britain under New Labour.[91] Globalisation is not something that has simply happened to Britain – or indeed, the rest of the world.[92] Rather, what appears as 'globalisation' is in fact the accumulation of a number of decisions made strategically by government ministers, who actually possess far more latitude to set policy than they might otherwise be prepared to admit.

Having re-established this agency, the lines of policy transmission between the domestic and the international begin to reappear and become a lot clearer. For globalisation to lift people out of destitution and end the vicious circle of poverty, developing countries had to adopt *the right set of policies*. The 'management' of globalisation, articulated by a number of New Labour ministers but emphasised in particular by Gordon Brown concerning matters of international development, in reality meant invoking the rhetoric of 'constraint' that appeared in New Labour's discourse at home. For New Labour officials, whether at home or abroad, globalisation remained, for all intents and purposes, 'a fact of life'. The opportunities it presented, however, could only be realised through the right mix of policies and increased participation and integration into the global economy. In an era of globalisation, New Labour understood the role of governments to be restricted to one of discretionary constraint; of orientating their national economies to meet the demands of the global economy. In resolving the paradox of 'challenge' and 'opportunity' evident in both the domestic and international dimensions of New Labour's political economy, 'opportunity' and 'constraint' appeared as two sides of the same coin. The 'opportunity' of globalisation could only be realised through the 'constraint' putatively imposed by globalisation upon policymakers.

This particular claim was reinforced by later remarks made by Tony Blair concerning the way in which globalisation was understood by officials and subsequently incorporated into policy strategies. This statement is particularly pertinent in light of the language of 'constraint' that appeared throughout New Labour's multiple discourses of globalisation:

> Occasionally we debate globalisation as if it were something imposed by governments or business on unwilling people. Wrong. It is the individual decisions of millions of people that is creating and driving globalisation. Globalisation isn't something done to us. It is something we are, consciously or unconsciously doing to and for ourselves.[93]

Blair here is both right *and* wrong, reflecting somewhat New Labour's contradictory and therefore problematic view of globalisation. Globalisation is the direct result of political and social activity. It is a performative act in that it is 'something we are and do'. When (and of course, if) millions of individuals do this on a global scale, then this leads to something that might be termed 'globalisation'. There might be nothing new in this sense, but technological advances have made us perhaps more aware of the ways in which these processes occur. What Blair does not acknowledge, however, – nor indeed did any of his cabinet colleagues – is the role that the various discourses of globalisation, articulated by his government ministers, play in shaping policy, and how these very statements acted as both an opportunity and constraint upon political activity. In this sense, it is misleading to suggest that globalisation is not something that is imposed by governments upon unwilling people.

The conventional wisdom of globalisation became a self-fulfilling prophecy for New Labour's policymakers. Policies designed for consumption both at home and abroad internalised the logic of 'opportunity-through-constraint', and since it was the perceived effects of globalisation that framed policies, officials duly imposed globalisation upon their respective polities. Therefore, while Blair is surely right to argue that 'it is the individual decisions of millions of people that is creating and driving globalisation', it is also the decisions of policymakers, pursuing a similar path, which perpetuate the effects – real or otherwise – of globalisation. Of Blair's own policymakers, none was keener to preach the virtues of globalisation than Gordon Brown.

Conclusions

Although articulated by almost all his senior colleagues, for Gordon Brown, the discourse of globalisation was central to his thinking concerning the political economy of New Labour. Questions over the way in which Britain's economy should be managed, what type of relationship the government should have with business, and the way in which the welfare state should be configured were just a handful of those that animated Brown in the light of the pressures that this 'new global economy' now placed upon policymakers. These would be particularly significant questions since their answers, certainly insofar as Gordon Brown was concerned, would shape how New Labour would respond to the very real challenges of poverty in the global South.

As the architect-in-chief of New Labour's political economy, and a politician personally imbued with a passion for social justice both at home and abroad, Brown took it upon himself to frame and offer credible answers to these questions. Here, carefully configured policies designed for domestic consumption were transported into the international realm to underpin the commitment of New Labour – and Brown in particular – to overseas development. Globalisation was writ large in each of these policies; providing the strategic context upon which policy choices were selected, and determining the parameters of the politically possible. Strikingly, however, these parameters were far from fixed, and globalisation was invoked by Brown and his ministerial colleagues in a number of different ways in an attempt to capture both the constraints that it was believed to impose upon policy, and the opportunities that it presented for improving social and economic outcomes.

As a discourse, globalisation was constructed in three different ways at home. Treated unquestioningly as an inevitable part of economic and social life, for senior New Labour officials, globalisation imposed a constraint upon policymakers and disciplined individuals alike. Yet abroad, within the realm of international development, the discourse of globalisation appeared to provide the altogether more positive rationale for New Labour's intervention within the developing world. Here, globalisation could be 'a force for good', and for Brown, as we shall see in later chapters, it was key to lifting millions out of poverty and delivering the global justice that was long overdue.

This appeared to present something of an inconsistency in New Labour thinking. How could globalisation be articulated as a constraint upon political agency at home, whilst being viewed as an opportunity within its international development policies abroad? This tension will become apparent over the following chapters, but closer inspection of New Labour's understanding of globalisation would suggest that 'constraint' and 'opportunity' were, in fact, two sides of the same coin; 'opportunity' could only be realised through careful management of the 'constraint' that globalisation was assumed to impose upon national governments in their policy choices. Even within the realm of international development, 'constraint' tempered the 'opportunity' that globalisation was supposed to deliver for those living in poverty. This had very real effects in that while Gordon Brown and his fellow officials spoke of the opportunity presented by globalisation to eliminate world poverty, it was deemed necessary to accept the constraints imposed by the 'conventional wisdom' of neoliberal globalisation, promoted within mainstream development circles.

This logic would be evident in each of Gordon Brown's policy interventions in the sphere of international development. Here, Brown strategically selected a set of policies that not only conceded the inevitability of globalisation but also accepted the necessity of these constraints for both state and citizen alike. While Brown claimed that this was necessary to take advantage of the economic prosperity promised by globalisation, the reality of this was somewhat different.

The political economy of Brown's strategic selectivity meant that his policies prioritised the preferences of those actors and institutions that were performing globalisation: the Washington-based institutions of global governance, and Western creditors, banks and transnational firms. While Brown's policies would all find favour with these actors, it was the operations and activities of these self-same actors that had contributed to and compounded the chronic underdevelopment and poverty experienced by many states in the global South. As we shall see in the following chapter, while this would not prevent Brown from orientating Britain within this global landscape, it would nevertheless undermine his mission to offer a radical solution to the poverty experienced by billions across the globe.

Notes

1. Hall and Jacques, *New Times*, 1989.
2. Hay and Rosamond, 'Globalisation, European integration and the discursive construction of economic imperatives', 2002, p. 148.
3. Fielding, *The Labour Party*, 2003, p. 150.
4. Smith, 'Tony Blair', 2007, p. 420.
5. Kenny and Smith, '(Mis)understanding Blair', 1997, p. 226.
6. Thompson, *Political Economy and the Labour Party*, 2006, p. 250.
7. Blair, *The Third Way*, 1998, p. 8.
8. Blair, speech delivered at the French National Assembly, 1998.
9. Blair, 'Doctrine of the International Community', 1999.
10. Blair, speech delivered at the annual CBI conference, 2001.
11. Blair, speech delivered in Tokyo, 2003.
12. Blair, speech on the economy delivered at Goldman Sachs, 2004.
13. Blair, 'Global Alliance for Global Values', 2006.

14. Short, 'Global Free Trade', 1997.

15. Cook, 'Britain in the World', 2000.

16. Darling, 'Our Economic Approach', 1998.

17. McIntosh, 'Globalisation', 2000.

18. Hoon, 'Foreign Affairs and Defence', 2001.

19. Hain, 'Business of the House', 2003.

20. Clarke, 'Identity Cards Bill', 2005.

21. Wicks, 'Steel Industry', 2007.

22. Alexander, 'Global Poverty', 2007.

23. Brown, 'Steering a Course for Stability', 1998.

24. Brown, speech delivered at the annual CBI conference, 1998.

25. Brown, speech delivered at the Smith Institute, 1999.

26. Brown, speech delivered at the TUC Congress, 2000, emphasis added.

27. Watson and Hay, 'The discourse of globalisation and the logic of no alternative', 2003.

28. Brown, 'Rediscovering Public Purpose in the Global Economy', 1998.

29. Ibid.

30. HM Treasury, *Building Long-Term Prosperity for All*, 2000, p. 115.

31. Lewis, 'The Treasury and the City', 2005, emphasis added; Balls, speech delivered at the Commonwealth, Middle East and North Africa Business Forum, 2006; Ainsworth, 'Departments: Lisbon Agenda', 2007; Darling, 'Maintaining Stability in a Global Economy', 2008.

32. Brown, speech delivered at the Royal United Services Institute, 2006.

33. Jessop, *State Theory*, 1990, pp. 9–10ff.

34. Cerny, 'Paradoxes of the competition state', 1997, p. 256.

35. Watson and Hay, 'The discourse of globalisation and the logic of no alternative', 2003, p. 292.

36. Labour Party, *Britain: Forward Not Back*, 2005, p. 18, emphasis added.

37. Mandelson, 'Post Office', 1998.

38. Blair, 'Doctrine of the International Community', 1999.

39. Ibid.

40. Blair, 'Helping People through Change', 2001.

41. Brown, speech delivered at the annual British Chambers of Commerce conference, 2003.

42. Ibid.

43. Brown, speech delivered at the Global Borrowers and Investors Forum, 2003.

44. Blair, 'The Modernisation of the Civil Service', 2004.

45. Ibid.
46. Friedman, *The World Is Flat*, 2005.
47. Browne, speech delivered at the British-American Business Council, 2005.
48. Driver and Martell, *New Labour*, 2006, p. 49.
49. Hay, *The Political Economy of New Labour*, 1999, p. 11.
50. Finlayson, *Making Sense of New Labour*, 2003, p. 118.
51. Darling, speech delivered at the CBI annual dinner, 2008.
52. Hay and Rosamond, 'Globalisation, European integration and the discursive construction of economic imperatives', 2002, p. 154.
53. Balls, 'Open macroeconomics in an open economy', 1998.
54. King, 'The Inflation Target 5 Years on', 1997.
55. Balls, 'Open macroeconomics in an open economy', 1998, p. 122, emphasis added.
56. Galbraith, *The Affluent Society*, [1958] 1999, p. 6.
57. Ibid. p. 9.
58. Krugman, 'Dutch tulips and emerging markets', 1995, p. 36.
59. Hay, 'Negotiating international constraints', 2001, p. 270.
60. Brown, speech delivered at the annual CBI conference, 1998.
61. Ibid.
62. Ibid.
63. Ibid.
64. Balls, 'Open macroeconomics in an open economy', 1998, p. 117.
65. Byers, 'Trade and Industry and Social Security', 1999.
66. O'Brien, 'Globalisation', 2004.
67. Darling, 'Maintaining Stability in a Global Economy', 2008.
68. Brown, James Meade Memorial Lecture, 2000.
69. Ibid.
70. Blair, speech delivered on welfare reform, 2002.
71. Blair, speech on the economy delivered at Goldman Sachs, 2004.
72. Ibid.
73. Timms, speech delivered at the South East England Development Agency Regional Employment Skills Summit, 2008.
74. DFID, *A Challenge for the 21st Century*, 1997, pp. 9–10.
75. Short, 'World Trade Organization', 1999.
76. Ibid.
77. Ibid.
78. DFID, *Making Globalisation Work for the Poor*, 2000, p. 15.
79. Brown, 'Globalisation', 2001.
80. Short, 'Globalisation White Paper', 2001.
81. Ibid.
82. Short, 'Can Africa Halve Poverty by 2015?', 2002.
83. Ibid.

84. Brown, 'Globalisation', 2001.
85. Ibid.
86. Hewitt, 'World Bank', 1999.
87. Hain, 'Social Summit: Geneva', 2000.
88. Blair, speech delivered in Tokyo, 2003.
89. Ibid.
90. Blair, speech delivered at the British Chamber of Commerce, Hong Kong, 2003.
91. Hay and Watson, 'Labour's economic policy', 1999, p. 155.
92. Coffey and Thornley, *Globalization and Varieties of Capitalism*, 2009, p. 25.
93. Blair, speech delivered at the Lord Mayor's Banquet, 2005.

3   Capitalising upon Globalisation

Faced with the both the opportunities and challenges of globalisation, Gordon Brown deemed it necessary to create what he would term a 'new economic architecture': a set of arrangements that would enable Britain to withstand the pressures and experience the benefits of this new global economy. This carefully calibrated model of political economy would provide Brown with the framework that he hoped would deliver a sustained assault on Britain's continuing economic underperformance and widening social inequality. This, however, was not simply a British model of political economy. Its blueprint would enable Brown to embark upon his personal crusade to address the matter of global poverty too, and the Chancellor set about establishing a clear line of transmission between the two previously separate spheres of domestic and international policymaking.

The focus of this chapter is upon those three central areas of domestic policy that Gordon Brown attempted to export into the realm of international development: (1) macroeconomic policy, (2) business, and (3) welfare. For Brown, these core areas of domestic policy were animated and driven by the strategic context of globalisation (mapped out in the previous chapter) and reconfigured accordingly. Crucially, however, for Brown, these policies could no longer be thought of in simply the domestic or national sense. Globalisation had resulted in a blurring between 'the domestic' and 'the international', necessitating the same type of 'global thinking' applied to one sphere as to the other. In this respect, globalisation provided Gordon Brown with a golden opportunity not simply to concern himself with matters at home (as important as these were to the Chancellor), but also to fulfil a personal desire to address issues concerning global poverty, debt and disease. This chapter therefore explores the hand of Brown in the design of these policies as they appeared in the British context, and highlights those themes and

motifs that would reappear in New Labour's international development policies examined in much greater detail later in this book.

The chapter unfolds as follows, tracing these three areas of policy in which Gordon Brown's influence was most clear. The first
of these concerns Brown's commitment to 'open, long-term economic policymaking' and its adherence to a set of clearly defined
rules and codes. Here, the Chancellor worked alongside his longstanding political ally and economic adviser, Ed Balls, to design
a model of political economy that prioritised the economic stability and market credibility that, the pair argued, was crucial to
deliver the growth and continued investment in Britain's economy.
Both this chapter and the next reveal just how pivotal Balls was in
partnering Brown in both the design and implementation of New
Labour's political economy. Indeed, Ed Balls's own influence was
writ large upon many of the key decisions taken by the Chancellor,
and through Balls, Brown was able to reach out to and convince
the City of London and other key financial actors as to the probity
and credibility of his policies.

Continuing the theme of credibility that dominated Gordon
Brown's approach to economic policymaking, the second area of
policy explores New Labour's relationship with business, and its
bid to dislodge the Conservatives' longstanding position as '*the*
party of business'. Partly to distance itself from 'old' Labour and
partly, again, to orientate itself as a party fit for office in an era of
globalisation, officials talked up New Labour's business credentials
so as to secure the credibility craved by Brown and his colleagues
in the Treasury. This second section traces the extent to which New
Labour, and Brown in particular, championed the virtues of business. Both as Chancellor and prime minister, Brown frequently
attempted to square Labour's traditional commitment to social justice with economic growth, efficiency and competitiveness. More
often than not however, these market imperatives were pursued at
the expense of the former. No more clearly did this occur than in
the government's relationship with the UK pharmaceutical industry.
While this partnership undoubtedly demonstrated New Labour's
embrace of the 'knowledge economy' and awareness of international shifts in drug research and innovation, it did – as Chapter 6
reveals – also create a series of tensions concerning the altogether
more urgent need for Brown and his colleagues to address the AIDS
crisis engulfing large parts of the global South.

The third area of policy explored in this chapter concerns welfare, and in particular, Gordon Brown's (new) 'New Deal'. At a rhetorical level, this was Brown's own personal homage to Franklin D. Roosevelt, one of the great liberal leaders whose achievements Brown would himself seek to emulate in office. In terms of the actual content of these policies however, Brown's 'New Deal' was a strategically selected response to a specific reading of globalisation. In order to address the challenges and make the most of the opportunities created by globalisation, welfare was to become a 'springboard' from which individuals could (re-) enter the labour market and obtain the necessary skills and training. This reworking of welfare however meant tweaking Labour's traditional emphasis upon equality, and focusing instead upon 'inclusion' and 'opportunity'. Central to these new values was a contract between the state and the citizen; one furnished with 'rights and responsibilities'. While the citizen, of course, retained the right to claim welfare from the state, the citizen could only do so if it met certain responsibilities. This allowed the state to act 'virtuously' whilst at the same time disciplining the citizen into working with the grain of globalisation so as to be able to take up the opportunities afforded by it. Crucially, as I shall show in Chapter 7, this thinking would undergird Brown's own 'global New Deal', the centrepiece of which would be his own International Finance Facility (IFF).

Creating a new economic and financial architecture at home: New Labour's management of the UK economy

As we saw in Chapter 2, globalisation did not simply provide a backdrop against which the New Labour project would unfold. Its spectre would have very material effects in terms of the way in which the political economy of New Labour would be primed. For Gordon Brown, the machine-minder and architect-in-chief of New Labour, globalisation would require a qualitatively new approach to economic management both in the UK and, as we shall see in the following chapter, abroad as well. Accepting the inevitability of globalisation, many of Brown's colleagues took a rather pessimistic view of the challenges that would confront Britain in an era of increased capital mobility, and cross-border flows of finance and labour. Gordon Brown, however, viewed globalisation in much more positive terms, frequently arguing for the opportunities that it presented for wealth creation and interdependency. For Brown, however, to seize these opportunities it was necessary to put in place the right institutional arrangements – a 'new economic architecture', one that would work with the grain of globalisation and secure its benefits. Working closely with his chief economic adviser, Ed Balls, the Chancellor therefore set about reorganising the way in which the British economy was managed.

'Working with the Grain of Globalisation': Locking in Macroeconomic Stability to Ensure Market Credibility

With globalisation providing the strategic context of Gordon Brown's political economy, 'stability' was a constant watchword throughout his chancellorship. Of course, the financial crisis meant that Brown's own premiership was racked with chronic economic *instability*, but for New Labour, and Gordon Brown in particular, stability was deemed crucial if Britain was to meet the challenges of globalisation.[1] As Ben Clift and Jim Tomlinson have remarked, there was a perception amongst policymakers 'of the inherent instability of a capitalist economy, and especially its inability unaided to deliver a full use of resources'.[2] This much was clear from New Labour's Janus-faced understanding of globalisation as both a 'challenge' and 'opportunity'. For all the opportunity and wealth that the global economy promised, it was by no means guaranteed to deliver. Furthermore, the increased interdependency that it brought about meant that the global economy was now, by its very nature, inherently and increasingly unstable. As Gordon Brown himself noted, 'however successful we aim to be at avoiding crises, we should recognise that shocks *will* occur'.[3]

These were understood to be the inexorable consequences of globalisation; consequences that national governments could only 'work with' and seek to ameliorate.[4] However, since it was neither possible nor desirable to retreat from these global processes, in order to mitigate the damage caused by this volatility, it became critically important to 'create an economic framework that would bring stability to the British economy and . . . promote investment, productivity and growth'.[5] Despite the challenges of globalisation, as Gordon Brown explained, there was a clear political and economic pay-off for implementing such a framework: 'Governments which . . . are judged by the markets to be pursuing, sound monetary and fiscal policies, can attract inflows of investment capital more quickly, in greater volume and at a lower cost than even ten years ago.'[6] Britain – or any other country for that matter – would only attract this capital, however, if the right economic architecture was in place. For Brown, 'over the long-term, investors will choose to invest for the future in a stable environment rather than an unstable one'.[7] For Ed Balls, this new framework would serve as the 'essential prerequisite for stability, economic growth and prosperity in a globalised world',[8] and underpin the credibility that the Treasury sought in order to encourage the continued flow of international investment into Britain. Put simply, the prosperity of a nation would depend on its ability to work *with* the grain of globalisation, and for the government to put in place a credible policy framework as a means of capturing its wealth and minimising its instability.

This stability, for Brown's colleagues in the Treasury at least, would consist of low and stable inflation and sound public finances. This 'monetary and fiscal stability', Brown added, was 'a necessary pre-condition for national economic success. In a global economy, funds will flow to those countries whose policies inspire confidence.'[9] Conversely, if governments got their policies wrong, then 'investors [would] punish mistakes more quickly and more severely than in the past'.[10] These perceived realities meant that development and poverty reduction could only be achieved through increased investment and economic growth.

As Balls had previously argued, however, stability was only a means to an end. The aim of the government's macroeconomic strategy 'was not simply to ensure low and stable inflation and sound public finances, but to deliver high levels of growth and employment by ensuring economic and employment opportunities for all'.[11] Delivering these three objectives would depend upon three pillars of policy, each one reinforcing the other. While the first of these pillars – long-term macroeconomic stability– would be necessary for investment, the second – a strong economy – was also necessary to embed this stability. However, the strength of this economy would only be sustained if it could generate both jobs and rising incomes.[12] As Gordon Brown made clear, however, stability was to be the essential precondition upon which everything else would rest.[13]

This stability could only be achieved 'through *constrained discretion*'.[14] Rejecting out of hand the fixed targets set previously by national governments, Balls called for instead a discretionary, counter-inflationary macroeconomic policy that could 'respond flexibly to different economic shocks – constrained, of course, by the need to meet the low inflation objective or target over time'.[15] This 'constrained discretion' was designed to appeal to market constituencies, as Colin Hay explains:

> Given a (belief in the) short-term trade-off between inflation on the one hand and unemployment and/or growth on the other, governments would seek to engineer a 'political business cycle', over-inflating the economy in the run-up to an election in order to reap the short-term electoral benefits of growth with little consideration to the longer-term consequences . . . In practice, governments could not be trusted to stick to any inflation target they had set for themselves. For it was rational for them to renege on any such bargain.[16]

As Ed Balls would later freely admit, 'an incoming government might declare that it wanted to achieve low inflation, but this government's incentive would always be to cheat and dash for growth, knowing that the resulting recession would only come along later'.[17] New Labour was acutely aware of the mistrust that market investors had of governments. Economic mismanagement was widely blamed for Labour's loss of power in 1979, while thirteen years later, the Conservative government suffered an irretrievable collapse of support after sterling's ignominious exit from the European Exchange Rate Mechanism.[18] The 'private discretion' exercised by government ministers in these two instances had precipitated a loss in confidence amongst markets. With investors left in the dark as to the real intentions of governments, the credibility of national policymakers was fatally undermined.

In response to these fears, 'credibility' became the touchstone of Brown's new architecture with 'constrained discretion' central in his efforts to reassure market actors. For the Chancellor, this 'constrained discretion' would be made credible through three stages: firstly, the alignment of policymakers' incentives with long-term objectives; secondly, the devolution of operational responsibility for decision-making to front-line agents (rather than politicians); and thirdly, increased transparency and the provision of clear, precise and publicly stated objectives, and the regular reporting of agents' performance against their objectives.[19] These three principles, Balls argued, would make private discretion more difficult and more costly to pursue. Taking monetary policy out of the hands of self-interested politicians, this new approach to policymaking would have at its centre processes that would be *long term*, *open*, *transparent* and *locked in*. These processes would form the basis of Gordon Brown's 'new architecture', a model of political economy that could be operationalised both at home and abroad:

> These principles, which stress the importance of open macroeconomic policymaking, apply to any small or medium-sized open economy. Indeed, this is why the UK was at the forefront in proposing that the International Monetary Fund draw up codes of good practice on openness and transparency covering several aspects of economic and social policy.[20]

Reiterating the purpose and the appeal of the political economy of this new architecture, the chief secretary to the Treasury (and future Chancellor of the Exchequer under Brown's own premiership), Alistair Darling, noted that 'stability will of course depend, to a large extent, on markets having confidence in the commitment of government to prudent and sound management of the economy'.[21] Brown stated that:

> If governments are judged to be pursuing sound long-term policies, then they will also be trusted to do what is essential – to respond flexibly to the unexpected economic events that inevitably arise in an increasingly integrated but more volatile global economy. Therefore, in the era of global capital markets, it is only within a credible framework that governments will command the trust they need to exercise the flexibility they require.[22]

For Ed Balls, even in a world of rapidly mobile capital, governments could retain policy credibility and maintain constrained policy discretion if they dealt with problems swiftly and reflexively, and if they pursued – and were seen to be pursuing – sustainable monetary and fiscal policies over the long term.

As Balls went on to suggest, however, while this would be a step in the right direction, certainly in terms of providing predictability to market investors, governments suffered from a time-lag, whereby new administrations were faced with the problem of 'proving' their competence and credibility. Clearly, within a post-monetarist framework, fixed policy rules were out of the question, so how might a new government – particularly one with a historical commitment to 'tax and spend' social democracy – assure market acta that it had changed its spots and that its qualitatively 'new' economic intentions were genuine? The solution put forward by Balls to solve this particular conundrum was 'credibility through maximum transparency'.[23]

According to Balls, market failure frequently occurred because investors lacked perfect information. If investors had complete information, then they could make better decisions concerning the market. Again, as Darling would go on to add, it was therefore important that economic policy was 'open and transparent' since 'openness builds confidence and credibility'.[24] In order to make the decision-making processes of government more accountable, it was deemed necessary by the Treasury to introduce a number of measures. *The Code of Fiscal Stability*, the publication of minutes of meetings held by the Monetary Policy Committee (MPC) together with the *Long-Term Public Finances Report*, were all noted by Alistair Darling during his time as Chancellor of the Exchequer as 'examples of increased transparency' that served to support the pursuit of macroeconomic stability and the Treasury's appeal for credibility amongst its core economic constituencies.[25]

However, while these were positive ways in which the problem of asymmetric information could be solved, they only went so far. For Balls, the answer was to put in place institutional mechanisms that would demonstrate *clearly* the government's intention to do the right thing; to make 'a strategic *pre-commitment*'.[26] Locking in the government's economic strategy would make it virtually impossible to sacrifice the long-term plan in favour of short-term electoral convenience. This thinking underpinned the decision to grant operational independence to the Bank of England. This move, and its wider implications for New Labour's political economy, is discussed in greater detail in the following chapter. In essence, however, it charged the newly set-up MPC with the independent responsibility of setting an interest rate baseline that it judged would enable the government's inflation target to be met. According to Balls, this transfer of power would have 'a decisive impact on both the international reputation of the government and on the wider credibility of Treasury', and send the message to the markets that this was a government 'not looking for short-termist quick fixes or to duck difficult decisions'.[27] In one swift move, there was an authenticity to the Treasury's claim of credibility amongst its key economic constituencies.

This was an economic framework designed explicitly by Gordon Brown to 'make Britain the best competitive environment for businesses in the world'.[28] Indeed, as Brown had argued, one of the reasons why many of Britain's rivals had enjoyed far higher levels of investment was because they had been able to deliver greater levels of economic stability.[29] This platform of stability would 'make Britain better equipped to face the new challenges of globalisation, with more competition, more business creation, more investment and a more skilled workforce'.[30] According to Nicholas Macpherson, the permanent secretary to the Treasury, this new approach to policymaking would 'underpin the UK's increased stability compared to other decades and other large economies'; and enable it to 'perform the role of "strategic friend" to the UK economy'.[31]

This 'strategic friendship' – illustrated in the following section concerning New Labour's relationship with business – was deemed by officials from across Whitehall to be essential in the light of globalisation. For Philip Arestis and Malcolm Sawyer, however, this 'new economic architecture', and its orientation towards securing increased business investment, signalled New Labour's intent to prioritise profits over wages.[32] Despite a clear need for investment, this would nevertheless preclude any commitment to fairness. Certainly insofar as Gordon Brown was concerned – given his own social democratic claims – one might have expected him to ensure that the gains of this investment accrued to the British people rather than the multinational enterprises.

This shift in emphasis reveals a further anomaly with even wider implications in the light of New Labour's welfare strategy discussed later in this chapter. As again Arestis and Sawyer have remarked, there was little reason to think that inward investment would create jobs in areas of high unemployment.[33] Targeting firms rather than people would do little to encourage local entrepreneurial activity, and paradoxically, was more likely to result in the *continuation* of a dependency culture that, as we shall see, Gordon Brown in particular was keen to eradicate. Understood in an altogether more global context, the pursuit of a similar type of investment in order to achieve growth was unlikely to succeed in areas that already suffered from high levels of poverty and under-development. Before exploring the further domestic and international implications of this framework, however, this chapter turns its attention to those rules, standards and codes that Brown introduced as a means of reinforcing this credibility amongst market constituencies.

Playing by – and Sticking to – the Rules of the Game: The Importance of 'Standards and Codes' in the Political Economy of HM Treasury

With this new architecture in place, Gordon Brown's commitment to credibility through a series of institutional 'lock-ins' was underpinned by a series of rules, standards and codes. This section explores specifically those rules that would appear in the 'new international economic architecture' discussed in Chapter 5, and those strategies that were evident in Britain's overseas aid commitment under New Labour, explored in Chapter 7. The pledges made by the Blair and Brown governments here to increase the amount of overseas aid and roll out immunisation programmes across the developing world would be predicated upon the same 'prudent' rule of 'borrowing only to invest' that the Treasury promised to stick to at home. This section concludes by drawing out two further policy measures that appeared in New Labour's domestic political economy: PFIs and PPPs. Linking in with the fiscal rules set out by the Treasury, these were mechanisms also evident in New Labour's commitment to increase aid, and latterly vaccines in the developing world, through the International Finance Facility (IFF).

Under the direction of Brown and Balls, Treasury officials had already outlined their commitment to credibility and transparency in the context of monetary policy. However, these measures were just as important when it came to setting fiscal policy, and it was in this context that the government deemed it necessary to introduce the Code of Fiscal Stability.[34] This code was designed to address past weaknesses in the fiscal policy framework by strengthening the openness, transparency and accountability of fiscal policy; features which of course mirrored the Treasury's monetary policy framework.[35] Reasserting the 'critical importance' that Brown and his colleagues in the Treasury placed upon stability, it was crucial that the conduct of fiscal policy matched that of monetary policy.[36] Ed Balls, together with Gus O'Donnell, argued that the code would provide 'valuable discipline on fiscal policy' and help 'rebuild trust in economic policy more generally';[37] trust that would be further enhanced with the alignment of the Treasury's own Code (Box 3.1), with the IMF Code of Good Practices on Fiscal Transparency (Box 3.2).

Box 3.1 The Treasury's Code for Fiscal Stability. (Source: HM Treasury, *The Code for Fiscal Stability*, London: HM Treasury, 1998, pp. 3–4.)

(1) Conduct fiscal and debt management policy in accordance with a set of specific principles

(2) State explicitly its fiscal policy objectives and operating rules, and justify any changes to them

(3) Operate debt management policy to achieve a specific primary objective

(4) Disclose, and quantify where possible, all decisions and circumstances which may have a material impact on the economic and fiscal outlook

(5) Ensure that best-practice accounting methods are used to construct the public accounts

(6) Publish a Pre-Budget Report to encourage debate on the proposals under consideration for the Budget

(7) Publish a Financial Statement and Budget Report to discuss the key Budget decisions and the short-term economic and fiscal outlook

(8) Publish an Economic and Fiscal Strategy Report outlining the government's long-term goals, strategy for the future, and how it is progressing in meeting its fiscal policy objectives

(9) Publish a specific range of information from its economic and fiscal projections, including estimates of the cyclically-adjusted fiscal position

(10) Invite the National Audit Office to audit changes in the key assumptions and conventions underpinning the fiscal projections

(11) Produce a Debt Management Report outlining the government's debt management plans

(12) Refer all reports issued under the Code to the House of Commons Treasury Select Committee

(13) Ensure that the public have full access to the reports issued under the Code

---

Box 3.2 The IMF Code of Good Practices on Fiscal Transparency. (Source: IMF, 'Code of Good Practices on Fiscal Transparency (2007)', <http://www.imf.org/external/np/pp/2007/eng/051507c.pdf>, last accessed 12 March 2012.)

(1) **Clarity of roles and responsibilities**
1.1 The government sector should be distinguished from the rest of the public sector and from the rest of the economy, and policy and management roles within the public sector should be clear and publicly disclosed
1.2 There should be a clear and open, legal, regulatory, and administrative framework for fiscal management

(2) **Open budget process**
2.1 Budget preparation should follow an established timetable and be guided by well-defined macroeconomic and fiscal policy objectives
2.2 There should be clear procedures for budget execution, monitoring, and reporting

(3) **Public availability of information**
3.1 The public should be provided with comprehensive information on past, current, and projected fiscal activity and on major fiscal risks
3.2 Fiscal information should be presented in a way that facilitates policy analysis and promotes accountability
3.3 A commitment should be made to the timely publication of fiscal information

(4) **Assurances of integrity**
4.1 Fiscal data should meet accepted data quality standards
4.2 Fiscal activities should be subject to effective internal oversight and safeguards
4.3 Fiscal information should be externally scrutinised

Although revised in 2007, the IMF's code retained the original four pillars of fiscal transparency that underpinned the 1998 code,[38] which the Treasury sought to assimilate into its own Code for Fiscal Stability. Policy consistency with the international institution whose very remit was to maintain global macroeconomic stability would seal New Labour's own credibility, and the integrity of its monetary and fiscal policies in the eyes of global market investors. It would ensure that actors were provided with the information they required to make 'correct' investment decisions, thereby squaring its commitment to stability with the principles of 'transparency', responsibility', 'fairness' and 'efficiency' that informed the conduct of its fiscal management.[39]

Gordon Brown operationalised the Code for Fiscal Stability through two rules governing public expenditure and borrowing. These rules, the Treasury argued, would 'deliver sound public finances and in doing so, assist greatly in restoring the credibility of fiscal policy':[40]

1. *The golden rule*: Over the economic cycle, the government will borrow only to invest and not to fund current expenditure.
2. *The sustainable investment rule*: Public debt as a proportion of national income will be held over the economic cycle at a stable and prudent level.

Although New Labour's monetary policy framework appeared to be reinforced by an equally rigorous fiscal regime,[41] neither of these rules actually restricted the capacity of the government to borrow to fund current investments.[42] This gave Brown considerable latitude, over the course of the economic cycle, to move the goalposts as he saw fit to ensure that these rules would be met. In keeping with the spirit of New Labour's monetary policy framework, what really was at stake was Brown's pursuit of credibility. These rules institutionalised and controlled government borrowing in a prudent (and therefore credible) fashion, in an attempt to reassure markets that the government would not run up an unsustainable level of debt.

Gordon Brown's 'golden rule' was justified on two grounds. Firstly, it distinguished between current and capital spending. According to Alan Budd, where governments had failed to do this in the past, the latter had often been sacrificed in an attempt to control public borrowing.[43] The second justification for the 'golden rule' was that it contributed to inter-generational equity. Current spending, the Treasury argued, would be paid for by those who would benefit directly from it, while the cost of capital spending would be spread over the lifetime of the assets.[44] There was a clear political appeal to this strategy as it enabled New Labour to present itself as 'a government of modernisation'; one that was both generous in its level of public investment and committed to improving Britain's social infrastructure. However, with the initial cost borne by private contractors, it also enabled the New Labour government to disassociate itself from the profligacy of 'old' Labour with what appeared to be, at least, a healthy balance sheet.

For John Grieve Smith, however, this second rule concerning the public-debt-to-GDP ratio was 'quite inappropriate in varying and unpredictable circumstances';[45] an observation quite striking in the light of the inherently unstable conditions that, as this chapter has already noted, Brown was determined to eradicate. Citing the work of the economist, Christopher Dow, who noted the lack of any correlation between the level of national debt and the economic performance of a country,[46] Grieve Smith argued that Brown's Treasury made 'a serious mistake' in applying rigid arithmetical rules to an area of policy where – even by the Treasury's own admission – greater flexibility is often required to mitigate against shocks and recessionary pressures that emerge from the global economy.[47]

Concerned by ballooning levels of government expenditure and debt, the Treasury used these rules to justify and increase the use PFIs and PPPs in order to fund New Labour's modernisation of the public sector. Such methods, however, had not always been popular amongst senior party officials. When the Major government launched the first PFI in 1992, it was denounced by Labour as 'privatisation by another name, the thin end of a commercial wedge that could only, over time, corrode the communal ethos of public service provision by commodifying the services provided'.[48] No more clearly was this being seen than in the National Health Service (NHS), where Labour warned of a 'creeping privatisation' that threatened to undermine the provision of public health in favour of private market interests.[49]

As Eric Shaw has suggested, however, Labour's initial hostility was soon replaced with 'the zeal of a convert',[50] and in its 1997 General Election manifesto, the party promised to 'overcome the problems that have plagued the PFI'.[51] True to its word, the Blair government rechristened the PFI, 'PPP', and between 1997 and 2004, New Labour signed off just over 600 such deals.[52] The government argued that these revised public-private arrangements would bring much- needed investment, skills and expertise to public sector provision.

Despite Labour's U-turn over the use of private finance, criticism of these PFIs and PPPs still remained. Increased private sector involvement locked public agencies into procuring private sector supplies; distorted clinical priorities; and diverted resources from frontline services,[53] while stories emerged of procurement processes heaping pressure on both private consortia and NHS trusts to depress the terms and conditions experienced by support staff.[54] These problems were compounded by a clear conflict in interest in the management of these consortia and their wider commercial instincts. Not only were many consortia seeking a voice in major management issues, a large number were using public health facilities to sell to patients insurance policies, long-term care and other health services.[55] Doubts were raised too as to the cost-efficiency of this type of finance. According to John Grieve Smith, for instance, a number of these PPPs put public investment in a 'double-jeopardy', imposing higher costs upon these public projects with less efficient management structures.[56]

These concerns, however, were simply sacrificed at the altar of the Treasury's fiscal rules. The money raised by PFIs in support of these PPPs allowed the two rules to square with one another. As well as keeping debt 'at a stable and prudent level', the PFIs and PPPs also allowed the Treasury's 'golden rule' to be met by increasing public expenditure over the life of a project, whilst also leading to an underestimation of current public liabilities.[57] In effect, these PFIs turned any item that would previously have been accounted for as capital expenditure by the government into current expenditure. The building of a new hospital, for example, using conventional government finance would have been accounted for as a capital cost incurred in the present, followed by interest payments on the borrowing. Under the terms of a PFI, however, the hospital would be financed by the private sector, and leased back to the government with only the leasing charges appearing as current expenditure. As a report by the Institute for Fiscal Studies suggested, in the absence of the PFI, the public sector would have had to fund the building itself, leading to higher debt if this was financed through borrowing.[58] Crucially, while the use of the PFI should make little difference to the 'golden rule', the reduction in public sector net debt makes the sustainable investment rule easier to meet.[59]

In strictly accounting terms then, these PFIs appeared to work – and for New Labour, this was all that mattered. In spite of the criticism levelled at these privately funded arrangements, they offered a pragmatic means of delivering much-needed levels of investment into Britain's social infrastructure in a manner that did not over-burden the public purse. Supporting the Treasury's fiscal rules, these borrowing initiatives linked directly into New Labour's 'new economic architecture'. As I demonstrate in Chapters 5 and 7 respectively, distinct aspects of this new blueprint would form the basis of Gordon Brown's own commitment to increase the amount of debt relief and aid to the developing world. As this section has shown, however, in domestic terms at least, this was a model of political economy based upon monetary and fiscal stability, designed explicitly to meet and accommodate the priorities of the government's core market constituencies.

Mirroring the emphasis that institutions such as the IMF placed upon stability, openness and transparency, this was a framework designed by Gordon Brown to maintain credibility amongst global investors and institutions of international finance. I will return to a number of these themes in the following chapter when I explore the institutionalisation of this new architecture, but it is in the two case study chapters mentioned above that I will assess the effects that the 'internationalisation' of this new architecture had upon New Labour's commitment to debt relief and overseas aid respectively. Since this architecture was so clearly geared towards meeting the expectations of market audiences at home, this would suggest that any direct transmission of policy abroad would similarly prioritise these economic actors over the most vulnerable individuals living in the world's poorest countries.

New Labour as 'the new party of business': securing knowledge and competitiveness in a global economy

International development relies on commerce to create the wealth and the jobs that will end poverty. That's why business is good for development and development is good for business.
The DFID policy paper, Business for Development[60]

Both prior to and throughout its time in office, New Labour sought to position itself as 'the new party of business', principally at home, but also abroad where it afforded business a key role in the fight against global poverty. The purpose of this section is to explore not simply New Labour's claim in this respect, but crucially the effects of such a claim upon the character of New Labour's political economy. For David Osler, if there was one theme that dominated Labour's politics under Blair and Brown, then it was the increased accommodation of business and the private sector.[61] New Labour's relationship with business would not merely offer opportunities for consultation, but grant special access for industry representatives to input directly into the policy process, both at home and, as I demonstrate in Chapter 6, abroad as well.

This section attempts to offer an explanation of New Labour's relationship with business and the effect that it had upon the government's domestic political economy. To frame these effects empirically, I explore New Labour's relationship with arguably the most powerful of these business constituencies, the pharmaceutical industry. Its centrality to the 'new' or 'knowledge economy' that the Blair and Brown government were keen to support gave the industry considerable leverage in dictating New Labour policy. Perhaps no more clearly was this leverage evident than in the relationship that I explore in Chapter 6 between the New Labour government and the pharmaceutical industry, and the attempts of the former to increase the availability of the antiretroviral treatments needed to fight HIV and AIDS in the developing world.

The Importance of Business to the New Labour Project

> The partnership we have tried to build with you over these past four years is one I am deeply committed to. It is a founding principle of New Labour and it will not change.
> *Tony Blair addressing the Confederation of British Industry*[62]

Throughout his time in office, the prime minister remained true to his word. As Eric Shaw has remarked, 'the Blair government, from its inception, demonstrated . . . a willingness to be attentive and obliging towards business needs'.[63] New Labour's relationship with business is frequently embodied in the premiership of Tony Blair – even forming the basis of a critically acclaimed film of the former prime minister, *The Killing$ of Tony Blair*. Yet even after Blair had left Downing Street, and Gordon Brown had moved into Number 10, this pledge continued. Announcing the remit of the newly formed Department for Business, Enterprise and Regulatory Reform in 2007,[64] its secretary of state, John Hutton, promised to give 'a strong voice for business at the heart of government' that would help British businesses become 'a powerful force for competitiveness and wealth creation in our country'.[65] Fêting business leaders as 'the wealth creators . . . the entrepreneurs . . . the innovators . . . the people who make a difference', Hutton applauded the activities that they carried out, which he argued 'contributed to the success of Britain'.[66] For the Brown government, there was 'nothing we can achieve as a nation without the dynamism and wealth that is created by business'.[67]

Of course, the Labour Party had not always had such a warm relationship with business. Yet, during its own period of reform – starting under Neil Kinnock and culminating with Blair – Labour moved from being a political party that once held firmly to the view that the state should play a leading role in the workings of a nation's economy to one that believed that little could be achieved without the active support of business.[68] In an era of globalisation, there was an obvious reason for this, as Stephen Gill and David Law have noted:

> Governments have to be concerned with the cultivation of an appropriate 'business climate', or else investment might be postponed . . . An elected socialist party with a radical programme would therefore be constrained in its policy choices by the nature of its 'business climate', because it would need tax revenue and/or loans to finance its ambitious spending plans.[69]

The welfare of society was therefore understood to depend upon a flourishing private sector, and, as such, there could or should be no antagonism between the private interests of business and the public good.[70] These statements capture not simply the key difference between New Labour and its predecessors but crucially the main reason *why* New Labour chose to position itself as a party that was so openly 'pro-market and pro-business'.[71] This section explores firstly how such a shift took place before interrogating the reasons behind such a shift. Chapter 6 discusses the effects of such a strategy within the sphere of international development.

New Labour's relationship with business was also crucial to Gordon Brown's pursuit of 'credibility'. Just as Brown sought credibility with financial markets, so too was securing the support of business central to New Labour's strategy prior to government, and the ongoing delivery of its policy commitments once elected. According to Leo Panitch and Colin Leys, the aim for officials was to win at least two successive elections, not just the next one, so that long-term policies, such as education and training policies, would have time to bear fruit.[72] To achieve this aim, it was believed that New Labour must win acceptance by 'business' as a suitable, and if possible a preferred, governing party, so that investment would be forthcoming to support the growth upon which everything else – namely, its social programmes – depends.[73]

As with the credibility of its wider macroeconomic reforms, New Labour officials appeared pessimistic as to the prospects of social democracy, should any strategy be chosen that was not met with the support of business constituencies. In order to acquire and retain this support, New Labour believed that it must prove its economic credentials. In practice this meant demonstrating extreme caution and sensitivity to the demands of business, and indeed, exercising discretionary constraint when formulating policy. Writing in the lead-up to New Labour's General Election victory in 1997, Will Hutton noted how 'the dominant discourse of political debate still prohibits the advocacy of public spending and higher taxes, however modest [whilst] the organisation of company law . . . is portrayed as "corporatist"'.[74] Despite an overwhelming rejection of the Conservative Party by the electorate, small 'c' conservative economic philosophy remained in the ascendancy. For Panitch and Leys, this was apparent in the very acute fear amongst officials of an adverse market reaction 'to almost any measure that might be represented as limiting market freedoms'.[75] As Colin Crouch has observed, 'nothing that might displease the neoliberal business community, especially the financial community, could be risked'.[76]

Obviating this fear meant recalibrating Labour's political economy, and recasting the 'means' and 'ends' associated with the ideology of 'old' Labour. This, according to Blair, was 'renewed social democracy'.[77] For Noel Thompson, however, this meant that any 'policies guided, and institutions informed, by the principles of equity, fraternity and justice' were 'seen as threatening growth, efficiency, profitability and thence national economic performance'.[78] In an era of increased globalisation, these 'old' values and ideals were simply unaffordable and unsustainable. They limited entrepreneurial freedom, jeopardised labour flexibility and created economic uncertainty. In their place, a new economic discourse emerged, one articulated in the language of individual choice and self-fulfilment; dynamism, entrepreneurialism and wealth creation; efficiency, competition, productivity and profitability. Bound up within the context of the market economy, these would become signifiers of New Labour's political economy, one designed to chime with the expectations of business constituencies.

This clearly appeared problematic for a senior figure such as Gordon Brown who maintained a commitment to a social democratic agenda of fairness, justice and opportunity. Strikingly, however, Brown seemed determined to reconcile economic efficiency with social justice. Underpinned and strengthened by institutional reform of the Treasury, these themes were frequently invoked in the annual budgets and spending announcements made by the Chancellor. Aiming to square these virtues, Brown spoke of 'building', 'investing in' and 'working for' a 'stronger and *fairer* Britain';[79] of 'building a Britain of economic strength and *social justice*';[80] and delivering '*fairness*' and '*opportunity* for all'.[81]

For Steve Buckler and David Dolowitz, what unified these claims was the central idea of *justice as fairness*, a term that systematically replaced *equality*, in New Labour's rhetoric.[82] Putting aside for one moment the apparent jettisoning of 'equality' from the New Labour lexicon, the unity of this approach is significant because it enabled the Treasury to claim in its economic policy pronouncements that the least well-off benefit in the long term from social arrangements in a manner consistent with market liberty.[83] As Simon Glaze has remarked, according to Brown, any provision of 'fairness' was contingent upon such a commitment to markets, competition and enterprise.[84] Benevolent interventions prompted by the Chancellor's moral sense, such as Child Trust

Funds, SureStart and the 'New Deal' initiatives were facilitated by New Labour's commitment to economic stability, low corporation tax and labour flexibility.[85] Put simply, greater economic efficiency through market liberalisation meant increased social justice. The concomitant 'socialisation' of New Labour's economic policy *and* the 'marketisation' of New Labour's social policy would enable the government to deliver on its dual and ostensibly socially democratic objectives concerning growth *and* fairness.

This would appear to signal, at the very least, a reformulation of social democracy under conditions of increased globalisation. For Richard Heffernan, however, quite how genuine New Labour's 'social democracy' was – and indeed that of Gordon Brown – remained a moot point. Although both Brown and New Labour were concerned, at a rhetorical level at least, with the promotion of social justice, the party was concerned principally with strengthening the power of capital and allowing competition within the market to secure social reforms. For Heffernan, Labour under Blair and Brown was, first and foremost, 'a party for and of business'. It was '"safe", "prudent" and "sensible" . . . a party of an ill-defined centre' – certainly not one that was radical and debatable even whether it remained on the Left.[86]

Evidence for Heffernan's claims emerges in a number of ways, and implicit in each was New Labour's overriding commitment to business, markets and capital. New Labour did not merely court or even engage with business, as one might expect any government to do, it was *wedded* to business. One needs only to glance through the pages of the Bibliography of this book to see where and to whom Gordon Brown delivered the majority of his speeches on a regular basis: the CBI, Mansion House, the Stock Exchanges in London and New York, business councils, chambers of commerce, economic forums and various other investment conferences. As Noel Thompson has remarked, 'it was not surprising, therefore, that on coming to power, it was leading entrepreneurs and City figures who were appointed to guide many of New Labour's policy reviews and policymaking committees'.[87]

This was a trend that continued during Brown's own premiership, as he sought to lead Britain's recovery from economic recession through a 'government of all the talents'.[88] Cabinet positions were filled by figures such as the former director-general of the

CBI, Digby Jones, and Paul Myners, who had made his name in the City as the chief executive of the pension fund manager Gartmore. Jones was appointed the minister of state for trade and investment, while Myners became financial secretary in the Treasury. Even international development did not escape such influence. Shriti Vadera, a former consultant at the investment bank UBS Warburg, was hand-picked by Brown to act as parliamentary under secretary of state at DFID. Tellingly, Vadera's previous work had included advising governments of developing countries, arranging debt relief and restructuring, and playing a prominent role in the partial privatisation of South African telecommunication firm Telekom. These appointments reflected a tacit understanding amongst senior New Labour officials that 'business knows best', and gave considerable weight to Charles Lindblom's observation concerning the perceived 'public value' of businesspeople to government officials.[89]

Of perhaps even greater significance was the *content* of the speeches that New Labour officials made to these business audiences. Despite a continued avowal of fairness and justice in the government's spending plans, these were themes that were downplayed in speeches made to business audiences. Officials used these opportunities instead to talk about the modern role of government in relation to business: 'the enabling state', cutting 'the red tape' and unleashing the creativity and entrepreneurialism of firms; increasing the skills of workers; and enabling firms to innovate and compete more effectively in the global economy. These speeches were clearly intended to reassure business that New Labour was speaking the same language, and that firms and business leaders had a unique position right at the decision-making heart of government. When one combines this rhetoric with the actual cuts that the Treasury made to the level of corporation tax; its efforts to maintain an economic environment attractive for inward investment; and the supply-side policies designed to increase labour flexibility, there was little doubt as to who New Labour saw as the primary beneficiaries of the improved economic performance it sought to deliver.[90]

Under the watchful eye of Gordon Brown, New Labour went beyond the rapprochement and co-operation with business interests to become simply a party of business.[91] Not only was this a hugely significant departure, it was deeply problematic, particularly in the global context in which New Labour located itself. As Michael Barratt Brown and Ken Coates have argued:

> today's transnational corporations suck profits out of employees stationed in every part of the world, and, if they are efficient in competition with their rivals, they will invest these profits in ways which will enrich them still further while diminishing or destroying the expectations of others.[92]

Such a stark assessment reveals the critical flaw in both New Labour's boast as *the* 'party of business' and its claim that 'business is good for development'. Undermining New Labour's commitment to social democracy, it also calls into question the way in which the government might respond to matters of global poverty.

Maintaining Global Competitiveness through the 'Knowledge Economy'

> Knowledge is the only source of competitive advantage . . . brainpower is more important than brawn; intelligence more powerful than energy; creativity more critical than raw materials; efficiency has to be combined with innovation.
> *Peter Mandelson addressing the Confederation of British Industry*[93]

Having begun to put in place the macro- and microeconomic framework deemed necessary for an era of increased globalisation, officials targeted Britain's own competitiveness as being 'the primary role' of the New Labour government.[94] In keeping with its commitment to the free market, this meant rejecting any notion of 'picking winners' or favouring certain industries over others,[95] but rather, in the words of Brown himself, making 'Britain the best competitive environment for business in the world'.[96] Competition was the driving force behind the Chancellor's linked reforms to boost enterprise and innovation,[97] and would dovetail with his bid elsewhere to secure 'credibility' in the eyes of financial investors both at home and abroad.[98]

In spite of this commitment to open competition, however, New Labour clearly did not want to be found guilty of backing 'losers'. This led officials to dismiss what it took to be the low-growth manufacturing sector.[99] British firms within this sector were simply unable to compete with the low-wage labour available elsewhere in the global economy. Here, as Steven Fielding goes on to remark, 'the global economy was deemed to have already spoken'.[100] This said as much about Labour's attitude to its past as it did its present. Historically, Labour had been recognised as the 'party of industry', with its core constituencies located in Britain's traditional mining and manufacturing heartlands. However, its transition to a 'party of business' would see New Labour embrace this 'new economy' and 'the competition state' with gusto.[101] The attendant imperatives of 'competitiveness', 'efficiency' and 'innovation' invoked by New Labour officials meant that very little was done to arrest the decline of firms in these 'old' industrial sectors.

In keeping with the claims of novelty applied to 'New' Labour, the Blair government set about instead placing Britain at the heart of the newly emerging 'knowledge economy'. As Alan Finlayson has noted, New Labour understood this new economy 'in a distinctly Schumpeterian way', one that laid to waste Britain's manufacturing base and instead was 'driven by creative, innovative and skilled individuals competing with each other for market advantage'.[102] Alongside Gordon Brown's 'new economic architecture', it would be this 'human capital' that would enable Britain to compete with other countries for investment from global economic enterprises. Together, this 'credible' macroeconomic framework and these supply-side reforms would enable Brown to meet his commitment to improve Britain's economic performance and adapt individuals to the exigencies of the global economy.

New Labour and the UK Pharmaceutical Industry

For Gordon Brown and New Labour to maintain both Britain's competitiveness in this changing global environment and its ability to attract foreign investment, then building partnerships with leading knowledge-based industries would be vital. For New Labour, globalisation and the 'knowledge economy' were inextricably linked. The secretary of state for trade and industry, Stephen Byers, viewed the 'knowledge economy' as being synonymous with the 'the changes taking place in markets across the globe'.[103] Indeed, for Tony Blair, if Britain was to navigate its way through this putatively new global economy, then this 'knowledge economy is our best route for success and prosperity'.[104] To this end, 'a successful pharmaceutical industry', Blair later argued, was 'a prime example of what is needed in a successful knowledge economy'.[105] Put simply, globalisation and Britain's international competitiveness provided the economic rationale for New Labour's partnership with the pharmaceutical industry.

Following a meeting in November 1999 between the prime minister and the CEOs of AstraZeneca, Glaxo Wellcome and SmithKline Beecham, the government heralded the pharmaceutical industry as the jewel in the crown of the British economy.[106] Yet its exalted place in New Labour's economic strategy was driven as much by fear as it was by admiration. This 'truly global' industry posed both an opportunity and a challenge to New Labour, not least because, as Blair realised, its firms had 'more choice than ever before when deciding where to place new investment'.[107] There appeared to be a genuine concern amongst officials that in an era of increased capital mobility, Britain's position as a leading site for the pharmaceutical industry could be in serious jeopardy. In a global economy where 'China's wage costs are 5 per cent of Britain's', the prime minister was for one deeply worried that the country could no longer compete on labour costs.[108] It was crucial therefore that Britain instead competed on those attributes essential in the emerging 'knowledge economy': intelligence, innovation and creativity.[109]

As well as prioritising these types of knowledge-based skills, it was deemed crucial by New Labour officials for Britain to retain the features that had made it an attractive location for investment in the past.[110] To achieve this, Blair argued that it would be necessary to establish an effective partnership at the highest levels between government and industry.[111] This arrangement was duly formalised through the Pharmaceutical Industry Competiveness Taskforce (PICTF). Set up to provide a forum for dialogue between business and government officials, the PICTF was designed to maintain and facilitate the ongoing competitiveness of the British pharmaceutical industry. New Labour's discourse of 'constraint' was writ large over the PICTF report, with government officials and industry representatives observing that:

> The conditions required for the industry to retain its competitive position are changing in the face of significant shifts in the global business environment. [The] rapid globalisation of markets, the ease of global

communications and the existence of an increasingly international and mobile pool of scientific and commercial talent mean that firms can serve more markets from fewer locations, while at the same time [having] greater choice than ever before about where to locate new investments.[112]

This argument was seized upon by the pharmaceutical industry. Giving evidence to the House of Commons Science and Technology Committee in 2004, representatives from AstraZeneca reminded MPs that 'as India and China develop their own pharmaceutical expertise, they will become very attractive locations for growth and investment compared with the UK and Europe'.[113] It therefore recommended 'that the UK acts to develop close links in science with these countries in order to provide us with greater access to their growing science base'.[114] For AstraZeneca, it was in the UK's best interests to continue to maintain the constraining logic of globalisation in order to secure future investment from the pharmaceutical industry.

The final report published by the Ministerial Industry Strategy Group (the new name for the PICTF) under Gordon Brown's premiership reflected the extent to which the economic expectations of firms continued to be accommodated by the New Labour government. It noted the perception by business leaders, across all sectors internationally, of the decline in UK labour regulations that Blair and Brown had overseen.[115] Although the US and Japan were perceived to have less obstructive market regulations, Britain continued to be seen as being more favourable to business than its biggest European rivals in Germany, France and Italy.[116] Noting how 'rates of taxation on company profits in different countries have a clear influence on international location decisions', the report provided some insight as to the thinking behind the Treasury's own fiscal policy.[117] From April 2008 (and throughout the rest of New Labour's time in office) the basic rate of corporation tax stood at 28 per cent. With only Switzerland, the Republic of Ireland and Singapore offering lower corporate tax rates, Britain's business-friendly tax regime and extensive provision of tax credits was designed to provide significant support for R&D activities carried out in the UK. In April 2008, R&D tax credits were raised from 150 to 175 per cent for small to medium-sized enterprises, and from 125 to 150 per cent for large companies.[118]

Despite a drop in the UK's share of global R&D expenditure from 10 per cent in 2000 to 9 per cent in 2007, Britain continued to see greater pharmaceutical industry R&D expenditure than any other country outside the US and Japan.[119]

In comparative terms, therefore, the UK remained 'a favoured site for research activity' with the productivity of UK pharmaceutical research considered to be 'good'.[120] For several years, UK-domiciled firms had produced around one-fifth of the world's leading seventy-five global medicines,[121] and continued to have more new medicines launched in each of the four major markets (the US, Germany, France and the UK) than any other country's companies apart from the US.[122] Under New Labour's watch, the UK continued 'to hold a strong position relative to most comparator countries, other than the US'.[123] Given the size and the dominance of the US pharmaceutical firms this was hardly surprising, but government officials would have been pleased to see the UK-based industry punch above its weight so effectively in international markets. Despite a difficult economic climate both at home and abroad, towards the end of its period in office, New Labour had managed to build up an attractive framework of conditions for the industry to invest and sustain its profitability.

New Labour's credentials as a 'party of business' were never in doubt. It frequently yielded to the demands of business, and although there was an intuitive appeal to this – after all, without the support of business, it was constantly reiterated that New Labour could not deliver on its 'social' commitments – the influence that business was able to exert went right to the heart of government. Indeed, there were times when the lines of division between government and business became extremely blurred, and the language of New Labour sounded more corporate than social democratic. This had very real effects for policy, none more so than when it involved the pharmaceutical industry. Domestically, pharmaceutical firms were afforded a unique place in New Labour's policymaking process, with their demands clearly accommodated in the government's strategy.

Abroad, however, New Labour was faced with a moral dilemma as to how to respond to a global health crisis that a lack of treatment provision by these pharmaceutical firms had only made worse. Chapter 6 assesses New Labour's response to this as a self-styled 'government of business' and its attempts to manage the economic expectations of an industry to deliver a policy outcome that would stand to benefit millions of the world's most vulnerable people.

A springboard not a hammock: 'rights and responsibilities' in New Labour's welfare policy

The third and final strand of New Labour's domestic political economy explored here concerns the employment and welfare strategies, again designed chiefly by Gordon Brown but articulated and implemented by a series of government ministers. The focus of this particular section is framed along the discourse of 'rights and responsibilities' that officials frequently talked about, both prior to and throughout New Labour's time in office. This dualism would underpin not only the take-up of welfare but also the provision of supply-side policy initiatives designed to encourage inclusion and participation in the labour market through increased skills and training. New Labour ministers were determined to end what they saw as the chronic welfare dependency that had built up in socially and economically deprived areas.

New Labour's welfare strategy was primed to 'make work pay', and to equip individuals with the skills required to participate and to compete in an increasingly competitive, global labour market. Under New Labour, welfare was to act not as a 'hammock' that it had become to this enclave of hardened, and now inter-generational benefit claimants, but rather as a 'springboard' into an increasingly global labour market. To this end, it was the responsibility of the individual to respond to the challenges and seize the opportunities of globalisation. For this goal of social and economic inclusion to be realised, however, and for this cycle of welfare dependency to be broken, it would be necessary to increase the opportunities available for individuals to participate in the labour market. The 'social investment state' would replace the old 'passive' entitlement state with a more contractual approach.[124] Senior officials made it clear that getting individuals off welfare and (back) into the workplace – what Norman Fairclough has termed the 'social integrationist discourse' – required a disciplinary framework.[125] The contractual discourse of 'rights and responsibilities' and of 'something for something', invoked through the threat of benefit sanctions and, ironically, further economic exclusion, would provide just that.

New Labour's domestic welfare strategy would go on to bear a striking resemblance to the government's commitment to increase overseas development aid (ODA) through the IFF mechanism explored in Chapter 7. The obvious contextual differences aside, New Labour officials treated welfare and overseas aid almost synonymously. Both were viewed as a *means* to an end, rather than an end in and of themselves, and both identified 'exclusion', or more specifically, exclusion from the global economy, as being the fundamental problem. As a result, New Labour emphasised the importance of increasing *opportunity* and *inclusion* as the means by which a greater sense of self-identity, financial independence and social mobility might be realised. However, for as much as these discourses emphasised positive values of self-fulfilment, both were framed in terms of an arrangement that would discipline and modify the behaviour of the recipient. In its analysis of the IFF, Chapter 7 draws out several of these parallels and assesses their implications for New Labour's aid commitment abroad.

It is this 'opportunity through increased inclusion' that opens this particular section, and which would underpin New Labour's welfare strategy. Yet it would also frame the contractual discourse of 'rights and responsibilities' that was rehearsed frequently by government ministers throughout New Labour's time in office. This will be discussed in the second part of this section. I take as my point of departure here, however, New Labour's changing commitment to the welfare state under conditions of globalisation. Despite its own historical achievements in establishing the NHS and the universal provision of social security, New Labour ministers believed that globalisation meant that the days of the state as a major provider of welfare were numbered. Of these officials, Gordon Brown was arguably the most influential in suggesting that welfare could no longer be delivered through traditional redistributive mechanisms but through the efforts of individuals. Under New Labour, the welfare state would have an altogether more 'virtuous' role; one of 'enablement', equipping subjects with the skills and the knowledge required to navigate the exigencies of the global economy.

Reconfiguring Equality: Achieving Social and Economic Inclusion through Increased Opportunity

Traditionally, 'old' Labour had prioritised full employment as the principle means by which its commitment to social justice could be achieved. Although this would continue to remain an aspiration of New Labour, it stopped short of enshrining this pledge in any historical sense.[126] Instead, Gordon Brown promised 'a new approach – employment opportunity for all – to face the challenges of today's dynamic labour market', which would create 'a modern definition of full employment for the 21st century'.[127] This restatement of 'full employment', cast in terms of 'opportunity', would be crucial for the delivery of New Labour's welfare strategy.

This redefinition of 'full employment' was a further attempt by Gordon Brown to demonstrate not simply his continued commitment to a credible form of social democracy but also his own overarching commitment to stability. In this respect, Brown's recalibration of 'full employment' actually put clear water between 'old' and New Labour. As Raymond Plant has remarked, the 'old' Keynesian techniques used by previous Labour governments to promote full employment were criticised as being inflationary and harmful to the prospects of business investment and growth that the current New Labour government was keen to promote.[128] In keeping with the Treasury's pursuit of credibility, Brown's redefinition of 'full employment' served to demonstrate the probity of New Labour's economic and welfare strategies, and reassure market constituencies that a Labour government would neither buckle under the demands of the welfare state nor be blown off course by inflationary pressures.

Linked in with this point, the emphasis upon 'opportunity' was also hugely significant because it served to reproduce the contours of *the* same strategic context of globalisation that Gordon Brown and his colleagues now believed they faced. As I remarked in the previous chapter, for all the challenging constraints that globalisation was understood to place upon governments and electorates alike, the global economy, along with its attendant processes, was also viewed as presenting a significant opportunity for wealth creation and increased standards of living. It was for this very reason that Brown and other ministers believed that governments should 'not retreat from globalisation', but actually 'work *with* the grain of globalisation' because of the economic benefits that it offered.

Of course, globalisation offered just the *possibility* of such benefits. In such an uncertain environment, these opportunities alone could not guarantee outcomes – let alone an equality of outcome. Nevertheless, it was deemed necessary for governments, operating under these conditions, to promote the potential opportunities offered by the global economy. Like a lottery, individuals – like countries – needed to be 'in it to win it'. This was certainly understood to be the case by Gordon Brown who argued that if the benefits of globalisation were to be realised, this should be done through 'inclusion' and, concomitantly, 'by asserting the responsibility of the individual'.[129]

The notion of 'opportunity' was understood by New Labour as an important means of contributing to the social and political environment in which the individual was located.[130] To achieve this, however, it was necessary for New Labour to place as much emphasis upon securing 'greater chances for those excluded from basic, minimum opportunities as on equalising opportunities'.[131] Here, the difference between 'old' Labour and New Labour was again stark. Whereas 'old' Labour's conception of equality was based on the assumption that 'capitalist societies by their nature create inequalities and conflicting interests', this was something that New Labour and its goal of increased social inclusion failed to acknowledge.[132] Therefore, rather than addressing the problem of inequality, tackling social exclusion was presented by the Treasury as a replacement for egalitarian concerns.[133]

Policies such as the 'New Deal', the National Childcare Strategy, individual learning accounts and baby bonds were all designed to promote social inclusion and enhance life chances, especially for the less well-off, to find work and to increase earning capacities.[134] Indeed, during his time as the education and employment secretary, David Blunkett argued that these forms of asset-based welfare could help deliver Labour's longstanding commitment to social mobility by helping children and their families make the most of the education system.[135]

Gordon Brown was, of course, instrumental in this commitment to social and economic inclusion, and the Treasury, under Brown's chancellorship, introduced a number of asset-based forms of welfare, such as the Child Trust Fund (CTF),[136] in order to encourage levels of saving and improve financial awareness.[137] Although officially launched in 2005, the idea had been circulating around the Treasury at the turn of the millennium.[138] The CTF was presented to the electorate as a welfare strategy based upon financial empowerment and independence. It was hoped that it would induce a behavioural change in the financial mindset of individuals towards one that encouraged economic and social development. If, as Rajiv Prabhakar has suggested, people were to have their way of thinking changed in this manner, then they were more likely to plan and invest in their future.[139] However, the work of Michael Sherraden is instructive here, for he argues that such a cognitive change does not come about by providing people simply with a flow of income.[140]

For Matthew Watson, these and other types of investment such as home ownership represented an attempt to turn people from passive recipients of welfare rights into active managers of assets.[141] Alan Finlayson argues that this transformation enabled asset-holders to become active, 'self-capitalising subjects . . . able reflexively to integrate themselves into a modernised economy'.[142] This newly acquired financial independence would enable individuals and their families to take greater responsibility for their own financial affairs, rely far less upon the state, and realise the opportunities that would foster greater inclusion in the new economy. What really lay at the heart of this strategy was the contractual 'something for something' approach that, according to the Treasury, undergirded these policies.[143] 'If you save', the Treasury promised, 'the government will reward you for your efforts.'[144] The opportunity that this form of 'independence for the long-term and intergenerational mobility' provided would only be available through a contractual arrangement between state and citizen.[145]

Beyond these monetary incentives, Gordon Brown also took steps to enhance Britain's skills base by introducing a series of supply-side reforms. Again, globalisation provided the strategic context for this. For Brown, 'in order to compete more effectively, an open and far more rapidly changing global trading economy, flexibility [and] the ability to respond quickly . . . is a necessary precondition of success'.[146] In order to make the most of the opportunities presented by globalisation, individuals needed to be flexible and willing to adapt. This in turn would secure skilled, well-paid employment. Early on in New Labour's time in office, Brown argued that 'the Britain that will succeed in the global economy will be the Britain that opens up the opportunity for employment and enterprise to all'.[147]

With 'emerging market countries ready to attract low value added, low investment and low skilled work', Brown warned that Britain now had 'to compete on ever higher levels of skill and technology rather than ever lower levels of poverty pay'.[148] To this end, the Chancellor promised to increase investment in further welfare reforms in order 'to give people, whether they are in work or out of work, the opportunity to get the skills necessary for them to succeed and for us to succeed in the new global economy'.[149] The justification for these reforms was rooted in Brown's belief that 'the way to respond to globalisation is to give people the skills and opportunities for the future'.[150] The state could only go so far. It would be up to the individual to take up these skills and make the most of the opportunities presented by globalisation. As Judi Atkins has remarked, what was striking about New Labour's commitment to education was not its intrinsic value or its potential to increase personal well-being but rather its potential for individuals to become active participants in the increasingly global job market.[151]

During Brown's premiership, his secretary of state for innovation, universities and skills, John Denham, proposed a raft of further changes to the benefits, skills and employment system to meet this very objective, again with the view of expanding Britain's skills base in light of the challenges and opportunities presented by globalisation. According to Denham, 'in an increasingly globalised and competitive world, we must use to the full the skills, talents and aspirations of all our people'. For Denham, 'the global changes threaten those who are least well equipped to respond. Those with low skills will find it harder to find work' and as a result, 'they and their families [will] struggle to share in the increasing prosperity of Britain'.[152]

A succession of government ministers echoed this sentiment. Brown's secretary of state for work and pensions, Peter Hain, spoke at length of the need to attach the provision of skills to welfare to enable individuals to participate in job markets, to become more flexible in their working practices, and to increase their skills.[153] These skills, Hain argued, would 'unlock the talents and skills of our people to equip them to compete in the globalised world'.[154] Another of Brown's most trusted lieutenants, Stephen Timms, as minister of state for employment and welfare reform, remarked that 'developing Britain's skills base [was] key for competing in the global economy'.[155] Again market logic trumped social concerns. If the UK as a nation was to retain or indeed increase its competitiveness within the global economy, and if individuals and their families were to reap the benefits of globalisation, then a broadened skills base would be integral to any welfare strategy.

Whether conceived as the Giddensian 'social investment state' or simply 'welfare-to-work', Gordon Brown's supply-side welfare reforms represented a clear departure from traditional social democratic thinking which, as Eric Shaw has remarked, had blamed structural factors and a lack of demand for labour. The 'old' welfare system had suffered from a weakening attachment to the labour market and had been further undermined by a lack of incentives to acquire skills or appropriate qualifications.[156] To overcome this problem, Gordon Brown oversaw a series of policies designed to increase the availability of educational and employment opportunities intended to promote human capital and enhance Britain's ability to compete in the global economy.[157] For a number of authors, this was further evidence of Adam Smith's influence upon Gordon Brown.[158] Like Smith, the Chancellor sought to identify the causes of the 'improvement in the productive powers of labour' that lay behind the contrast that Smith had observed between the 'miserably poor' nations on the one hand and those that were 'civilized and thriving' on the other.[159] This Smithian focus on the proportion of the population in employment and the productivity of their labour was central to the thinking of Gordon Brown not only at home but, as later chapters will show, abroad as well.

Disciplining Opportunity: 'Rights and Responsibilities' in New Labour's Welfare Conditionality

Central to New Labour's welfare strategy was Gordon Brown's 'New Deal', a series of initiatives designed to get more individuals into work and training. As Chapter 7 will show, the Chancellor would later export this strategy abroad through the 'global New

Deal', but at home his 'New Deal' programme was designed to improve the long-term job prospects of young people. Running alongside this flagship strategy, for those unable to work, Brown's Treasury announced a series of measures including £195 million to support disabled people, £190 million for lone parents, and the first ever national child care strategy.[160] This initial outlay in government spending was followed up with the introduction of the Minimum Wage and a series of tax credit schemes.

For each of these initiatives, however, there was a sting in the tail. This welfare programme did not come with a set of automatic rights or entitlements but rather a series of punitive conditions. In return for the money that the Treasury was prepared to spend on increasing benefits, it was expected that the recipient took on increased responsibilities and met their duties as citizens, as parents and as employees. Alistair Darling, for example, argued that it was 'reasonable that people of working age – lone parents, the unemployed and people claiming incapacity benefits – should be required to attend an interview to discuss their options for work'.[161] In 2002, Gordon Brown extended these measures through the introduction of the StepUp scheme, which obliged 'the long-term unemployed to accept a guaranteed job'.[162] This new programme, Brown announced, would be matched by 'mandatory work preparation courses for the long-term unemployed'. Those who were recurrently in and out of work would now come within the same 'rights and responsibilities' of the 'New Deal'. To ensure that work paid more than benefits, only to those who met these new obligations would the government offer new opportunities.[163]

There was no option of non-participation in these schemes.[164] If a job was turned down, then the claimant would incur a benefits sanction. Initially this took the form of a two-week benefit withdrawal but if the recipient continued to refuse further offers of employment, then this would result in repeated four-weekly withdrawals.[165] New Labour did not shy away from meting out these sanctions, disciplining young people with children, carers, those with disabilities and pregnant mothers.[166] Despite his own experiences growing up in a town scarred by unemployment, Gordon Brown reinforced the stigma of joblessness by boasting of his government's record of 'tightening up sanctions for the unemployed' and 'compelling young people into training and work' to an audience of business leaders and investors.[167] Rather than focusing upon the structural conditions that create unemployment, the Chancellor took aim at the individuals who found themselves out of work. Quite simply, for Brown, a life on benefits was not an option.[168]

Under Gordon Brown's watch, claimants were compelled into accepting responsibility for their own participation in the global economy. His skills minister, John Denham, announced that 'when people sign on for benefits, they should sign up for skills', promising to 'make it easier for those on benefits to gain new skills' and provide both 'the tailored support that people need in order to get into work' and the 'new opportunities for people to train'. However, 'with those rights come responsibilities', Denham warned, 'responsibilities to upskill and to work'.[169] For the minister for science and innovation, Malcolm Wicks, the opportunities of globalisation would only come to 'those willing to reach out to embrace them'.[170] Brown believed that although 'the prize for Britain is great',[171] there was still nevertheless 'a duty on the inactive to take up those opportunities'.[172] Again, placing this policy within the strategic context of globalisation, the prime minister differentiated between the 'old' economy, and the 'new, global economy'. 'In the old days', Brown argued, 'the obligation was on the unemployed to find a job.' 'In the new world', however, 'the obligation on the unemployed should be not just to seek work but to train for work.'[173] Cranking up the pressure upon the individual to participate within the global economy and seize its opportunities, Brown was adamant that opportunities, like rights, were no longer universal but contingent upon whether 'we choose to seize them', or whether we are willing to fulfil our responsibilities.[174]

Adopting a far more active approach to welfare, New Labour demonstrated its commitment to address social exclusion through employment and increased social and economic opportunity. However, it also signalled what even one government insider called 'the strongest ever attack on the workshy'.[175] New Labour's authoritarian attitude to joblessness echoed that of the former Conservative employment minister, Norman Tebbit, who believed that unemployment was due to people simply being unwilling to 'get on their bike'.[176] As secretary of state for education and employment, David Blunkett, maintained, 'jobs were there for the taking'.[177] Yet as John Grieve Smith has remarked, 'unemployment is primarily determined by the strength in demand for labour ... People in areas of high unemployment are not more reluctant to work than people elsewhere: they are victims of job shortage'.[178] This fundamental deficiency ran right through the heart of the 'New Deal' programme, and fatally undermined any social commitment that Brown might have claimed in respect of his reconfiguration of the welfare state.

Much can be read into Gordon Brown's use of the supply side as a welfare strategy to drive up skills and competitiveness. Mark Bevir argues that it represents a clear shift from Labour's traditional emphasis upon 'equality' to one of 'efficiency', and the way in which redistribution only took place when industrial competitiveness was not under threat.[179] Colin Hay agrees. Under New Labour, welfare expenditure was no longer justified principally in terms of its contribution to social justice but rather in terms of its contribution to *competitiveness*.[180] This is a crucial point for it suggests that while New Labour did not jettison completely 'social justice' from its political economy – both at home and abroad, it evidently remained committed to the spirit of this at least – it clearly believed that social justice could *only* be achieved within the context of an efficient and competitive market economy.

Gordon Brown's reordering of the welfare state, like the other areas of policy explored in this chapter, emerged as a result of the challenges that globalisation was understood to impose upon national governments. This prompted a reconceptualisation of Labour's traditional commitment to equality and social justice. A greater emphasis was placed upon social and economic 'inclusion' as opposed to 'equality', and increasing 'opportunity' was deemed to be far more effective in achieving this aim than redistributive means, such as 'tax and spend'. This approach, however, required far greater responsibility to be exercised on the part of the individual.

New Labour's approach to welfare was clearly based upon the third discourse of globalisation discussed in the previous chapter; a discourse that viewed globalisation as a constraint upon policy, but one that if appropriately managed, could present an opportunity, in this instance for greater economic and social integration. This, however, would entail a shift in responsibility away from the state and onto the individual, and fit neatly into the narrative of 'competitiveness' that New Labour deemed necessary in an era of globalisation. However, where this was talked about in terms of Britain's competitive advantage, it was inflected here for consumption at an individual level. To realise the government's commitment to global competitiveness, officials deemed it necessary to issue a coercive warning of 'no rights without responsibilities'. Participation in the job market would be mandatory. Those who could work should work, and those out of work should acquire skills and undertake training in order to equip themselves to meet the demands of the increasingly global labour market.

Chapter 7 explores the implications of such a strategy when exported abroad through New Labour's aid policies. Since globalisation was understood to present significant opportunities for wealth creation at an individual level, so too would there be a clear imperative for developing countries to participate fully within the global economy in order to benefit from these self-same processes. The case study examining the IFF analyses how New Labour, in its commitment to tackling poverty, would address this issue of 'inclusion', what 'responsibilities' it would demand of aid recipients, and how these would be orientated. Just as this section has demonstrated how responsibilities at home were geared towards 'the logic of no alternative' imposed by the market, Chapter 7 assesses how this contractual arrangement was pursued abroad.

Conclusions

Having considered in the previous chapter the assessment made by Gordon Brown and his colleagues of globalisation and the strategic context it provided for New Labour's political economy, this chapter turned its attention to those areas most affected by these changes in the global economy. It was in each of these areas that the influence of Gordon Brown was most evident, and it was Brown – principally as Chancellor but also as prime minister – who took it upon himself to ensure that Britain's economic and social frameworks were robust enough to not simply withstand the pressures of globalisation but capitalise upon the opportunities that it presented to the British people.

This thinking was evident in each of the subsequent three areas of New Labour's political economy explored throughout the course of this chapter. Placing considerable emphasis upon stability, openness and transparency, the macroeconomic architecture drawn up by Gordon Brown was designed to maintain credibility amongst investors and IFIs. As I will go on to demonstrate in the following chapter, the pillars of this framework would form the basis of the 'new global economic architecture' that Gordon Brown in particular was keen to promote abroad, and in doing so, underpin efforts towards increased levels of debt relief and more sustainable forms of financing for development explored in Chapter 6.

The second area of New Labour's political economy discussed in this chapter examined the party's rebranding as the 'government of business'. Again derived from New Labour's understanding of globalisation, Brown and his colleagues argued that if Britain was to compete successfully in the global economy, it needed a strong 'knowledge economy'. At the heart of this 'knowledge economy' was the pharmaceutical industry, dominated by a handful of powerful and potentially 'footloose' firms. Consequently, New Labour ministers afforded the industry a unique place within government in terms of setting domestic policy. Yet, as I shall show in Chapter 6, the closeness of this relationship at home would prove problematic when New Labour sought to engage with the industry over its commitment to tackling the so-called 'diseases of poverty' and in particular the provision of antiretroviral drugs in the developing world.

The third and final area of New Labour's domestic political economy addressed by this chapter concerned its welfare policies. Under New Labour, Britain's welfare state, along with the Labour Party's own, traditional conceptions of social justice, underwent a significant change, again largely as a result of the constraints that globalisation was understood to impose upon governments and electorates alike. These changes brought about a change in discourse and policy, with a focus upon 'opportunity' and 'inclusion' replacing traditionally Labourite values of 'redistribution' and 'equality'. Recipients of welfare were expected to take far greater responsibility of their lives in order to increase their employability in an increasingly global market. As I show in Chapter 7, where New Labour officials spoke of the opportunities of globalisation to developing countries, these new values of 'inclusion' and 'responsibility' would be transmitted abroad in Britain's aid programme.

These three areas of policy not only formed the basis of Gordon Brown's model of political economy at home but would, as the following chapters reveal, provide the blueprint for the Chancellor's interventions in the field of international development. Yet it would not be enough for Brown to simply roll out a 'British' model of international development. Brown's vision was far greater than that, and the new architecture that he had constructed at home had a much wider purpose. It was designed to be hard-wired into and ultimately reform the existing institutions of global governance based in Washington. The following chapter explores how Gordon Brown sought to align these institutional arrangements so as to enable there to be a clear path of policy transmission between the national and international levels of economic governance.

Notes

1. Labour Party, *New Labour*, 1997.
2. Clift and Tomlinson, 'Credible Keynesianism?', 2007, pp. 50, 51.
3. Brown, 'The conditions for high and stable growth and employment', 2001, p. 42, emphasis added.
4. Blair, 'New Britain in the Modern World', 1998.
5. Driver and Martell, *New Labour*, 2006, p. 69.
6. Brown, 'The conditions for high and stable growth and employment', 2001, p. 34.
7. Brown, speech delivered at the Lord Mayor's Banquet, 1997.
8. Balls, 'Preventing Financial Crises', 2003.
9. Brown, speech delivered at the News International Conference, 1998.
10. Ibid.
11. Balls, 'Key principles for policy making in an open economy', [1997] 2002, pp. 28–9.
12. Ibid. p. 29.
13. Brown, 'The Central Economic Objectives of the New Government', 1997; Brown, 'The conditions for high and stable growth and employment', 2001, p. 31.
14. Balls, 'Key principles for policy making in an open economy', [1997] 2002, p. 30, emphasis added.
15. Ibid. pp. 32–3.
16. Hay, 'Negotiating international constraints', 2001, p. 274.
17. Balls, 'Open macroeconomics in an open economy', 1998, p. 120.
18. Glyn and Wood, 'Economic policy under New Labour', 2001, pp. 50–1.
19. Lee, *Best for Britain?*, 2007, p. 79.

20. Balls, 'Key principles for policy making in an open economy', [1997] 2002, p. 28; see also IMF, 'Communiqué of the Interim Committee of the Board of Governors of the International Monetary Fund', 1997.
21. Darling, 'Our Economic Approach', 1998.
22. Brown 'The conditions for high and stable growth and employment', 2001, p. 34.
23. Balls, 'Key principles for policy making in an open economy', [1997] 2002, p. 38.
24. Darling, 'Our Economic Approach', 1998.
25. Darling, 'Maintaining Stability in a Global Economy', 2008.
26. Balls, 'Key principles for policy making in an open economy', [1997] 2002, p. 41, emphasis added.
27. Balls, 'Delivering Economic Stability', 2001.
28. Brown, speech delivered at the British-American Chamber of Commerce, 2000.
29. Brown, speech delivered at the Lord Mayor's Banquet, 1997.
30. Brown, 'Economy and Trade and Industry', 2002.
31. Macpherson, 'The Treasury', 2005.
32. Arestis and Sawyer, 'New Labour, new monetarism', 1998, p. 41.
33. Ibid. p. 41.
34. Balls and O'Donnell, *Reforming Britain's Economic and Financial Policy*, 2002, p. 136.
35. HM Treasury, *The Code for Fiscal Stability*, 1998, p. 3.
36. Ibid. p. 3.
37. Balls and O'Donnell, *Reforming Britain's Economic and Financial Policy*, 2002, p. 137.
38. IMF, 'IMF launches revised transparency Code and Manual', 2007.
39. HM Treasury, *The Code for Fiscal Stability*, 1998, pp. 4–5.
40. Balls and O'Donnell, *Reforming Britain's Economic and Financial Policy*, 2002, p. 155.
41. Coates, *Prolonged Labour*, 2005, p. 62.
42. Broadbent and Laughlin, 'The role of PFI in the UK government's modernisation agenda', 2005, p. 83.
43. Budd, 'Fiscal policy under Labour', 2010, p. 36.
44. Ibid. p. 36.
45. Grieve Smith, *There Is a Better Way*, 2001, p. 14.
46. Dow, *Major Recessions*, 1998.
47. Grieve Smith, *There Is a Better Way*, 2001, p. 15.
48. Coates, *Prolonged Labour*, 2005, p. 122.
49. Labour Party, 'Renewing the NHS', 1996, pp. 279–80.
50. Shaw, *Losing Labour's Soul?*, 2007, p. 82.
51. Labour Party, *New Labour*, 1997.

52. Driver, 'New Labour and social policy', 2008, p. 58.
53. Ibid. p. 58.
54. Ruane, 'Acts of distrust?', 2007, p. 75.
55. Leys, *Market Driven Politics*, 2003, pp. 200–1.
56. Grieve Smith, *There Is a Better Way*, 2001, p. 42.
57. Sawyer, 'Fiscal policy under New Labour', 2007, p. 889.
58. Emmerson et al., *The Government's Fiscal Rules*, 2002, p. 6.
59. Ibid. p. 6.
60. DFID, *Business for Development*, 2008, p. 1.
61. Osler, *Labour Party PLC*, 2002, p. 45.
62. Blair, speech delivered at the annual CBI conference, 2001.
63. Shaw, *Losing Labour's Soul?*, 2007, p. 192.
64. The creation of BERR was a result of the changes by Gordon Brown made to the machinery of government when he became leader of the Labour Party and prime minister in June 2007. BERR replaced the old Department of Trade and Industry (DTI).
65. Hutton, speech delivered at the CBI President's Dinner, 2007.
66. Ibid.
67. Ibid.
68. Falconer and McLaughlin, 'Public-private partnerships and the "New Labour" government in Britain', 2000, p. 122.
69. Gill and Law, 'Global hegemony and the structural power of capital', 1989, p. 481.
70. Shaw, *Losing Labour's Soul?*, 2007, p. 192.
71. Gamble and Kelly, 'New Labour's economics', 2001, p. 172.
72. Panitch and Leys, *The End of Parliamentary Socialism*, 2001, p. 242.
73. Ibid. p. 242.
74. Hutton, *The State to Come*, 1997, p. 105.
75. Panitch and Leys, *The End of Parliamentary Socialism*, 2001, p. 251.
76. Crouch, 'The terms of the neo-liberal consensus', 1997, p. 358.
77. Blair, speech delivered at the Civil Service Conference, 1998.
78. Thompson, *Political Economy and the Labour Party*, 2006, p. 252.
79. HM Treasury, *Prudent for a Purpose*, 2000b; HM Treasury, *Building a Stronger, Fairer Britain in an Uncertain World*, 2001; HM Treasury, *The Strength to Make Long-Term Decisions*, 2002; HM Treasury, *Steering a Steady Course*, 2002, emphasis added.
80. HM Treasury, *Building a Britain of Economic Strength and Social Justice*, 2003, emphasis added.
81. HM Treasury, *Opportunity for All*, 2004; HM Treasury, *Investing for Our Future*, 2005; HM Treasury, *Britain Meeting the Global Challenge*, 2005; HM Treasury, *Building Britain's Long-Term Future*, 2007, emphasis added.

82. Buckler and Dolowitz, 'Can fair be efficient?', 2004, p. 24, emphasis in original.
83. Ibid. p. 24.
84. Glaze, 'The Gordon Brown problem', 2008, p. 382.
85. Ibid. p. 383.
86. Heffernan, *New Labour and Thatcherism*, 2001, p. 73.
87. Thompson, *Political Economy and the Labour Party*, 2006, p. 274.
88. Number 10, 'Her Majesty's Government', 2007.
89. Lindblom, *Politics and Markets*, 1977, pp. 170–88.
90. Thompson, *Political Economy and the Labour Party*, 2006, p. 274.
91. Crouch, 'The parabola of working-class politics', 1999, p. 80.
92. Barratt Brown and Coates, *The Blair Revelation*, 1996, p. 32.
93. Mandelson, speech delivered at the annual conference of the CBI, 1998.
94. Fairclough, *New Labour, New Language?*, 2000, p. 29.
95. Blair, 'Doctrine of the International Community', 1999.
96. Brown, speech delivered at the British-American Chamber of Commerce, 2000.
97. Coates, *Prolonged Labour*, 2005, p. 70.
98. Hay, 'Credibility, competitiveness and the business cycle in "Third Way" political economy', 2004, p. 41; see also Hay, 'Negotiating international constraints', 2001.
99. Fielding, *The Labour Party*, 2003, p. 159.
100. Ibid. p. 160.
101. Cerny and Evans, 'Globalisation and public policy under New Labour', 2004.
102. Finlayson, 'Did Blair advance social democracy?', 2010, p. 13.
103. Byers, 'The Importance of the Knowledge Economy', 2000.
104. Blair, 'The Knowledge Economy: Access for All', 2000.
105. Blair, 'Foreword by the Prime Minister', 2001.
106. Department of Health, 'Pharmaceutical Industry Competitiveness Task Force', n.d.
107. Blair, 'Foreword by the Prime Minister', 2001.
108. Blair, 'Our Nation's Future – Science', 2006.
109. Ibid.
110. Blair, 'Foreword by the Prime Minister', 2001.
111. Ibid.
112. PICTF, *Pharmaceutical Industry Competitiveness Task Force*, 2001, p. 20.
113. AstraZeneca, 'Memorandum Appendix 54', 2004, p. 258.
114. Ibid. p. 258.
115. Department of Health (with the Association of the British Pharmaceutical Industry), *Pharmaceutical Industry*, 2009, pp. 5, 10.

116. Ibid. pp. 5, 10.
117. Ibid. pp. 5, 11.
118. Ibid. p. 5.
119. Ibid. pp. 6, 16.
120. Ibid. p. 7.
121. Ibid. pp. 7, 26.
122. Ibid. pp. 7, 27.
123. Ibid. p. 7.
124. On the 'social investment state', see Giddens, *The Third Way*, 1998, p. 117–18.
125. Fairclough, *New Labour, New Language?*, 2000, p. 57.
126. McKnight, 'Employment', 2005, p. 23.
127. HM Treasury, 'Employment Opportunity for All', 1997.
128. Plant, 'Political thought', 2004, p. 25.
129. Brown, James Meade Memorial Lecture, 2000.
130. Ellison and Ellison, 'Creating "opportunity for all"?', 2006.
131. Driver and Martell, *Blair's Britain*, 2002, p. 77.
132. Fairclough, *New Labour, New Language?*, 2000, p. 65.
133. Goes, 'The Third Way and the politics of community', 2004, p. 116.
134. Driver, 'North Atlantic drift', 2004, p. 32.
135. Blunkett, 'Enabling Government', 2000.
136. Under the Child Trust Fund scheme, vouchers were issued to parents of all children born after September 2002. Families earning less than £13,230 a year and eligible for the child tax credit would receive £500, while families with a larger income received £250. These vouchers could then be deposited in a special tax-free account, to which parents could add a maximum of £1,200 a year. The government pledged to top up these funds when the child reached the age of seven and then eleven. At the age of eighteen, the account would mature, and the child would be able to access this account and use the cash in whatever way they chose.
137. Hodge, 'Chancellor and Minister for Children launch Child Trust Fund', 2005.
138. HM Treasury, *Saving and Assets for All*, 2001.
139. Prabhakar, 'What is the future for asset-based welfare?', 2009, p. 52.
140. Sherraden, *Assets and the Poor*, 1992.
141. Watson, 'Constituting monetary conservatives via the "savings habit"', 2008, p. 301.
142. Finlayson, 'New Labour', 2008, p. 105.
143. HM Treasury, *Saving and Assets for All*, 2001, p. 2.
144. Ibid. p. 2.

145. Ibid. p. 12.
146. Brown, speech delivered at the Global Borrowers and Investors Forum, 2003.
147. Brown, 'Enterprise and Employment Opportunity for All', 2000.
148. Brown, speech delivered at the annual British Chambers of Commerce conference, 2003.
149. Brown, 'Pre-Budget Report', 2003.
150. Brown, 'Pre-Budget Report', 2006.
151. Atkins, *Justifying New Labour Policy*, 2011, p. 85.
152. Denham, 'Welfare and Skills', 2007.
153. Hain, 'Next Steps to Full Employment', 2007.
154. Ibid.
155. Timms, speech delivered at the South East England Development Agency Regional Employment Skills Summit, 2008.
156. Shaw, *Losing Labour's Soul?*, 2007, p. 44.
157. Atkins, 'Assessing the impact of the Third Way', 2011, p. 41.
158. For further accounts of Adam Smith's influence upon Gordon Brown, see Brown, 'State and market', 2003; Lee, 'Gordon Brown and the "British Way"', 2006; Glaze, 'The Gordon Brown problem', 2008; Watson, 'The split personality of prudence in the unfolding political economy of New Labour', 2008; Watson, 'Gordon Brown's misplaced Smithian appeal', 2009.
159. Smith, *The Wealth of Nations*, [1776] 1999, p. 105, cited in Cammack, 'The shape of capitalism to come', 2010, p. 264.
160. Darling, 'Welfare Reform', 1998.
161. Ibid.
162. Brown, 'Budget Statement', 2002.
163. Ibid.
164. Bochel and Defty, *Welfare Policy under New Labour*, 2007, p. 19.
165. Blundell et al., 'The impact of the New Deal for young people on the labour market', 2003.
166. King and Wickham-Jones, 'Bridging the Atlantic', 1999, p. 273.
167. Brown, speech delivered at the Global Borrowers and Investors Forum, 2003.
168. Fielding, *The Labour Party*, 2003, pp. 198–9.
169. Denham, 'Welfare and Skills', 2007.
170. Wicks, 'Department of Trade and Industry', 2007.
171. Brown, speech delivered at the annual CBI Scotland dinner, 2008.
172. Brown, speech delivered at the annual CBI conference, 2007.
173. Ibid.
174. Brown, speech delivered at the annual CBI Scotland dinner, 2008.
175. Lister, 'To RIO via the Third Way', 2000, p. 12.

176. Tebbit, speech delivered at the Conservative Party conference, 1981.
177. Blunkett, 'No hiding place for fraudsters', 2001.
178. Grieve Smith, *There Is a Better Way*, 2001, p. 55.
179. Bevir, 'New Labour', 2000, p. 290.
180. Hay, 'Credibility, competitiveness and the business cycle in "Third Way" political economy', 2004, p. 47, emphasis added.

4   Building a 'New Jerusalem'

Having established the domestic policies that were to be transmitted into the realm of international development, Gordon Brown set about putting in place the institutional arrangements that would be crucial to meet New Labour's commitment to eliminate world poverty. Despite its recent incarnation, Brown clearly felt that it was not enough for the Department for International Development (DFID) to simply roll out these policies. His vision was much bigger than that, and the Chancellor set about forging links with a number of key international financial institutions (IFIs) in order to build what Brown himself termed a 'new Jerusalem'. Invoking the biblical imagery found in the Book of Revelation, for Brown, this 'new Jerusalem' represented a 'new world', one free from poverty, debt and disease.

This 'new Jerusalem' was to be built upon the same 'building blocks of prosperity' that Gordon Brown had put in place in Britain; building blocks of stability and 'sound' policies that would, according to Brown, enable developed and developing nations alike to realise the opportunities of globalisation and deliver global prosperity for all. Embedding his vision into the orthodoxy of the 'post-Washington Consensus', Brown took his blueprint to a galaxy of international institutions of economic governance abroad. This would ensure that there was not only a clear transmission of policy but also a distinct *institutional* transmission from the domestic to global spheres of economic governance. This policy and institutional transmission between the domestic and international levels would lock in the Chancellor's 'new economic architecture' and provide the basis for the specific policies explored in the following three chapters.

This institutional transmission is striking for it represented a clear departure from the criticism expressed by 'old' Labour concerning the 'free-market' monetarist policies constituted in the original 'Washington Consensus' and pursued by the International Monetary Fund (IMF) and other IFIs.[1] As the party began the long road back to power at the start of the 1980s, Labour warned that these policies could 'inflict economic damage of such severity as to cause the destruction of democratic governments'.[2] Seeking radical reform of the institutional ideas and practices that kept countries locked in an unequal and unjust global economic system, the party called upon the IMF and World Bank to reverse their hugely damaging commitment to trade and financial market liberalisation.[3] According to Labour figures, such policies would leave the global economy in the unaccountable and avaricious hands of the multinationals, the currency and the commodity speculators, and the international financial institutions.[4]

As the decade wore on, the social and economic apocalypse predicted by Labour unfolded. With indebtedness, hunger and disease at catastrophic levels, dozens of economies across sub-Saharan Africa collapsed. By 1990, the continent's gross national product per capita stood at just US$440. Millions of Africans were left living on barely a dollar a day, the poorest of whom, in the least developed of these countries, were living on less than 60 cents a day.[5]

Many countries across the global South – not simply in Africa – saw their terms of trade slip to well below the levels that they were experiencing in 1980. For countries such as Cameroon, Congo, the Dominican Republic, Ecuador, Egypt, Gabon, Malawi, Peru, Trinidad and Tobago, and Uganda, these diminished by up to a third, while others, including Bolivia, Nigeria and Venezuela, saw their terms of trade almost halve.[6] Sluggish growth rates and hyperinflation were problems that afflicted large parts of South America throughout much of the decade. Bolivia, for instance, experienced a staggering 601.8 per cent annual rate of inflation, while Argentina and Brazil saw inflation increase at an annual rate of 298.7 and 166.3 per cent respectively during this same period. Other countries, both in Latin America and sub-Saharan Africa, suffered from particularly high levels of inflation, including Uganda (95.2 per cent), Nicaragua (86.6 per cent), Zaïre (53.5 per cent), Sierra Leone (50.0 per cent) and Ghana (48.3 per cent). Combined with their negative growth rates, each of these economies experienced chronic stagflation.[7] If they did not directly cause the human crises, such as famine, HIV and AIDS, and conflict that emerged during the 1980s, then these economic problems certainly exacerbated them, critically undermining any effective response to this lost decade of development.

Appalled by the scale and the severity of this crisis, Labour labelled the way in which Western creditors (including Britain) were handling this chronic underdevelopment, 'a travesty of economic justice'.[8] And for good reason. Heavily indebted countries in the global South were paying out more to Western banks and governments than they were receiving in new investment, while the cost of servicing these debts was taking money away from development projects, social welfare, food production and the finance needed to build the base for future economic growth. Furthermore, the monetarist, deflationary austerity measures, or Structural Adjustment Programmes (SAPs), imposed by the World Bank and IMF, were shifting the burden of debt directly onto the poor, cutting deep into wages, welfare benefits and food subsidies.[9]

Politically too, these SAPs undermined the autonomy of national governments, forcing them to implement highly prescriptive deregulatory policies in order to accommodate the market-orientated form of development promoted by Washington. Not only did these SAPs serve to discourage governments from seeking funds before budgetary deficits reached crisis level, these policies were fundamentally asymmetric in the demands that they placed upon indebted countries. Clearly, economic reform was indeed necessary for some countries to achieve sustainable levels of development – yet for many, these regressive policies served only to increase the poverty experienced by these countries. For its part, Labour promised not to withhold aid from countries unwilling or unable to meet the demands of the IMF. Instead, the party would 'provide additional aid to countries that refuse IMF austerity measures' and support those countries that would use the aid for anti-poverty initiatives.[10]

Prior to New Labour, 'institutional reform' was a key part of the party's distinct commitment to international development. In Labour's eyes, these institutions were presently doing little to resolve the crisis, merely postponing it. According to Labour, it was the World Bank and the IMF who held 'the keys to debt management' and who had a central role in arranging 'for debt to be rescheduled, for payments to be deferred . . . and provide some

97

money themselves to tide the debtors over'.[11] Yet the interests of the developing world were woefully under-represented in these institutions. For Labour, neither the World Bank nor the IMF was fit for purpose. Pre-dating Gordon Brown's call for a 'new international economic architecture', as early as 1987, Labour were arguing for 'a new financial system and new financial arrangements to deal with today's economic problems'.[12] Labour made it clear that it did not want these institutions to be scrapped. It did, however, promise that, if elected into government, it would 'use its influence in the World Bank and IMF to press for changes in their policies and structures, and put development back on top of their agenda'.[13] For Labour, this would mean these institutions giving developing countries a greater say in how the global economic system worked, and undertaking joint action with governments in the developing world to help them pursue democratic development strategies that had been rejected by the institutions.[14]

Labour, of course, would not arrive into power for another decade but its commitment to 'eliminating world poverty' as the first DFID White Paper put it, remained clear. What was far less clear, however, is how the New Labour government would manage its relationships with those IFIs that in the past it had been so critical of. The international development policies of 'old' Labour had been guided principally by the party's instinctive orientation towards social democracy. Having stripped much of this away, however, in its own bid to restore its economic credibility and become the self-styled 'party of business', New Labour appeared far more willing to work with the grain of these global institutions rather than call for their ideological reform. Accepting the neoliberal orthodoxy of globalisation preached by the IFIs, these institutions were quickly afforded a much more central role in Britain's international development policies.[15]

This alignment with the policies supported by these IFIs immediately put government ministers on a collision course with Labour's altogether more 'traditional' and increasingly vociferous caucuses who had continued to campaign hard against poverty in the developing world. Indeed, the year after New Labour's election triumph, some 50,000 people – including many longstanding Labour MPs, rank-and-file party members, alongside other NGOs, activists and church groups – joined hands in Birmingham as part of a seven-mile chain organised by the Jubilee 2000 coalition to call for the cancellation of debt in the developing world. Coinciding with the G8 summit being hosted in the city, at which several senior New Labour figures were present, including Brown, the campaign brought into sharp focus the significance for many of a development programme imbued with equality and social justice.

For Gordon Brown, however, as we shall see in the next chapter, this represented not so much an accommodation of the much-maligned Washington institutions but rather a golden opportunity to deliver on Labour's longstanding commitment to reform them. Rather than simply launching his attack upon global poverty from his office in Whitehall, Brown could also build the foundations of the 'new Jerusalem' from an ostensibly 'reformed' Washington as well. The successful transmission of Brown's political economy from the domestic into the realm of global development, however, would require a matching-up of the institutional arrangements at both the national and international levels. As this chapter will show, it was this 'institutional' as well as 'policy' tie-in that Brown hoped would ensure that his 'new global architecture' was credible enough to be embedded within the economic system.

This chapter therefore begins by examining the central role that Gordon Brown played in directing and implementing government policy at a national level through his position as Chancellor of the Exchequer. Although the Treasury extended its tentacles across all areas of Whitehall, the chancellorship of Brown saw the Treasury take a particular interest in matters of international development. To demonstrate this claim, this chapter explores the domestic origins of the control exerted by the Treasury, before tracing this back to the theme of 'credibility' explored in the previous chapter. It is this commitment to credibility that leads me on to discuss the Chancellor's claim of 'prudence' and latterly, 'prudence for a purpose', and how this was realised both domestically and in terms of the government's international development policies.

I then turn my attention beyond Whitehall to examine the 'internationalisation' of the Treasury under Gordon Brown's stewardship. Here, I reveal how Brown's model of political economy was hard-wired into the framework of the 'post-Washington Consensus'. As a means of tying this section up and opening the case study chapters that follow, I conclude this particular part of the chapter by analysing the stamp of 'Treasury preference' upon New Labour's international development policies.

Tanks on the lawn: Gordon Brown and the institutional dominance of HM Treasury

Arguably the clearest difference between 'old' and New Labour, or indeed that of any of New Labour's predecessors in government, was the latitude afforded to Gordon Brown, as Chancellor of the Exchequer, in the setting of policy that would normally fall outside the traditional economic policymaking duties of the Treasury. This difference has been summarised pithily by one of Brown's biographers, William Keegan, who remarked: 'previous Labour governments had felt captured *by* the Treasury. Brown *captured* the Treasury'.[16] This section examines how the Chancellor achieved this and the policy influence that Brown's Treasury was subsequently able to exercise over other Whitehall departments and DFID in particular.

As Chancellor, Gordon Brown was not simply content to hold the strings of the public purse. Of much greater interest to Brown were the opportunities for social and economic reform that his place at the heart of the New Labour machine afforded him. Brown therefore used his position to pepper his annual budget speeches, spending review announcements and other statements with frequent references to education, welfare and social policy. However, it was in the area of international development that Brown devoted most of his attention. For Brown to realise his ambitions in this regard, however, it was necessary to oversee a revolution in the Treasury; one that would give the Chancellor unparalleled scope to shape New Labour's international development policies to an even far greater degree than DFID's own secretary of state.

The evidence of Gordon Brown's imprint upon New Labour's international development policies is writ large over each of the case studies explored in the following three chapters. As a means of contextualising these three areas of policy however, I begin by exploring the institutional reconfiguration of the Treasury under Brown's chancellorship.

Prior to New Labour's arrival into office, some debate existed over the significance of the Treasury within Whitehall. For Martin Smith, although formally the Treasury was an economic, rather than a co-ordinating department, the importance of its functions, the status of its ministers and the impact it has upon all other departments gave it a unique position in its ability to affect the operation of the core executive as a whole.[17] Nevertheless, as Colin Thain and Maurice Wright have argued, despite this power, the Treasury could not simply dictate to departments or impose its will upon them.[18] Nicholas Deakin and Richard Parry agree with this, adding that 'whatever its apparent strength, Treasury power is less than absolute'.[19] For these authors, irrespective of the dominance that the Treasury might have been able to claim in terms of its control over the resources of central government, Whitehall departments were still able to enjoy relative autonomy in the way policy was formulated.

Gordon Brown's arrival into the Treasury changed these claims almost overnight. Under Brown's chancellorship, the Treasury enjoyed unparalleled dominance, not simply in terms of budgetary or fiscal control, but crucially through the centralisation of the Treasury as *the* pilot agency of New Labour's political economy and its economic modernisation.[20] For both Simon Lee and John Hills, the particular type of dominance in Whitehall exercised by Gordon Brown in the Treasury was both new and striking. For Hills:

> Not only have most of the significant developments [concerning New Labour's welfare and social policies] been made as part of its budget and spending announcements, but the tax system is also being used as an explicit instrument of social policy. It has also greatly increased its power by making any additional spending by departments in cash terms over the next few years conditional on convincing the Treasury that agreed reforms have taken place.[21]

All this was made possible by the crucial decision that Brown made right at the start of his chancellorship to cede responsibility for monetary policy to the MPC at the newly reformed Bank of England. Although it was a decision taken initially to establish a monetary policy framework that would, in the terms of the chief economic adviser to the Treasury, Ed Balls, 'command market credibility and public trust' through an altogether more 'prudent' approach to spending,[22] it was a move that would give the Treasury unprecedented scope to intervene in social as well as economic policy arrangements, both at home and abroad.

The power that this gave to the Treasury enabled New Labour to pursue an altogether more 'joined-up' programme of government.[23] 'Joined-up government', as policy officials articulated it, was a meta-governmental response to the problem of separate compartmentalised Whitehall departments attempting to deal with 'cross-cutting issues'.[24] Several issues faced by the government fell, directly and indirectly, within the remit of several Whitehall departments, which, historically, had led to inter-departmental conflict and a less than consistent set of policies. In order to prevent various government ministers and officials attempting to assert their own stamp of authority upon policy, New Labour sought to govern far more cohesively, designing and delivering policy in a far more integrated manner. However, for New Labour's policy-making process as a whole to take on the appearance of a single, 'joined-up' entity, it required an institutional agency at its core as a means of steering government policy.

It was to be the Treasury – and Gordon Brown in particular – that would fulfil this role, and this enabled Brown and his colleagues to extend their reach concerning the policy decisions taken by other ministers in Whitehall. Crucially, as Matthew Watson has remarked, although 'the outcome might well be more consistency across different policy outputs . . . it is also likely that all policies [would] be inflected with a clear stamp of Treasury preference'.[25] No more clearly was this demonstrated than in the policies of DFID, in whose work Brown took a particular interest. The section explores how, rooted in the Chancellor's reforms of Britain's economic policymaking at home, the pursuit of 'prudence for a global purpose' enabled Brown and his colleagues in the Treasury to achieve this, and establish considerable control over New Labour's international development policies as a result.

Reforming the Treasury: institutionalising and locking in macroeconomic credibility

'In order to do what a Labour government should do', Ed Balls is reputedly said to have said to Gordon Brown, 'you've got to earn credibility first.'[26] For Brown, it had always been clear what a Labour government should do. As we saw in Chapter 1, from a very young age Brown's politics had been inculcated with the Christian values of neighbourly compassion and civic duty of his Presbyterian parents. Whilst shadow Chancellor, Brown promised delegates at the Labour Party conference 'that we in the Labour Party will not leave our conscience at the Treasury door: we will take moral purpose to the heart of government'.[27] As Brown waited to take charge of the Treasury, his moralism would be central to the political economy of a New Labour government.

Brown understood, however, that in order to pursue this 'moral purpose', both in Britain and overseas, it was necessary to put in place a credible macroeconomic framework. The problem was, as Andrew Rawnsley has remarked, that Brown himself was less interested in operating the levers of macroeconomic management than any previous incumbent at the Treasury.[28] Brown was concerned not with the day-to-day intricacies of economic policymaking but rather the bigger picture: how such a framework might deliver the social justice that Brown craved. It would therefore fall to his long-time ally and confidante, Ed Balls to set out such a policy framework that would allow the Chancellor of the Exchequer to become, in the terms of Robert Peston, a 'credible socialist'.[29]

Accounts of the post-1994 New Labour project, understandably, focus upon the Blair–Brown nexus and afford other players, such as Peter Mandelson, John Prescott, Robin Cook, Alastair Campbell and Bryan Gould, roles in the supporting cast of varying prominence.[30] Rather surprisingly, Ed Balls features very little. Yet he was instrumental in Gordon Brown's efforts to secure credibility with the financial markets: a central objective of the party, both in opposition and in government. It was the ideas of Balls, and in particular his argument concerning the need to build a credible monetary framework based upon stability, low inflation and institutional reform, that underpinned the macroeconomic reforms initiated by Gordon Brown as Chancellor of the Exchequer. Without the support of the financial markets that this credibility would secure, both Balls and Brown felt unable to achieve the economic and social aims of New Labour.

Through his role as Brown's chief economic adviser, Ed Balls was able to exert considerable influence upon the formation of New Labour's domestic economic policy. Moreover, given the centrality of the Treasury in dictating New Labour's international development policies, Balls's influence also extended far beyond the British polity to an altogether higher spatial scale of governance. No more clearly was this evident than in Gordon Brown's appeal for a 'new global financial architecture' which was derived from the same policy narrative of macroeconomic stability, policy transparency, and clear and binding rules that Balls had frequently argued was necessary for the Treasury to instil at home.

Ed Balls was uniquely positioned in order to capture the credibility that Gordon Brown craved. His position at the *Financial Times* gave him an array of important contacts in the City of London, which in turn provided him with an insight into what the financial markets were thinking. Politically too, although critical of 'old' Labour's stance over the European Exchange Rate Mechanism (ERM), Balls was a leading member of the progressive, centre-left Fabian Society and a proponent of alternative economic strategies. In a paper written in the wake of the ERM debacle, Balls criticised the failures of the incumbent Conservative government to address the underlying structural weaknesses of the UK economy and called for 'a credible and predictable macroeconomic policy framework' – one that could deliver 'economic stability combined with active government measures to promote growth and full employment'.[31] Brown, for one, was impressed with Balls's critique, and in a single statement, Balls had distilled what Brown would attempt to achieve as Chancellor of the Exchequer.

Although senior party officials had sought to engage with the City and financial constituencies, since the launch of the so-called 'prawn cocktail offensive' in November 1989,[32] it was only after Balls's appointment in 1994 that New Labour adopted an altogether new approach to securing this credibility. From this point onwards, Gordon Brown and his colleagues started to stress the importance of 'predictability' and 'stability', and how this would be achieved through a framework of fixed rules, constrained government discretion and increased openness in macroeconomic policymaking.

These touchstones would become central to the macroeconomic framework of the New Labour government. For Gordon Brown, however, they served a far deeper purpose. They gave the Chancellor the latitude to fulfil what he saw as his own moral purpose as a Labour politician. Leaving Balls to engineer New Labour's macroeconomic strategy,[33] the Chancellor could realise his own commitment to social justice through the pursuit, both at home and abroad, of a series of microeconomic policies and supply-side reforms.

The final piece in securing this credibility – the masterstroke for which Brown is frequently credited – was the decision to grant 'the Bank of England operational responsibility for setting interest rates, with immediate effect'.[34] Announced within days of Brown being elected into office, it was a move that caught many by surprise, both for the speed and the manner in which the decision appeared to have been taken. However, it was a move that should not have taken anyone aback. In a speech to business leaders in London in May 1995, Brown had expressed his belief that:

> The Bank [of England] should establish a new monetary policy committee, which would decide on the advice given to the government on monetary policy. The committee could comprise of the Governor and the Deputy Governor of the Bank, both appointed by the government, [and] six directors including the Chief Economist. These six also appointed by the government following consultation with the Governor and the Deputy Governor . . . I believe that these reforms, together with our suggestions about more openness and transparency, and the conduct of decision-making including the budgetary process will make a positive impact on the way policy is made and greatly improve the credibility of the current process.[35]

Although widely understood as a personal triumph for Brown, it was in fact, Ed Balls whose influence was writ large in this decision. In his 1992 Fabian pamphlet, Balls had argued that 'an independent central bank, charged to deliver low and stable inflation, is a better way to achieve macroeconomic stability'.[36] Indeed, as he went on to argue, 'a carefully reconstituted and statutorily controlled central bank, empowered to pursue low and stable inflation, would make policy more representative and more accountable than at present'.[37] Although when he was writing in 1992, Balls was quick to point out that the Bank of England in its current form lacked the institutional capacity to fulfil such a task,[38] by the time Brown made the announcement a little less than five years later, the necessary preparatory work had been completed, leaving the door open for central bank independence.

Although the government would continue to set economic policy through the Treasury, it would be the Bank of England, through the MPC, whose responsibility it would be to ensure that the government's monetary targets were met. For Balls, the logic of this move was clear. The creation of an independent central bank would boost the credibility of the Chancellor and strengthen the hand of a Labour government: 'Freed from debilitating market doubts about the government's anti-inflationary resolve, a Labour chancellor would be free to concentrate on many other aspects of policy, including fiscal policy.'[39] Depoliticising monetary policy in this fashion was essential in reassuring both the financial markets and the electorate that this was a very different kind of Labour government. According to Brown, the monetary policy decisions taken by his predecessors had been 'dominated by short-term political considerations',[40] which Ed Balls later argued had contributed to 'the violent boom-bust economic cycles of the past twenty or so years'.[41] Balls's reading of the British economy in the past was one that had been punctuated by recession, joblessness and high inflation, all of which had reduced Britain's economic capacity and the willingness of firms to make long-term investment commitments. Having internalised this narrative of Britain's recent economic crises, Treasury officials concluded that the political manipulation of monetary policy undermined not only the government's aim to secure the macroeconomic stability necessary for investment[42] but crucially the very credibility of this commitment in the eyes of market investors.

Taking these decision-making processes out of the hands of politicians and placing them with a small group of non-elected, ostensibly independent economists at the Bank of England would, the Chancellor claimed, benefit both 'business, which wants to plan ahead with confidence', and 'families, who have suffered enough from the uncertainties of short-term economic stability'.[43] An altogether more credible set of economic policies would be more likely to convince voters that a New Labour government would not be blown off course by the kinds of financial pressures that had wrecked its predecessors.[44]

Again, the views of Ed Balls dictated Gordon Brown's position on this issue. Depoliticising the setting of interest rates would signal to markets New Labour's commitment to make its macroeconomic policy as open and as transparent as possible. According to Balls, British economic policymaking up until this point was 'shrouded in secrecy', and any pre-existing notions as to the 'absolute' power of the Treasury were 'inefficient and out of date. Successful developed economies, including left of centre governments . . . have realised that an independent central bank, charged to deliver low and stable inflation, is a better way to achieve macroeconomic stability.'[45] By locking in an altogether more transparent policy process, the Treasury could present far more demonstrably a credible set of policies, commensurate with the preferences of international financial investors. Explaining and justifying this particular approach to policy, in the wider context of the global economy, Balls would later argue that: 'In a world of global capital markets . . . credibility in modern open economies requires three ingredients: a reputation for following long-term policies; maximum openness and transparency; and new institutional arrangements, which guarantee a long-term view.'[46] These new institutional arrangements locked in the government's commitment to pursue a long-term macroeconomic strategy that incentivised global capital, and, as Matthew Watson has argued, demonstrated by their very presence that no alternatives would be possible to the pre-announced policy.[47] This new institutional arrangement put in place a formal apparatus that, from the government's perspective, would run policy on automatic pilot and reassure the global financial markets of the credibility of Gordon Brown's policies.[48] By putting macroeconomic policy out of the reach of meddling ministers, New Labour could make a decisive break from both its own past reputation as a 'tax-and-spend' party and the economic misfortune that had befallen previous Labour and Conservative governments.

Yet what was designed as an economic strategy to demonstrate the credibility and the financial probity of the Treasury's macroeconomic strategy under New Labour would also prove to be beneficial for Gordon Brown in a number of other political ways. For Peter Burnham, granting the Bank of England the power to set Britain's monetary policy could, politically, enable the New Labour government to 'evade direct responsibility for high interest rates and the high value of sterling, thus establishing its credibility with markets whilst, at the same time, [increasing] the pressure on labour and capital to become more competitive'.[49] Developing these observations further, Simon Lee suggested that this apparent 'loss of power' was little more than a political con-trick:

> The Bank of England is not independent. The Monetary Policy Committee . . . exercises a degree of administrative autonomy over the setting of interest rates but only within the monetary policy framework and inflation target laid down by the Treasury and the Chancellor of the Exchequer. What Brown presented as a devolution of political power was, in practice, a delegation of administrative responsibility that provided Brown with an institutional alibi for unpopular economic policies.[50]

Gordon Brown and his officials in the Treasury did little to reject these claims. Indeed, the depoliticisation of monetary policy was deemed to be a useful tool in a wider strategic context of globalisation in which the role of national politicians had supposedly been eviscerated. Since globalisation was understood by policy-makers to have restricted the latitude of politicians to pursue only those policies that worked 'with the grain' or accommodated the demands of global capitalism,[51] the handing over of power to an agency more attuned to the preferences of the market, rather than short-termist political actors, could usefully refine and even downgrade public expectations concerning the capacity of politicians in setting policy.[52]

Freed from the shackles of monetary policy, Gordon Brown was able to undertake a series of microeconomic reforms to tackle the barriers to productivity growth and to close the productivity gap.[53] These reforms were intended to boost the supply side, to enable markets to function more efficiently, and to allow firms and workers to maximise their productive potential by targeting five historical weaknesses that had undermined Britain's productivity. They included strengthening the competition regime; promoting enterprise; supporting science and innovation; improving skills through better education; and encouraging investment to improve the stock of physical capital.[54] Brown was also able to enter new areas of policy such as healthcare, education, welfare, poverty and international development – areas that, spending concerns aside, would traditionally have fallen outside the remit of the Treasury.

To both of these ends, the Chancellor frequently took it upon himself to make specific announcements relating to each of these areas of policy and tie them into the Treasury's broader economic framework. In 1998, for instance, Brown announced a series of supply-side measures designed to boost the quality of education, skills and training as a means of 'improving productivity, expanding opportunity and investing in our future'.[55] Under previous governments such policies would have been announced by either the secretary of state for education and employment or the secretary of state for trade and industry. Brown, however, while giving the impression of 'joined-up government', made only a passing mention of the input of these ministers and their departments. Rather, these were policies taken over by the Treasury, and presented as reforms designed to 'achieve our long-term goals for growth and employment' and support the 'radical modernisation of our *economic policy* in favour of opportunity, enterprise and work'.[56] This would signal the socialisation of economic policy that, under the chancellorship of Brown, the Treasury would roll out across Whitehall and, as the following case study chapters demonstrate, beyond into the developing world.

Even these policy announcements, however, were constrained, initially at least, by the Treasury's overarching commitment to credibility. A credible macroeconomic strategy meant a credible *microeconomic* strategy based upon what was presented to the electorate as 'prudent' levels of public spending. To this end, Gordon Brown chose to accept, for the first two years of office, the punitive expenditure targets set by the outgoing Conservative administration; to maintain a 'tough inflation target'; to keep 'mortgage rates as low as possible'; and to 'stick for two years within existing spending limits'.[57] This prudence would be governed by the self-imposed 'golden rule' of borrowing and spending; a fixed rule – again reinforced by the perceived need for predictable government policies – that would permit the Treasury to spend only what it could afford, and to borrow only as a means of financing future investment. As Robert Peston has argued, this initial prudence or 'hair-shirtism' would be 'crucial to acquiring economic credibility, to restoring the strength of the public finances and averting the kind of economic crises that undermined all previous Labour governments'.[58]

This prudence, however, had significant payback once credibility amongst the financial markets was assured. Having stuck assiduously to these spending levels in the first two years of being in office, the Chancellor moved to the next stage of this prudence, thereby revealing its *purpose*.[59] This prudence would enable the government to:

> target tax cuts on hard-working families and to release for our public services in the coming year alone additional resources of £4 billion. These extra resources are not at the expense of our prudence; they arise *because* of our prudence.[60]

With a little over a year to go before the next General Election, the prudence that Brown had exercised in a bid to secure macroeconomic credibility would now enable the Chancellor to pursue an election-winning programme of tax cuts and increased investment in public services.

With the fundamentals of macroeconomic stability locked in place through its monetary policy framework and prudent set of fiscal policies, Gordon Brown was now in a position to meet his 'prosperity goal' of closing the productivity gap; his 'full employment goal' of employment opportunity for all; his 'education goal' of 50 per cent of young people in higher education; and his 'anti-poverty goal' of halving child poverty by 2010 and ending it by 2020.[61] In 2002, the purpose of Brown's prudence was health. By 'cutting debt, unemployment and waste' and pursuing 'prudent management and economic stability and growth', the Chancellor was able to announce significant increases in spending on the National Health Service.[62] While in 2001 the Treasury invested £2,370 for the average household on the NHS, by 2007–8 the Chancellor promised it would increase this investment to £4,060 per household; a 48 per cent increase in real terms after inflation.[63]

Ironically for Brown – or more directly, his successor in the Treasury, Alistair Darling – once this prudence had been relaxed and levels of government spending started to rise towards the middle of New Labour's time in office, it was difficult to retrieve. When Britain became exposed to the global financial crisis during Brown's premiership, his own largesse as Chancellor, incorrectly, became a stick with which to beat him as prime minister. For a Conservative Party languishing in opposition, Brown's perceived imprudence provided a foothold to reclaim some ground on the New Labour government, and a means by which they could finally attack his hard-won credibility. Nevertheless, insofar as it lasted, Brown's prudence enabled the Treasury to place its considerable imprimatur upon these other Whitehall departments.

It was widely held by Brown's Treasury staff and other senior government officials that without a credible and prudent monetary and fiscal policy framework, none of the Whitehall departments concerned with New Labour's social policy commitments – the Department for Trade and Industry, the Department for Education and Skills, the Department for Work and Pensions, or the Department for Health – could deliver their objectives. It was therefore essential that the New Labour project retained the Treasury at its centre to drive through Brown's carefully designed model of political economy. His position at the heart of the Whitehall machine enabled Brown to strengthen his grip upon these departments, not simply in terms of the money that his Treasury provided as the *de facto* ministry of finance, but crucially concerning the content and outcomes of policies in these areas. No more clearly was this achieved than in the area of international development.

'Prudence for a global purpose': establishing the dominance of the Treasury in DFID

Brown's passion – perhaps his overriding passion – lay in the field of international development. Upon arrival into office in 1997, New Labour made good on its promise to establish a separate department from the Foreign Office for matters relating to global poverty and overseas development. The creation of DFID, however, did not prevent Gordon Brown from setting the tone for the policy outputs of this new department. Indeed, the decision to hand over the setting of interest rates to the MPC enabled Brown to pursue his very personal commitment to the alleviation of poverty in the developing world.[64] Whilst Chancellor, Brown made frequent references to international development in his numerous announcements concerning public spending. Where Brown had claimed 'prudence for a purpose' in relation to increased spending in domestic policy areas such as education, skills, welfare, productivity and health,[65] there was a distinctly 'global' purpose to his prudence concerning matters of international development. Tackling global poverty became central to the political economy of the Treasury under New Labour, and issues relating to international development featured heavily in subsequent spending announcements made by Brown as Chancellor.

As we shall see in the following chapters, Gordon Brown placed a clear emphasis upon the core areas of debt relief, access to antiretrovirals and other essential medicines, and increasing aid to developing countries. Debt relief was to be achieved through the Heavily Indebted Poor Countries (HIPC) Initiative but the Chancellor was also keen to extend debt relief through other mechanisms that he had designed, such as the 'Mauritius Mandate' and the Multilateral Debt Relief Initiative (MDRI). Access to the antiretrovirals, vaccines and other medicines required to combat the 'diseases of poverty' would be subject to a series of supply-side measures, such as tax credits to incentivise pharmaceutical firms into scaling up levels of R&D. Brown also sought to increase the amount of aid that was available for developing countries to finance their growth. A specific International Development Trust Fund was suggested initially but this was replaced by an International Finance Facility that would frontload aid money borrowed from private markets.

Gordon Brown even went as far as to propose a new compact – a 'global New Deal' – between rich and poor countries. If developing countries implemented 'pro-poor' policies, that is, policies that maintained economic stability, good governance, trade liberalisation and open markets, then developed countries would open up their markets to exports from developing countries and continue to meet their commitments. Elsewhere, four steps were identified by the Chancellor as a means of achieving global prosperity: new codes and standards; an increased role for the private sector and business within the development process; a freer and fairer global trade regime; and increased finance. These were areas that were clearly central to New Labour's commitment to the developing world, and crucially, areas that Brown would retain full control over.

Despite a pre-election commitment to increase Britain's aid spending sufficiently to meet the longstanding 0.7 per cent/GDP target, Brown in his prudence was reticent to finance this aim straightaway. The Chancellor instead elected to stick to his principle of 'prudence for a purpose', believing that this would enable the newly formed department to deliver on its aid target and attendant policy programmes in the longer term. Yet this commitment to prudence meant that the Treasury was bound by hard economics rather than any moral sentiment to dictate the amount of money

Britain was willing to spend on aid. Indeed, as the Treasury's chief secretary, John Healey, would later remark, although the government remained committed to making progress towards meeting the 0.7 per cent/GDP target, it would do so only 'as the fiscal climate permits'.[66] Therefore, although overseas aid did increase under Brown's watch, there were times when it fell back quite considerably. In 1999, for example, Britain's ODA actually dropped to its lowest level during the forty-year period between 1970 and 2010. Although this figure did climb up to 0.51 per cent/GDP in 2006, it slipped back again to 0.36 per cent in 2007. It was this cut in particular – a cut almost as great as that made by Thatcher's Conservative government in 1980 – that put back New Labour's initial commitment to meet the 0.7 per cent/GDP target by 2009,[67] to 2013 instead.[68]

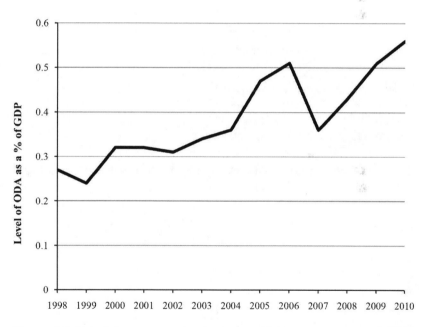

Figure 4.1 Britain's overseas development aid as a percentage of GDP, 1998–2010. (Source: OECD, 'DAC1 Official and Private Flows', 2011, <http://stats.oecd.org/Index.aspx?DatasetCode=TABLE1>, last accessed 23 August 2011; DFID, *Statistics on International Development 2005/06–2009/10*, London: DFID and the Office of National Statistics, 2010, p. 25.)>

Brown's global prudence was exercised in two ways: firstly, by creating a tax relief scheme to encourage British taxpayers to increase their giving; and secondly, by selling off the government's majority stake in the Commonwealth Development Corporation (CDC). The creation of the tax relief scheme was designed to shift away, or at least share the burden of, responsibility for development aid from the government onto the British taxpayer. The sale of the government's share of the CDC paved the way for it to become initially a PPP and then a public limited company in 1999. Both these decisions enabled the Treasury to prudently increase Britain's commitment to international development, and in particular its level of overseas aid, two years after entering office.

During the first two years of New Labour's time in government, spending limits were imposed across all Whitehall departments. Therefore, although clearly supportive of DFID's commitment to addressing matters of global poverty, Treasury officials were left to look for alternative, yet prudent ways in which to support the financing of this commitment. To do this initially, Gordon Brown urged British taxpayers to increase their contributions to projects in the developing world by introducing a 'gift aid' or tax relief scheme designed, symbolically at least, to mark the new millennium. The money raised by this policy would support the work, not of DFID itself but of charities and NGOs working within developing areas that, as Brown would later claim, shared New Labour's own commitment to debt reduction, poverty relief and development. In policymaking terms, this statement fitted in with the government's openness to working with a plurality of outside actors and matched the importance that DFID had already afforded to 'building partnerships' in its own White Paper.[69]

As with the Treasury's decision to cede responsibility for other aspects of New Labour's economic policy, this 'Millennium Gift Aid' scheme enabled the Chancellor to depoliticise the government's initial forays into international development. By incentivising British taxpayers to increase their contributions to the work of the charities and NGOs that had 'led the crusade to combat Third World poverty', the Chancellor deliberately imputed to those agencies a principal role in the delivery of the government's own international development goals. This strategy shifted the spotlight away from the government and onto a set of actors understood to be far better placed to address the issues faced by developing countries. During a period of self-imposed fiscal rectitude, this would be useful since it would rein in any expectations that civil society might have of the government itself and buy government ministers more time to build an altogether more fiscally 'credible' set of development policies.

The second means by which the Treasury sought to prudently finance its commitment to international development, and in particular Britain's level of overseas aid, was through the sale of the government's majority stake in the CDC. The CDC was set up as the UK's own development finance institution to 'create and manage new business and act as a catalyst for other investors'.[70] Using its own resources, the CDC invested in a number of private equity funds that subsequently enabled it to help finance the development of countries in Asia, Africa and Latin America. Upon entering office, New Labour officials called the CDC 'an under-utilised asset' and one that could play a more prominent role within the development process.[71] However, rather than increasing the government's stake in this public corporation, policy officials decided to retain just a minority holding in the CDC and transform it into a PPP. This would enable an injection of private capital that would increase the resources at the CDC's disposal, and enable its proceeds to be recycled into the government's aid budget.

This CDC would come to embody New Labour's new-found commitment to working in partnership with the private sector, and typify its new, altogether more 'market-orientated' approach to development.[72] For New Labour, the new 'dynamic government/private sector partnership' that underpinned the CDC would enable the Treasury to increase Britain's aid commitment overseas, whilst at the same time balancing the books at home. With this money, New Labour could finance its healthcare, education and anti-poverty programmes in the developing world, as well as offer debt relief for the poorest countries. This, in and of itself, represented a significant break from 'old' Labour. For New Labour officials, the party could and should no longer be held hostage to the *means* by which development should be achieved. What was important was the *outcome*; and addressing issues of international development was all that mattered. The loosening of these ideological constraints and, concomitantly, New Labour's acceptance of the private sector as being vitally important in the development process, allowed Brown to meet the demands of both his own party and wider civil society in a prudent, 'fiscally responsible' manner.

Combined with the Chancellor's 'Millennium Gift Aid' initiative, the selling-off of the government's majority stake of the CDC (and its subsequent transformation into a PPP) provided Brown with the prudence that he sought in sticking to the Treasury's spending commitments during New Labour's first few years in office. This spending strategy would provide the platform for Gordon Brown to intervene in the setting of New Labour's international development policies. From 2001 onwards, the Chancellor's parliamentary announcements became less about the financing of development (although, clearly, in the spending reviews this remained the case), and more about the *substance* of the policies themselves. Traditionally, the secretary of state would make such policy announcements but Brown took it upon himself to outline the significance of these policies in terms of New Labour's political economy, offering explanations as to the way certain policies had been formulated, and the role of particular actors, both in and outside of government, within the policy process.

The 'internationalisation' of the Treasury and its emergence as an institutional focal point for global development

Under Gordon Brown's chancellorship then, the Treasury became the institutional mechanism at the heart of New Labour's policy process. However, it mediated, influenced and engaged not only Whitehall departments but external policy constituencies as well. Brown's spending announcements relied upon an ongoing dialogue with institutions of global financial governance such as the World Bank, the IMF and the WTO; transnational business elites; and non-governmental actors such as charities, development agencies and faith groups. The Treasury retained a unique role in being able to talk directly with each of these constituencies, giving Brown considerable leverage in directing and co-ordinating New Labour's international development policies both at home and abroad.

As well as becoming the longest-serving and most senior finance minister within the G7/G8 group of countries, Gordon Brown also served as the chair of the powerful International Monetary and Financial Committee (IMFC) in Washington. This gave the Chancellor unparalleled scope to impress upon his fellow finance ministers his proposals – for instance, to establish a 'new global economic architecture', or introduce policy mechanisms such as a Multilateral Debt Relief Initiative and the International Finance Facility in a way that the secretary of state simply could not do. As well as these 'market-orientated' audiences, Brown was also keen to engage in dialogue with representatives from faith groups and NGOs. Throughout his chancellorship, Brown delivered far more speeches and lectures to these audiences than any secretary of state for international development. Indeed, very rarely did the likes of Clare Short or Hilary Benn speak to these constituencies without the Chancellor present. Keen to micro-manage New Labour's international development programme in a similar way as he had in other areas of government spending,[73] Brown would frequently use such opportunities to explain and justify the rationale for the policy decisions that had been made in an attempt to secure support amongst these altogether more 'socially orientated' constituencies for the government's own position.

Even in areas of policy where the Chancellor was not afforded quite such a high profile, such as the Prime Minister's High Level Working Group on Increasing Access to Essential Medicines in the Developing World (the secretary of state, Clare Short, chaired this particular group), there was a sufficiently strong Treasury presence in the Group to ensure that Gordon Brown's preferred strategy of supply-side measures such as tax credits and other incentives was incorporated into the government's strategy.[74] As Chapter 6 demonstrates, Short favoured a more 'demand-side' approach based upon creating the right 'market conditions' in developing countries for pharmaceutical firms to invest. Brown, on the other hand, believed the government's priority should be to incentivise firms to undertake far more research into the 'diseases of poverty'. It would be this research, combined with more equitable pricing strategies, that the Chancellor argued would increase the amount of vaccines and treatments available in the developing world and enable the government to meet its commitment to securing universal access to essential medicines. Short's departure from the government in 2003 and the subsequent appointment of Hilary Benn as secretary of state for international development merely made this approach to policy a formality. As a backbencher, Benn had already sided with the position taken by Brown, arguing that 'the pharmaceutical companies have a moral obligation to make [life-prolonging] drugs available to the people of Africa at a price they can afford'.[75] Benn's later promotion allowed DFID's strategy in this area of policy to be far more aligned, or in New Labour-speak, 'joined-up' with that of the Treasury.

The scope of the Treasury to intervene in the setting of government policy was strengthened further by the extensive role that Brown played *beyond* Whitehall within what Robert Cox (and latterly, Andrew Baker) has termed the '*nébuleuse*' of global financial institutions: the World Bank and IMF, or more specifically the IMFC.[76] The Chancellor's longstanding status as one of the world's leading finance ministers gave Brown a prominent voice within these institutions. The 'complex, reciprocal' relationship between the global agencies of this *nébuleuse* and national governments to which Baker refers[77] enabled New Labour's own development policies to be 'internationalised' and embedded within these institutions in an unprecedented manner. This meant that although New Labour was undoubtedly influenced by the party's own historical commitment to addressing matters of global poverty, its policies were also framed and mediated by the contemporary 'conventional wisdom' of these international institutions. Crucially, this left New Labour's international political economy much closer to New Right economics than to its traditional commitment to social democracy, and bearing more than a passing resemblance to the so-called 'post-Washington Consensus'.[78]

Hard-wiring New Labour's political economy into the 'post-Washington Consensus'

Coinciding with the arrival of New Labour into office in 1997, the emergence of the 'post-Washington Consensus' was supposed to mark a decisive break from the failures of structural adjustment and the chronic underdevelopment experienced in large parts of the developing world. As I have already remarked, 'old' Labour had been hugely critical of the neoliberal policies of privatisation, deregulation and liberalisation that many developing countries had been forced to undergo during the 1980s. Although further denunciation of the old 'Washington Consensus' came from economists such as Paul Krugman,[79] the real tipping point came with the financial turmoil experienced in South East Asia, Russia and parts of Latin America in the mid to late 1990s. It was in the aftermath of the Asian crisis in particular that IMF-led reforms came under attack,[80] prompting senior officials at the Fund, such as the managing director, Stanley Fischer, to reassess how it as an institution might respond to future market crises.[81]

Crucially, it was this crisis that flagged up to Treasury officials in the UK 'the need for action'.[82] These financial crises highlighted the ways in which the global economy had changed the environment for domestic policymaking, and the need for 'a shift in the focus of global financial governance away from *ex post* crisis resolution and toward strengthened *ex ante* procedures for crisis prevention and containment'.[83] Treasury officials noted that: 'At the heart of this new approach lies an enhanced mechanism for international economic surveillance based on a framework of internationally agreed codes and standards of best practice and embodying a greater degree of openness and transparency.'[84] Within the pre-existing neoliberal orthodoxy, the expansion of the market had meant reducing the role that the state had to play in the economy. As Ziya Öniş and Fikret Şenses have noted, however, although the 'post-Washington Consensus' maintained the importance of market liberalisation, it now conceived states and markets as 'complementing rather than substituting for each other'.[85] This fundamental shift in emphasis was underpinned by the publication by the World Bank of the 1997 World Development Report, *The State in a Changing World*. It argued that: 'An effective state is vital for the provision of goods and services – and the rules and institutions that allow markets to flourish and people to lead healthier, happier lives. Without it, sustainable development, both economic and social, is impossible.'[86] Where there had been what Craig and Porter term 'an over-withdrawal of the state ... paradoxically, a strong and capable state was [now] required to implement the neoliberal reform agenda'.[87] The World Bank, for instance, argued that the 'liberalisation of the business environment can be a powerful catalyst, setting off a virtuous spiral whereby each reform makes the next one easier'.[88] The challenge, however, was 'finding a way to set this virtual spiral in motion'.[89] The Bank argued that through better regulation, institutional reform and increased capability, the state was best placed to meet this challenge, and to this end, it offered a template of responsibilities that governments should take up in order to make markets work. Countries should put in place 'commitment mechanisms that credibly restrain arbitrary government action', and demonstrate to markets 'the ability to respond quickly to surprises, a competitive business environment and a track record of public-private partnership'.[90]

Crucially, this narrative also underpinned Brown's design of New Labour's political economy and its understanding of contemporary state–market relations, both at home and abroad. In its first White Paper, DFID made it clear that 'only governments can create the right political and economic framework within which the march of poverty can gather momentum'.[91] Officials claimed to have learnt the lessons from the shortcomings of post-war development thinking. An over-reliance upon the state in certain areas had led to inefficiency and corruption that only served to create distortions in the market. The free-market approach had fared little better, failing to deliver sustainable economic growth, and giving rise instead to an increase in inequality across the developing world.

This assessment of international economic policy mirrored that of New Labour's own 'Third Way' project at home, and specifically Tony Blair's personal 'pursuit of a "Third Way" between the *laissez-faire* of the last twenty years, and the model of statist and corporatist policies that used to be fashionable on the Left'. Neither of these policies, 'New Right' or 'Old Left', Blair argued, fitted the modern world.[92] New Labour's 'Third Way', however, gave governments a new role: 'not as a director but as enabling of wealth generation. Not trying to run industry or protect it from proper competition; but stepping in, where the market fails, to equip business and industry compete better in that market [sic].'[93] For New Labour, government had an ostensibly new role: to create 'the right political and economic framework'. Rejecting out of hand a return to 'big government' – after all, 'leverage, not size, is what counts',

Blair maintained – in a modern society, what was more important was 'what government does, and how well, not how much'.[94]

Whatever personal differences may have existed between Tony Blair and Gordon Brown, there was an unmistakeable similarity in the way that they understood the role of the modern state. It was within New Labour's broader framework of international development that this newly defined role for government presented 'an opportunity to create a new synthesis which builds upon the role of the state in facilitating economic growth and benefiting the poor'.[95] This 'Third Way' thinking led officials to argue that both states and markets make good servants and bad masters. Consequently, it became the aim of the New Labour government to create what DFID labelled 'the virtuous state'; one that might start the World Bank's 'virtuous spiral' necessary to create the conditions attractive to business. There are parallels here with the shift from the 'safety-net state' to the 'enabling state' that Mark Bevir has argued occurred under New Labour.[96] This 'virtuous' or 'enabling' state would support the 'economic arrangements, which encourage human development, stimulate enterprise and saving, and create the environment necessary to mobilise domestic resources and to attract foreign investment'.[97]

With their own emphasis upon credible economic decision-making, prudent approach to monetary and fiscal policy, and commitment to working in partnership with the private sector, Treasury officials set about institutionalising the framework supported by the World Bank, both domestically and at an international level too. At home, in line with the World Bank's wish to see national governments introduce 'commitment mechanisms that credibly restrain arbitrary government action',[98] Gordon Brown set about introducing new measures including a Memorandum of Understanding between the Treasury, Bank of England and Financial Services Authority, and Code for Fiscal Stability. These new rules and codes were designed to make the decision-making processes of the government and British financial institutions more transparent and accountable to market actors.

For both the World Bank and New Labour, the 'post-Washington Consensus' and its attendant model of political economy was to be implemented through a strategy of specifying the content of policy in precise rules, locking in those rules using mechanisms that made it costly to reverse course, working in partnership with firms and citizens, and, where appropriate, shifting the burden of implementation entirely outside government.[99] This strategy would form the basis of the 'new global financial architecture' that Brown himself was keen to introduce. Underlying this new strategy was the unwavering belief that capitalism could be made to work for the good of all. For this to occur, however, it was necessary to introduce a series of institutional reforms to mini-mise the inherent instability of market activity and make economic policies responsive to the needs of global capital. Under the terms of the 'post-Washington Consensus', the problem rested not with markets but with national governments. By emphasising and insti-tutionalising the principle of 'good governance', this new 'post-Washington Consensus' could restrict the profligacy of national and local politicians, and orientate government policy towards the exigencies of the international economy.

Although this new paradigm for development represented a considerable improvement of the terms of the crude neoliberal understanding of development that underpinned the earlier Wash-ington Consensus, its policy arrangements nevertheless remained problematic. For Ben Fine, the 'post-Washington Consensus' shared the same 'intellectual narrowness and reductionism' of its predecessor,[100] while Öniş and Şenses highlighted its continued 'systematic bias towards domestic reforms as opposed to systemic or global reforms'.[101] Although this new emphasis upon institu-tions represented an important recognition that markets do not function unless they are socially embedded, the focus of the 'post-Washington Consensus' towards regulatory and institutional reform was designed principally to improve the performance of the market. Gordon Brown frequently championed such mea-sures, particularly in respect of banking and finance, as part of moves towards this new global economic and financial architec-ture. For the Chancellor, increased transparency and a more effec-tive supervision of government policymaking, together with a more robust set of standards and codes were understood to be key elements in maintaining macroeconomic stability. The platform of stability that Brown was careful to stake out both at home and abroad would be essential in creating the right investment climate for economic growth and development.

Despite the Chancellor's fulsome endorsement of the 'post-Washington Consensus' and the way in which the Treasury embedded both its domestic and international policies within an IFI-approved model of political economy, it did not always follow that Brown's own proposals concerning international development were met with the backing that he or his party would have liked. Clearly, it gave the Chancellor considerable scope to hard-wire his ideas within this institutional *nébuleuse*, yet there were times in which his proposals hit a roadblock. Attempts to build support for faster and deeper levels of debt relief were often made in vain, whilst the International Finance Facility, proposed as a means of increasing the amount of finance for development, was met with a decidedly lukewarm response from the United States and other leading OECD countries. Indeed, US President George W. Bush brusquely dismissed the idea out of hand, telling reporters that the IFF did not fit the budgetary processes of the United States.[102] Unperturbed by this, the Chancellor's unique position within both Whitehall and Washington meant he retained unparalleled influence at both a national and an international level in the formulation of strategies designed to address the most pressing issues facing the developing world. Back home, such was the influence of Brown that in spite of the independence granted to DFID upon its institutionalisation in May 1997, its policies were imprinted with a clear stamp of Treasury preference.

Conclusions

The central pillars of New Labour's strategy for addressing global poverty – debt relief, improved access to medicines and increased aid – all displayed the hallmark of 'Treasury preference' in that the content and the delivery of these policy proposals borrowed extensively from Gordon Brown's political economy at home. Just as the Chancellor frequently argued that monetary policy stability and prudent government spending should be at the heart of New Labour's reforms of Britain's economic policymaking, so too should this 'new global architecture' be based upon these same principles in order to stabilise the global economy and relieve the world's poorest countries of their debt. Furthermore, just as

Brown sought to raise Britain's productivity and competitiveness through a series of supply-side reforms, the Chancellor introduced similar policies in order to incentivise pharmaceutical firms to increase access to essential medicines in the developing world. By the same token, Brown's ideas concerning welfare, and in particular the 'New Deal' programme introduced to tackle youth unemployment, found their way into the formation of 'a global New Deal', the centrepiece of which was the IFF and the delivery of aid, or welfare, to the global poor.

Bearing the considerable imprimatur of Gordon Brown, such was the dominance exerted by the Chancellor in this area of policy that other government departments, including DFID itself, were simply either assimilated into New Labour's policymaking process and the Treasury's way of thinking – or excluded altogether. Similarly, for those audiences beyond Whitehall, although Brown gave the impression of engaging in open policy dialogue with these groups, when their demands did not match the priorities of the Chancellor, their voice too within government policy was silenced. Due in no small part to some institutional chicanery of his own, this approach to policy gave Brown unparalleled scope to design and direct policy as he saw fit, and crucially to embark upon his personal mission to save the developing world.

The institutional dominance that Gordon Brown's Treasury was able to exert across Whitehall and into the international arena tells us a great deal about the Chancellor's vision of a 'new Jerusalem'. As we shall see over the coming chapters, this 'new Jerusalem' would be a city that Brown would claim to be built upon social justice and a moral impulse. In reality, however, its foundations would be the self-same 'pro-market' orthodoxy espoused by the institutions of international finance responsible for so much of the social and economic damage that had been wreaked across the developing world. Prioritising credibility amongst these institutions, it would also be a city built to maintain the cloistered interests of transnational corporations rather than to lift up and protect the global poor. Laudable in its scope and ambition, Brown's 'new Jerusalem' would therefore ultimately fail to take into account the systemic and structural causes of underdevelopment and poverty experienced across the global South.

Notes

1. Williamson, 'What Washington means by policy reform', [1989] 1990.
2. Labour Party, *A Socialist Foreign Policy*, 1981, p. 4.
3. Ibid. p. 3.
4. Ibid. p. 4.
5. UNDP, *Human Development Report 1990*, 1990, p. 171.
6. Ibid. p. 165.
7. Ibid. p. 171.
8. Labour Party, *Modern Britain in a Modern World*, 1987, p. 22.
9. Ibid.; Labour Party, *Meet the Challenge*, 1989, p. 83.
10. Labour Party, *Modern Britain in a Modern World*, 1987, p. 24.
11. Ibid. p. 24.
12. Ibid. p. 24.
13. Ibid. p. 24.
14. Ibid. pp. 24, 25.
15. DFID, *A Challenge for the 21st Century*, 1997, pp. 34–7.
16. Keegan, *The Prudence of Mr Gordon Brown*, 2004, p. 247, emphasis in original.
17. Smith, *The Core Executive in Britain*, 1999, p. 145.
18. Thain and Wright, *The Treasury and Whitehall*, 1995, p. 5.
19. Deakin and Parry, *The Treasury and Social Policy*, 2000, p. 2.
20. Lee, 'The British model of political economy', 2008, p. 20, emphasis added.
21. Hills, *Thatcherism, New Labour and the Welfare State*, 1998, pp. 32–3.
22. Balls, 'Stability, Growth and UK Fiscal Policy', 2004.
23. HM Government, *Modernising Government*, 1999. Interestingly, 'policy consistency' was also a cornerstone of DFID's first White Paper, *A Challenge for the 21st Century*, 1997, pp. 50–76.
24. Clark, 'New Labour's big idea', 2002, p. 108.
25. Watson, 'Planning for a future of asset-based welfare?', 2009, p. 48.
26. Cited in Keegan, *The Prudence of Mr Gordon Brown*, 2004, p. 131.
27. Brown, speech delivered at the Labour Party conference, 1995.
28. Rawnsley, *Servants of the People*, 2001, p. 32.
29. Peston, *Brown's Britain*, 2005, p. 112.
30. See, for example, Anderson and Mann, *Safety First*, 1997; McSmith, *Faces of Labour*, 1997; Gould, *The Unfinished Revolution*, 1999; Rawnsley, *Servants of the People*, 2001.
31. Balls, *Euro-Monetarism*, 1992, p. 3.
32. Wickham-Jones, 'Anticipating social democracy, pre-empting anticipations', 1995, p. 476.

33. It is notable that it was Ed Balls who in 1997 delivered what was arguably the definitive statement on the New Labour government's macroeconomic strategy at the Scottish Economic Society/Royal Bank of Scotland annual lecture.
34. Brown, 'The Central Economic Objectives of the New Government', 1997.
35. Brown, speech delivered to business leaders, 1995.
36. Balls, *Euro-Monetarism*, 1992, p. 16.
37. Ibid. p. 17.
38. Ibid. p. 18.
39. Ibid. p. 18.
40. Brown, 'The Central Economic Objectives of the New Government', 1997.
41. Balls, 'Open macroeconomics in an open economy', 1998, p. 115.
42. Ibid. p. 115.
43. Brown, 'The Central Economic Objectives of the New Government', 1997; see also Balls and O'Donnell, *Reforming Britain's Economic and Financial Policy*, 2002, p. 93.
44. Annesley and Gamble, 'Economic and welfare policy', 2004, p. 147.
45. Balls, *Euro-Monetarism*, 1992, p. 16.
46. Balls, 'Open macroeconomics in an open economy', 1998, pp. 114–15.
47. Watson, 'The split personality of prudence in the unfolding political economy of New Labour', 2008, p. 580.
48. Ibid. p. 581.
49. Burnham, 'New Labour and the politics of depoliticisation', 2002, p. 139.
50. Lee, *Best for Britain?*, 2007, p. 139.
51. Balls, *Euro-Monetarism*, 1992, p. 19.
52. Flinders and Buller, 'Depoliticisation', 2006, p. 308.
53. Balls et al., *Microeconomic Reform in Britain*, 2004, p. 9.
54. Ibid. pp. 9–10.
55. Brown, 'Pre-Budget Report', 1998.
56. Ibid., emphasis added.
57. Labour Party, *New Labour*, 1997.
58. Peston, *Brown's Britain*, 2005, pp. 150–1.
59. Brown, 'Budget Statement', 2000.
60. Ibid., emphasis added.
61. Ibid.
62. Brown, 'Spending Review', 2002.
63. Ibid.
64. Keegan, *The Prudence of Mr Gordon Brown*, 2004, p. 244.

65. HM Treasury, *Prudent for a Purpose*, 2000a.
66. Healey, 'Overseas Aid', 2004.
67. HM Government, *The UK's Contribution to Achieving the Millennium Development Goals*, 2005, p. 39.
68. HM Treasury, *Meeting the Aspirations of the British People*, 2007, p. 126.
69. DFID, *A Challenge for the 21st Century*, 1997, pp. 22–47.
70. Ibid. p. 46.
71. Ibid. p. 46.
72. Ibid. p. 41.
73. Heffernan, 'Perhaps, over to you, Mr Cameron . . .?', 2008, p. 285.
74. The financial secretary, Paul Boateng, was the Treasury's sole representative on this working group.
75. Benn, 'Engagements', 2001.
76. Cox, 'Global *perestroika*', [1992] 1996, p. 298.
77. Baker, '*Nébuleuse* and the "internationalization of the state" in the UK?', 1999, p. 92.
78. Williams, *British Foreign Policy under New Labour, 1997–2005*, 2005, p. 110.
79. Krugman, 'Dutch tulips and emerging markets', 1995.
80. Sachs, 'The IMF and Asian flu', 1998; see also Bullard et al., 'Taming the Tigers', 1998; and more famously, Stiglitz, *Globalization and Its Discontents*, 2002.
81. Fischer, remarks made during a panel discussion titled 'Macroeconomic Policies and Poverty Reduction', 2001.
82. Balls and O'Donnell, *Reforming Britain's Economic and Financial Policy*, 2002, p. 300.
83. Ibid. p. 302.
84. Ibid. p. 302.
85. Öniş and Şenses, 'Rethinking the emerging post-Washington Consensus', 2005, p. 275.
86. World Bank Group, *The State in a Changing World*, 1997, p. 1.
87. Craig and Porter, *Development beyond Neoliberalism?*, 2006, p. 98.
88. World Bank Group, *The State in a Changing World*, 1997, p. 63.
89. Ibid. p. 63.
90. Ibid. p. 75.
91. DFID, *A Challenge for the 21st Century*, 1997, p. 12.
92. Blair, speech delivered at the CBI National Conference, 1997.
93. Ibid.
94. Blair, *The Third Way*, 1998, p. 15.
95. DFID, *A Challenge for the 21st Century*, 1997, p. 12.
96. Bevir, *New Labour*, 2005, p. 42.

97. DFID, *A Challenge for the 21st Century*, 1997, p. 12.
98. World Bank Group, *The State in a Changing World*, 1997, p. 75.
99. Ibid. p. 75.
100. Fine, 'Neither the Washington Consensus nor the post-Washington Consensus', 2001, p. 4.
101. Öniş and Şenses, 'Rethinking the emerging post-Washington Consensus', 2005, p. 278.
102. Bush, cited in 'Mr and Mrs Blair go to Washington', *The Independent*, 2005.

5   A Matter of Life and Debt

Addressing the issue of 'Third World' debt was central to Gordon Brown's commitment to eliminate global poverty. The first of many forays into the realm of international development made by the New Labour government upon its arrival into office, it would become a hugely important instrument in freeing up the financial resources urgently required to meet this aim. Alongside the other means of development finance, such as increases in bilateral aid and the Treasury's own proposals for an International Finance Facility (IFF) discussed in Chapter 7, debt relief would provide an important means by which the most heavily indebted of these poor countries could restructure their economies and finance the projects needed for development and growth.

Eligibility for debt relief, like the aid that would be made available through the IFF, would be dependent upon recipient countries meeting a certain set of conditions laid out by the international community. However, where the IFF sought to reconcile the disbursement of aid with the discourse of 'rights and responsibilities' articulated by Gordon Brown and his colleagues at home, the approach to debt relief discussed here explores what these global 'responsibilities' looked like in practice. This chapter argues that the 'responsibilities' laid out by Brown and other New Labour officials were designed to embed the economies of heavily indebted poor countries (HIPCs) into a qualitatively 'new' international economic and financial architecture: an arrangement of state–market relations based upon the framework of the 'post-Washington Consensus'. Although designed principally for the global polity, this new architecture was derived from a similar set of reforms that Gordon Brown as Chancellor of the Exchequer had introduced at home in order to reduce Britain's own exposure to market volatility and global instability.

Indeed, as at home, Gordon Brown's approach to management of the global economy was derived from an almost unwavering belief in market liberalism. Here, he and other Whitehall colleagues time and again reiterated their commitment to open markets and to pursuing policies that facilitated, rather than hindered, the expansion of international market activity. It was widely believed that by opening up the global economy still further, increased flows of international capital could reach developing countries, encouraging growth and reducing poverty. This acceptance of free market activity was complemented by a tremendous enthusiasm to work closely alongside the existing Bretton Woods and other international financial institutions (IFIs) to introduce an ostensibly 'new', rules-based architecture that would enable global capitalism to work for the world's poor. For Gordon Brown, this new set of financial arrangements was required to maintain the stability that he viewed as being essential for market-led development. This macroeconomic stability was to be achieved through national governments adhering to internationally agreed codes of conduct relating to standards of fiscal and monetary discipline, market openness, accountability and transparency. Granting the IFIs the power to monitor the policymaking activities of national economies, these measures would lock in the economic 'prudence' and 'discipline' discussed in previous chapters, and provide market actors with the context in which they could now make more informed investment decisions.

This chapter argues that the mechanisms designed in support of Brown's new architecture provided the opportunity for the IFIs to discipline much more extensively the governments of these HIPCs. Debt sustainability would only be granted to those countries prepared to orientate their economies towards the demands of this new financial architecture; whether they were willing or not to open up their borders to the global economy, and whether they were prepared to create an appropriate institutional policy framework to maintain the stability that market investors sought. Therefore, although the HIPC process and latterly, the Multilateral Debt Relief Initiative (MDRI) were created under the pretext of poverty reduction, both were in fact based upon market-reinforcing reforms designed to encourage a process of 'market civilization'.[1] Embedding these reforms into this new global architecture through a clearly defined system of standards and codes enabled IFIs and other market actors to deepen their surveillance of national governments, and to monitor their performance and policy activities.

Since the market-led development sought by both Whitehall and Washington relied upon the flows of trade and inward investment, this architecture was designed to attract those market actors whose capital could finance anti-poverty strategies. In meeting this particular set of policy objectives, however, these IFIs simultaneously restricted the policy activities of debtor governments, further undermining their economic sovereignty and autonomy as they embarked upon the process towards debt relief. The role of Gordon Brown was crucial in this for it was the Chancellor's own proposals that sought to coerce these debtor countries into undertaking a distinct set of economic policies that met the criteria of this new global financial architecture, while at the same time giving the IFIs increased scope to discipline and punish the 'inappropriate' or 'unsound' monetary and fiscal activities of national governments. Rather than addressing the systemic inequality present in the global economy, this architecture was designed merely to recreate the conditions for capital accumulation, masking the relations of power and exploitation that continued to underpin it. It would in effect serve as a form of political discipline; one that would ensure the balance of power would remain skewed heavily in favour of the economic elites in the global North.

Two key issues emerge from this line of argument. Firstly, there were strong linkages between the formation of New Labour's macroeconomic strategy at home and the design of this new financial architecture abroad. At home, as I have already shown, Gordon Brown set about building a model of political economy sensitive to the perceived demands of the global economy and founded upon a 'rules-based' system of openness and accountability. The emphasis upon transparency was crucial since Brown himself understood instability to occur when market actors lacked full information. To secure the Treasury's principal goal of macroeconomic stability, policy officials, already committed to increased market liberalisation, deemed it both logical and necessary to provide market actors with the information they required to make the appropriate investment decisions that would maintain this stability.

Through the creation of a series of binding standards that investors could rely upon, New Labour pursued a two-fold strategy of maintaining open markets and creating an institutional framework that would support macroeconomic stability and policy credibility both at home and abroad; indeed, this was a strategy created to meet the expectations of domestic market investors and consolidate this new international financial architecture. As this chapter will show, this was to be achieved through a strong and distinct transmission of policy between Whitehall and Washington that embedded the New Labour project squarely within a constellation of international economic institutions. Crucially, however, this left New Labour's response to the debt crisis – led by Gordon Brown – merely reinforcing the disciplinary forms of debt relief such as the HIPC process and MDRI across the developing world already pursued by these self-same institutions of international finance.

Following this line of argument raises important questions concerning New Labour's commitment to the *moral* dimension of debt relief, and the extent to which concerns centred upon ideas of global justice and equality, articulated by Brown himself, made any difference to the commitment made by the New Labour government in respect of debt relief. A rapidly expanding civil society coalition, which drew together not only NGOs, faith groups and celebrities but also core Labour constituencies such as grassroots party members and trade unions, viewed the continued indebtedness of poor countries as at best a form of Western usury, or at worst, 'economic slavery'.[2] Both collectively and individually, these groups were unanimous in singling out the IFIs as being to blame for their mismanagement of the crisis. Rather than a further round of debt rescheduling, they argued that what was required was outright debt forgiveness, root-and-branch institutional and ideological reform of the IFIs, greater representation of the global poor, and a (re)orientation towards a form of development that was focused less upon market-led growth and more upon those most at risk from the systemic failures present in the global economy.

The argument made by civil society posed New Labour officials with a dilemma. Government ministers could not ignore this increasingly vociferous coalition, yet as this chapter shows, this new financial architecture remained embedded within the existing institutional and ideological framework of these heavily criticised IFIs. This is not to say that Gordon Brown and other government ministers completely sidelined the civil society coalition. Indeed, the Chancellor frequently met with senior figures of different parts of this movement, often going so far as to borrow the language and the imagery of these constituencies to signal his personal commitment to deeper and faster debt relief. However, although Brown was careful in how he framed his own commitment to debt relief, selectively using the language of his personal faith in the management of these particular expectations, it was ultimately only those narratives that fitted the Chancellor's appeal for a new global financial architecture which were included. Those that were included would be used as signals of social justice and morality that would legitimise the government's debt relief policy to this particular audience. Those elements that challenged the government's received economic orthodoxy were either simply ignored or criticised as being out-dated and out of step with the assumed realities faced by states in the new global economy.

To demonstrate these arguments, this chapter proceeds by tracing the evolution of New Labour's debt relief policies from the legacy of the HIPC Initiative that the party took up upon arrival into office in 1997. Gordon Brown's own 'Mauritius Mandate' launched in 1997 and the G8 summit in Birmingham the following year provided the first of many opportunities for New Labour to take its proposals for a new approach to debt relief to an international audience. The summit also placed the issue firmly within the public arena since it gave civil society, under the umbrella of the Drop the Debt/Jubilee 2000 coalition, an increased opportunity to press for much greater levels of debt relief. Gordon Brown, alongside Tony Blair and the secretary of state for international development, Clare Short, their counterparts in the G8 and the IFIs all signalled a willingness to reform the initiative with the agreement of the Enhanced HIPC Initiative at the Cologne G8 summit in 1999. This, it transpired, paved the way for the formation of the MDRI introduced at the 2005 G8 summit in Gleneagles. These policies tell us a great deal, not simply about New Labour's debt relief strategy but, more broadly, about the attempts made by Gordon Brown to locate his carefully calibrated model of political economy within the existing economic orthodoxy of the 'post-Washington Consensus'. Brown believed that rather than responding directly to those voices within civil society demanding a fairer and more just resolution to the debt crisis, a solution could be found through the redesign of the existing global financial architecture and the building of a 'new Jerusalem'.

The Heavily Indebted Poor Countries Initiative

Arguably the most significant, and certainly the most durable, set of debt relief measures proposed by the international community was the Heavily Indebted Poor Countries (HIPC) Initiative, agreed in 1996. Although this initiative pre-dated New Labour's time in office, it nevertheless provided the framework within which Gordon Brown's own approach to debt relief strategy would be situated. It is appropriate therefore that before exploring the terms upon which New Labour animated its own debt relief policy, the HIPC Initiative itself is explored. It was within this framework that, as the latter part of this chapter demonstrates, Brown set about incrementally reforming the HIPC debt relief process by institutionalising at a global level the financial architecture that underpinned his own model of political economy.

Emerging in part out of a proposal in the mid 1990s by John Major's Conservative government, the HIPC Initiative laid out a commitment by multilateral organisations and governments to work together in order to reduce to sustainable levels the external debt burdens of the most heavily indebted poor countries. It was designed to ensure that 'no poor country faces a debt burden it cannot manage'.[3] By ruling out straightaway the idea of debt *forgiveness*, this statement of intent by the IMF polarised those groups with whom New Labour officials would engage when forming their own response to the debt crisis. Much to the chagrin of debt activists, the HIPC Initiative did not promise to cancel the debts of poor countries, but rather consolidate and reduce the debt burden to a sustainable or more manageable level. Rejecting out of hand any notion of debt cancellation, the deputy director of the IMF's African Department, Goodall Gondwe, asked supporters of debt forgiveness to consider:

> Who would lend again to recipients of such cancellation? . . . Why should countries that have misused resources more than others have more of their debt cancelled? . . . and what guarantee was there that the money saved would be put to effective use?[4]

The IMF minister went on to argue that moves towards total debt write-off would be 'sadly mistaken' for debt, he argued, was 'only one of many problems that Africa must grapple with' and 'the pressures to misallocate money are strong'. Unconditional cancellation, Gondwe argued, could risk debt relief being squandered on corruption, military expenditure or grandiose projects with little, if any, benefit in terms of sustainable growth or poverty reduction.[5] Similar sentiments were expressed by the president of the World Bank Group, James Wolfensohn, who, as well as voicing concerns over corruption and the misappropriation of resources, also pointed to the large losses that the Bank itself was likely to incur if these debts were written off. These losses, Wolfensohn argued, would undermine the financing of the International Development Association (IDA) whose lending activities support the poorest countries by providing interest-free loans and grants.[6]

Such arguments reveal the paradox of the lending practices of the World Bank. Although Wolfensohn suggests that these repayments were needed for the Bank to continue to underwrite the development in these countries, it almost goes without saying that *if* these funds were in fact retained by the debtor countries, then this money could have been used by these countries to self-finance their development. Under the existing terms of the initiative, however, HIPCs were in effect paying the Bank to finance their development. Rather than supporting the 'national ownership' of development as the IFIs had promised under the terms of the Poverty Reduction Strategy Paper (PRSP), this recycling of repayments continued to give the Bank leverage to dictate the terms of development.

The other side to the 'debt sustainability' discourse was supported by the IMF's principal mandate to maintain international financial stability. Without this stability, 'the sustained global growth' upon which economic development was believed to rest 'would not be possible'.[7] The IMF framed the debt crisis of the 1980s in terms of the threat that it posed to the stability of the global economy and the prospects for global growth. Consequently, the HIPC Initiative was designed not to address directly the poverty experienced by those countries crippled by debt but rather to maintain global macroeconomic stability. The HIPC Initiative would ensure that borrowing countries locked in the reforms necessary to prevent the accumulation and default of unsustainable debt in the future; maintain fiscal responsibility; and, as Ben Thirkell-White has argued, act as a catalyst for private capital flows in an era of increased financial globalisation.[8]

To secure this debt sustainability, the HIPC Initiative was designed as a two-stage process: the initial 'decision point' and final 'completion point'. In order to successfully reach the first of these two stages, the indebted country must fulfil four criteria. By virtue of their orientation towards the neoliberal framework laid out in both the 'Washington Consensus' and the 'post-Washington Consensus', these criteria was designed by the IFIs to discipline and 'civilise' developing countries into undertaking the appropriate market and institutional reforms at the national level. For the IFIs, these criteria remained important, not simply as a means of securing debt sustainability, but more broadly, to enable developing countries to participate far more fully in the global economy and in doing so, benefit from globalisation.

In order to meet the first criterion, the HIPC must be facing an unsustainable debt burden that cannot be addressed through traditional debt relief mechanisms. For their part, the Bank and the Fund consider a debt burden to be unsustainable when it exceeds a debt-to-export ratio of 150 per cent. Since it is, by definition, a 'poor country' initiative, in order to meet the second criterion, the debtor country must also be eligible – that is, poor enough – to borrow from the IDA arm of the World Bank and the IMF's Extended Credit Facility (ECF).[9] Yet even this level of poverty (measured by per capita income) is not enough. Since the IDA and ECF act, in effect, as lenders of last resort, the country's creditworthiness for market-based borrowing from both the commercial sector and the International Bank for Reconstruction and Development (IBRD) is also considered.[10]

Countries unable to access borrowing from these public and private lenders and deemed poor enough to qualify for assistance must still meet the 'appropriate standards of performance' laid out by the IDA and ECF. Eligibility for support from the IDA is still contingent upon countries meeting certain criteria – 'of which macroeconomic stability is an important one' – before funds are released.[11] Similarly, under the terms of the ECF, countries must agree to implement a set of policies that will help them support significant progress toward a stable and sustainable macroeconomic position over the medium term.[12]

This emphasis upon macroeconomic reform is supported by both the third and fourth criteria, both of which are interlinked through the conditionality imposed upon debtor governments. For

HIPCs to secure relief, there must be a firmly established track record of reform and 'sound' policies through IMF and World Bank supported programmes. The emphasis upon 'sound' policies is a recurring theme both of policy documents and in the speeches made by IFI officials. Publicly at least, very little is ever given away as to what these 'sound policies' actually look like, yet representatives from these IFIs have frequently stated *why* such policies are important. Horst Köhler, the one-time managing director of the IMF, for instance, identified 'sound macroeconomic policies and domestic and international financial stability' as being the 'preconditions for sustained growth'.[13] Köhler's successor at the Fund, Anne Krueger, emphasised – without a hint of irony – the *democratic* basis of such policies, arguing that 'sound fiscal policies give governments and citizens more choice', making it easier 'for society to decide on its priorities'.[14] A few years later, in her role as the Fund's first deputy managing director, Krueger claimed that 'better policies' deliver 'stability at the national level' thereby 'greatly reducing the risk of instability at the global level'.[15] These claims echo with the continued claims made by the IMF that 'sound' economic policies are both desirable and necessary since they create 'the room for fiscal stimulus without jeopardising economic stability',[16] and in doing so support economic growth.[17]

In the midst of these appeals for 'sound' policymaking, few clues are offered as to what these, or indeed 'unsound', policies actually look like. Despite this absence, this rhetoric nevertheless formed an integral part of contemporary development narrative and the importance of these institutions in managing and reproducing this orthodoxy. An implicit understanding – or perhaps even a straightforward disinclination – amongst IFI officials might have precluded a discussion of what these 'sound policies' actually entail but obviously, clarity as to what these 'sound' policies look like in practice is necessary. Here the work of prominent World Bank economists, Craig Burnside and David Dollar, is instructive. In their influential work on aid and growth, they spell out quite explicitly what these policies should look like in practice, and how these are to be embedded institutionally in an era of liberal market reforms. Put simply, Burnside and Dollar argue that 'sound policies' are those measures 'that have been shown in a wide range of studies to promote growth: open trade regimes, fiscal discipline, and avoidance of high inflation'.[18]

There is a clear link between the analysis offered by Burnside and Dollar and the broader narratives of the IFIs concerning the importance of achieving and maintaining stability through 'sound' macroeconomic principles. If developing countries create the right policy framework, that is, 'if they stabilise their macroeconomic situations and liberalise their trade, they can create a sound environment for investment and growth'.[19] Although these policies could produce improved results even without an increase in a country's receipts of aid (which may also be read as debt relief), Burnside and Dollar argue that growth and poverty reduction would occur 'significantly faster' in those countries to which aid/debt relief is increased since these increasing inflows of foreign aid, in and of themselves, increase the confidence of private investors in a country's economy. In a sound policy environment, Burnside and Dollar go on to suggest, aid attracts private investment, whereas in a poor policy environment, it displaces private investment.[20]

Burnside and Dollar's logic underpins what Jeremy Gould has termed the 'new conditionality' that supported both the HIPC Initiative and the 'new global financial architecture' that Brown himself was keen to promote.[21] Rather than simply focusing upon policy outcomes – that is, poverty reduction and debt relief – this 'new conditionality' sought to influence the policy- and decision-making *processes* designed to secure these outcomes. At the heart of this 'process conditionality', therefore, are the institutions themselves. If aid donors, creditors and market actors are confident in the institutional capacity of a state to maintain market discipline and stabilise the macroeconomic environment, then that state would be more likely to attract the flows of aid, debt relief and/or private investment necessary to support poverty reduction strategies. Conversely, poverty is more likely to remain in those areas with weak institutions since they are not able to sustain market confidence.

This appeal for developing countries to pursue 'sound policies' squared with the emphasis placed upon more state-led forms of development mapped out under the terms of the 'post-Washington Consensus'. Within this framework, institutional reform is required to make aid and debt relief 'work', and attract private investment. However, rather than offering any radical move away from market-led development, this framework – and, concomitantly, the HIPC Initiative – remained wedded to an approach to development designed primarily to accommodate the preferences of global finance. Although framed within reformist language, the continued emphasis upon macroeconomic stability and processes designed to tackle budgetary deficits and inflation merely locked in the neoliberal fundamentals demanded by the IFIs to support greater integration into the global economy. Echoing the mantra of 'prudence' and 'stability' pursued by Gordon Brown during his chancellorship in Britain, these institutions prioritised the need for debtor countries 'to pursue cautious borrowing policies and strengthen their public debt management',[22] rather than addressing the systemic faultlines upon which debt had been allowed to accrue.

This emphasis upon 'sound' economics, poverty reduction and a new, 'process'-orientated form of conditionality underpinned the fourth criterion that debtor countries were required to meet in order to reach the 'decision point' of the HIPC process. When the initiative was first launched in the mid 1990s, HIPCs were expected to have undertaken a Structural Adjustment Programme (SAP) in order to restructure their economies. Towards the end of the decade, however, these SAPs started to be phased out and replaced with PRSPs, and debtor countries have since been required to develop a 'home-grown' strategy paper through a broad-based participatory process in the country.

These new PRSPs promised to work in 'partnership with the poor' and offer increased 'country ownership' of poverty reduction programmes.[23] In many respects then, PRSPs reflect the shift in emphasis from the old, *policy*-orientated 'Washington Consensus' to the newer, more *process*-orientated 'post-Washington Consensus'. What did remain, however, was a commitment to neoliberal ideas, reproduced in the narrative of 'sound policies' concerning open markets, macroeconomic stability, and monetary and fiscal discipline. Under the terms of the 'post-Washington Consensus', much greater emphasis was placed upon the role of the state in poverty reduction strategies. The failure of SAPs to secure local ownership of policy had undermined efforts towards economic development. By stressing the importance of processes and institutions, PRSPs offered a putatively new means by which the overall aim of poverty reduction might be achieved. As Ben Thirkell-White has observed, macroeconomic theory began to place an increasing emphasis upon 'the economics of information'.[24] Development practitioners and economists in Washington were becoming more interested in how institutional factors, particularly those promoting transparency and information provision, could ensure efficient capital allocation. With a renewed emphasis upon the state, these PRSPs could instil the 'correct' institutional processes needed to increase and support flows of finance into the economy, whether through aid, debt relief or private investment.

However, the underlying commitment to deflationary policies in these PRSPs would present a problem for this 'process' conditionality. A clear conflict existed between, on the one hand, the monetary and fiscal discipline that was an integral part of both the HIPC process and the broader framework of the 'post-Washington Consensus', and the high levels of government spending that poverty reduction programmes required on the other. Policy officials feared that increased government expenditure could lead to the inflationary pressures that might jeopardise the 'stability' and 'sound policies' sought by the IFIs, donors and market actors. As the World Bank made clear, 'Stability requires a monetary and fiscal policy stance consistent with maintaining public sector solvency at low levels of inflation, while leaving some scope for mitigating the impact of real and financial shocks on macroeconomic performance.'[25] Even the explicitly more development-orientated United Nations Development Programme argued that 'an expansion of public expenditures is only desirable when it does not compromise short-term macroeconomic stability'.[26] Both statements suggest that macroeconomic discipline was to be prioritised over any spending plans a government might have, leaving indebted countries facing a decision as to whether to play by the strict deflationary rules of the neoliberal game or to cut loose and make the necessary investments in poverty reduction and development. Such a scenario, of course, presented developing countries with a further dilemma since it was the self-same institutions that set the rules of the game but who also held the purse strings for the funding required for development. Framed in these terms, any commitment to 'increased country ownership' appeared to be very hollow indeed.

Even having met these criteria – and therefore reaching the 'decision point' – it still remained up to the Executive Boards of the IMF and World Bank to formally decide whether or not the country in question was eligible to receive debt relief. Should these institutions be satisfied with the progress made by the debtor country, they will recommend that its creditors commit to reducing debt *to a level that is considered sustainable*. Once a country successfully reaches this 'decision point', it may immediately begin receiving interim relief on its debt servicing as it falls due, and start to take the second step towards 'completion point'. This second stage ensures that the debtor country receives full and irrevocable debt reduction. To achieve this second stage, however, the country still needs to meet three further policy conditions to reassure its creditors of its commitment to the 'sound' policies pursued prior to the 'decision point'. Firstly, the debtor country must continue and establish a further track record of good performance under programmes supported by loans from the IMF and the World Bank; secondly, it must implement satisfactorily key reforms agreed at the 'decision point'; and thirdly, the country must adopt and implement its PRSP for at least a further year. When, and only when, a country meets these criteria does it reach its 'completion point', which allows it to receive the full debt relief agreed at the earlier 'decision point'.

Embedded in the political economy of the 'post-Washington Consensus', the HIPC Initiative attempted to move countries away from a policy-led form of development to one more orientated towards the processes and institutions that promote poverty reduction and economic growth. This change in direction enabled the IFIs to rebrand the HIPC process as one that gives countries a greater sense of 'ownership' over their development. However, these attempts to institutionalise neoliberal reforms resulted in a strong tendency to discipline and 'civilise' these countries into pursuing a series of market-based reforms reflecting the preferences of international finance and capital. This can be seen most clearly in the prioritisation of 'sound policies': monetary and fiscal discipline, open markets and, crucially, macroeconomic stability. Promoted vigorously both by the IFIs and by Gordon Brown himself, these principles would shape not simply New Labour's domestic political economy but the 'new global financial architecture' in which the government's debt relief strategy would be embedded.

Sustainability, stability and 'sound policies': New Labour's formative debt strategy

New Labour talked up its early development credentials by promising in its 1997 General Election manifesto to 'reduce the debt burden borne by the world's poorest countries'.[27] An early test of this commitment came at the meeting of the Commonwealth finance ministers in Mauritius the following September, during which Gordon Brown set out his 'Mauritius Mandate'. This five-point plan, the Chancellor promised, would lead to every eligible poor country in the Commonwealth having at least started to embark upon the process of securing a sustainable exit from debt by the year 2000. To meet this target, Brown committed the UK to: (1) helping countries meet the conditions to escape from the debt trap; (2) cancelling the remaining debt due to the UK from lower income Commonwealth countries, on the condition that they remain 'committed to the "pro-poor" policies, transparent and accountable government and sound economic policies'; (3) financing technical assistance to poor countries in the Commonwealth; (4) providing unconditional finance to the IMF Trust Fund; and (5) ensuring that export credits for poor, highly indebted countries would only support 'productive expenditure'.[28] There was, however, a catch. Only those countries 'with the strongest reform programmes, including a focus on transparency and productive expenditure, should get the maximum possible relief needed to ensure their debt burden is sustainable'.[29]

As a statement of intent it was ambitious to say the least, but the Mandate did at least confirm that the issue of developing world debt would be an important priority for the New Labour government. Although question marks remained over some of the Chancellor's proposals, the Mandate was, by and large, welcomed by most NGOs. After all, it demonstrated the government's commitment to go a considerable way in addressing the longstanding problem of debt in a relatively short space of time. Where NGOs did express a concern, it was that the government's approach remained reformist rather than revolutionary.[30] Like the HIPC Initiative, Brown's 'Mauritius Mandate' emphasised the central importance of debt *sustainability*, rather than debt relief, and conditionality based upon the self-same 'sound' economic policies advocated by the IFIs. For Brown and his colleagues in Whitehall, policies that encouraged 'human development' were considered important. Crucially, however, this normative commitment could only be realised through the pretext of 'sound' economic reforms.

Despite the maelstrom of economic and social upheaval that debt had wreaked across the developing world over the previous two decades, New Labour officials remained convinced that borrowing was, in principle at least, a sound investment strategy. DFID's first White Paper, for instance, acknowledged that nearly all developing countries need to import from abroad the capital necessary for development,[31] suggesting that the government was quite content for low-income countries to pursue a development strategy financed by borrowing on international capital markets. Such an assessment would also suggest that New Labour was dismissive of the claims made by some debt activists that it was precisely this present system of continued borrowing which was keeping developing countries locked in a cycle of dependency and poverty. For government officials, however, borrowing only became problematic when money was wasted or spent unproductively, when loans began to accumulate and developing countries were faced with an increasingly unsustainable debt burden. As DFID's 1997 White Paper argued, it was this 'overhang of unpayable foreign debts' that acted as a long-term barrier to development by discouraging the new investment necessary to promote growth. Policymakers believed that countries could avoid this scenario by managing their loans more effectively, investing in capital productively, and pursuing beneficial and transparent economic policies.

Clear similarities can be drawn between the analysis put forward by Whitehall officials and that of Burnside and Dollar at the World Bank. Locating these claims within the broader political economy of the emerging 'post-Washington Consensus', a causal link was made between the weak economic governance of a country, its unsustainable debt burden, macroeconomic instability, and a subsequent lack of development. For lasting poverty reduction to be achieved, national government institutions needed to pursue policies that would maintain this macroeconomic stability. As a means of securing this economic and financial stability, New Labour's principle goal was to achieve debt 'sustainability'.[32]

For New Labour, the party had in Gordon Brown a Chancellor committed to delivering these very same objectives at home as well as abroad. 'High and stable levels of growth and employment' were the central economic objectives of his Treasury and the New Labour government.[33] 'Stability with low inflation', the Chancellor would later argue, would form the first of five 'building blocks of prosperity' needed to deliver Britain's 'national economic purpose'.[34] However, this could 'only happen *if* we build from solid foundations of prudent economic management and sound finance'.[35] Both at home and abroad, the link between maintaining macroeconomic stability and pursuing prudent or 'sensible economic policies' was unmistakeable. While domestically, the high levels of national economic growth and employment sought by the Treasury could only be achieved through prudent economic decisions, so similarly, within the field of international development, poverty reduction strategies would only work if they were underpinned by 'sound' economic reforms.

The character of these 'sound' reforms matched those that had been tacitly appealed to by IFIs: a continued orientation towards an open economy, macroeconomic stability, low inflation, market discipline, and monetary and fiscal rectitude. Treasury ministers were adamant that any commitment made by the international community towards debt relief must be matched with an equal commitment by the debtor countries to adopt and adhere to appropriate economic and structural reforms.[36] Clare Short was similarly clear on this point. 'Governments must have a good [economic] track record to qualify for their first stage of debt relief, and their record must continue to be good.'[37] As those in charge of the HIPC process had argued, debt relief would not take place until countries had taken on board and institutionalised the neo-liberal policy reforms required to sustain the poverty reduction strategies.

This raised suspicions amongst civil society that these reforms were too heavily geared towards 'process conditionality' and penalising 'poor macroeconomic performance'. Oxfam, for instance, noted that these conditions continued to give insufficient regard to their impact on the poor,[38] while the international think-tank, the South Centre, argued that the PRSP programme merely constituted a 'rebranded' form of the conditions to the old structural adjustment policies.[39] Crucially, for debt campaigners, unsustainable debt was not a macroeconomic problem, but rather a human tragedy exacerbated by the greed and profiteering of Western lenders. The Jubilee Debt Campaign criticised the HIPC process as being entirely controlled by creditors not accepting responsibility for their part in creating and maintaining the debt crisis, and not allowing poor countries to have a say.[40] These processes of macroeconomic discipline and 'market civilisation' not only meant that government policies reflected and accommodated the expectations of market constituencies, but they actually undermined the ability of debtor countries to invest in adequate levels of healthcare, education and other forms of social welfare. As World Vision noted, indebted countries were allocating less than 15 per cent of their budgets to the provision of basic services such as health, education and water, while more than 40 per cent was being spent on repaying debts.[41]

Despite the clear emphasis in the White Paper linking 'debt sustainability' to 'macroeconomic stability', the significance of the 'human' dimension to the debt crisis was not entirely lost on New Labour officials. Tony Blair acknowledged that some countries 'spend a vast proportion of the public money they spend simply on debt repayment, so that, of their overall expenditure, only a small percentage is left for trying to develop their countries'.[42] Similarly, Clare Short recognised that policies and processes concerning debt should be designed to benefit the needy and the poor since they are the ones who suffer the consequences of debt.[43] Gordon Brown even went so far as to argue that debt was a social, rather than simply an economic, issue: 'Millions of people in the world's poorest countries are suffering because money that could be spent on health and education and on ensuring economic self-sufficiency is currently going to repay debt.'[44] In its response to a report published by the Commons Select Committee on International Development, the Treasury reiterated the claims made by Brown by stating that 'unsustainable debt is a *moral* as well as an economic issue'.[45] The assimilation of these two distinct narratives revealed how New Labour intended to frame its own debt strategy at this early stage, and how this enabled the government to appeal to the two main policy groups with whom Whitehall ministers were in dialogue.

To meet the government's commitments towards debt and poverty reduction, it was considered necessary to orientate the processes of institutions in developing countries towards 'the market' as a means of stabilising their economies and setting them on the path towards development. Focusing upon the *outcome* rather

145

than the means enabled Whitehall officials to justify these policies as being 'pro-poor'. Of course, to audiences in Washington the policies themselves represented 'sensible' policies and 'sound' reforms. The outcome, however – the 'pro-poor' narrative – was used as a discursive device to appeal to those voices from within civil society concerned at the way in which the 'social' or 'moral' dimension to the debt crisis had been overlooked in favour of Western and economic interests. That New Labour could claim these policies as being 'pro-poor' would be useful as government officials set about addressing – albeit selectively – the expectations of civil society, and in particular the nascent Jubilee 2000 Coalition (out of which the subsequent Drop the Debt and Jubilee Debt Campaign would later emerge), as it gathered momentum in the lead-up to the crucial G8 summit in Birmingham. Ahead of this summit, the Coalition gave evidence to the Parliamentary Select Committee for International Development, in which it called on the prime minister to exert maximum pressure on other G8 leaders at the summit to take a significant step towards the cancellation of the unpayable debt of the world's poorest countries by the year 2000.[46]

For their part, Gordon Brown and Clare Short convened a joint Treasury–DFID seminar, the headline outcome of which was the announcement that the British government was prepared to cover 10 per cent of Mozambique's debt owed to the Paris Club. Strikingly, however, Brown chose *not* to play the 'moral card' but instead suggested that his decision was based upon the fact that Mozambique had 'a strong track record of economic reforms' yet still faced 'a growing debt burden'.[47] Brown, of course, did not problematise the failure of these 'sound economic reforms' to address Mozambique's struggling economy. Nevertheless, this did signal to the debtor countries, faith groups and NGOs represented at the seminar that hard economics, rather than any moral imperative, would continue to dictate the decisions of Western creditors.

Despite this decision, the rhetoric of senior New Labour officials appeared to suggest that the government was on the side of the debt campaigners. Clare Short praised the churches and Jubilee 2000 who had 'done a glorious job in mobilising support in this country and internationally for debt relief for the poorest countries'.[48] For his part, Gordon Brown actively encouraged MPs to work with the churches in their areas to ensure that there would continue to be strong public opinion in favour of action.[49] This groundswell of public opinion, Brown believed was already making a difference internationally and would help secure the necessary debt reductions. This public activism even led some Treasury ministers to believe that the debt campaigners were on the side of the government. The economic secretary, Helen Liddell, for instance, told the House of Commons that the Treasury had received many thousands of letters *supporting* the government's position on the 'Mauritius Mandate'.[50] Given the evidence that the NGOs involved in the Jubilee movement had presented to the Parliamentary Select Committee earlier in the year, and the public policy work that these organisations had undertaken themselves, Liddell's claims appeared somewhat disingenuous. While there had been extensive and open dialogue between the government and civil society, and a shared commitment to debt reduction, it was clear that there were still distinct differences between the two as to *why* and *how* debt should be reduced. The New Labour government remained committed to the economic case for debt sustainability, disciplining heavily indebted countries with market reforms, while civil society pressed the moral case for deeper and faster debt cancellation to allow these countries to develop on their own terms.

Much to the disappointment of the 60,000-strong crowd of demonstrators that had gathered in Birmingham in May 1998, the G7 summit itself failed to provide any real progress towards finding a solution to the debt crisis. New Labour's proposals to modestly extend the 'Mauritius Mandate' to a new, global Multilateral Debt Relief Initiative were blocked by Germany, the United States, Japan and Italy, and all the final communiqué contained was a broad and indeterminate agreement supporting 'the speedy and determined extension of debt relief to more countries, within the terms of the HIPC initiative'.[51] The usual disclaimers applied. Debt relief would be made available *if* 'all eligible countries take the policy measures needed to embark on the process . . . so that all can be in the process by the year 2000'. Creditors were encouraged to ensure that 'when they qualify, [debtor] countries get the relief they need to secure a lasting exit from their debt problems'.[52] Therefore, although Tony Blair would claim that the summit would mark 'a significant step forward',[53] it was clear that a great deal more still needed to be done. How the government would go about meeting this challenge would form the second phase of New Labour's debt strategy.

Towards a new global financial architecture: New Labour and the Enhanced HIPC Initiative

Despite Blair's arguments to the contrary, Birmingham had unquestionably been a huge setback for those campaigning to secure a fairer deal for those living in highly indebted countries. The response to this from both the Treasury and DFID in particular was to implicitly blame the developing countries for the poverty in which they found themselves immiserated. If these poor countries refused to adopt the necessary 'sound' policies that were required to lift themselves out of poverty, then the creditor countries could not be expected to agree to more debt relief. As Clare Short reminded the Commons, 'countries must have a track record of such economic management both before and after they sign on for debt relief' and 'no country will receive debt relief unless it is being very responsible in its economic management'.[54] The Treasury was similarly clear on this point, even going so far as to argue that debt relief was not the principal issue at stake:

> Debt relief is not enough in itself. It might be a necessary precondition for economic growth and development, but it is essential in the long term that the indebted countries implement policies that will lead to economic growth and development, so that they never again return to the high levels of debt that exert such a drag on their economics and create the conditions in which poverty becomes endemic.[55]

This refusal to budge over sound economic reforms was leading to a growing conflict between the position of the government and that of the Jubilee campaign:

> Sometimes it [the Jubilee movement] talks as though all debt should be relieved unconditionally. We do not agree with that. There are countries with high levels of debt that have spent their money on luxuries or have excessive military expenditure. We believe that debt relief should be linked to a commitment to poverty reduction and sensible economic management. We believe in implementing HIPC more flexibly, not in cancelling all debt unconditionally.[56]

Clearly agitated by the increasing public pressure surrounding debt, Short later disingenuously claimed that much of the talk surrounding debt relief was 'media-driven, and driven by people who do not understand debt'.[57] As the case for debt forgiveness continued to be pressed by NGOs and faith groups, however – the same groups whom the government had welcomed during the first phase of its debt strategy – the international development secretary was forced to declare that it was 'not in the government's power to call for a moratorium' on multilateral debt.[58] Rather than displaying the political leadership that one might expect, Short capitulated and maintained that if these countries were to be helped, there needed to be far greater levels of international co-operation instead.[59]

Strengthening this international co-operation and locking in the 'sound' economic reforms at a global level underpinned the second phase of New Labour's debt strategy, with its focus shifting to the creation of what Gordon Brown initially called 'new global structures for the new global age'.[60] While Brown and other government ministers continued, as they had in the first phase of their debt strategy, to talk to fellow parliamentarians, NGOs and faith groups about the need to base debt relief upon sound economics and 'pro-poor' policies,[61] the Chancellor spent the second phase delivering a series of speeches and lectures to principally international economic elites and financial audiences across the world, in order to build up support for a 'new global financial architecture'. These addresses were designed to showcase Brown's proposals for a broad set of global mechanisms that would offset the risk of financial crises emerging and support the debt relief process. In this second phase, Brown's new global architecture would shape New Labour's commitments concerning debt relief and become central to its relationship with the HIPCs.

In a clear sign of Brown's own policy imprint, DFID's 1997 White Paper had already spoken about developing a 'well-managed and regulated set of international mechanisms, such as increased IMF surveillance and banking supervision to support beneficial regulation and stability'.[62] However, it was only during this second phase that the details concerning this new global financial architecture began to emerge. These details would prove to be instrumental in securing the agreement for an Enhanced HIPC Initiative at the G7 summit in Cologne in 1999, and latterly in the third phase of policy, when at the 2005 G8 summit in Gleneagles, Brown himself would push for the introduction of the Multilateral Debt Relief Initiative.

Brown argued that the combination of this new architecture and measures to reduce the levels of unsustainable debt would go beyond the existing HIPC process, and offer 'new hope to the poorest and most heavily indebted countries'.[63] To this end, Brown transposed his own macroeconomic strategy for Britain into this new architecture for the global economy:

> I believe that, just as through central bank independence we set down a new rules-based system in the UK . . . we should, in pursuit of the objectives of stability, development and prosperity, consider also a new rules-based system of economic governance for the community of nations. This new system should be founded on clear procedures, with all countries, rich and poor, pursuing agreed codes and standards for fiscal and monetary transparency, and for corporate and social standards.[64]

These global policies squared neatly therefore with both the existing economic orthodoxy of the 'post-Washington Consensus' and New Labour's own domestic political economy. For Brown, the lessons that he as Chancellor had learnt in terms of monetary and fiscal policy were lessons critical to the future of emerging markets across the world.[65] It made sense to apply policy ideas intended initially for domestic consumption to this new global architecture and Brown duly set about joining up New Labour's macroeconomic strategy for the UK with its commitment to addressing the debt crisis in the developing world.

Brown had sought to build British economic success upon the solid rock of 'prudent' and consistent economic management, as opposed to the shifting sands of the 'boom-and-bust' approach of his Conservative predecessors.[66] Although the global financial crisis a decade later would leave this claim in tatters, it was, nevertheless, from this early blueprint that Brown sought to create a new global financial architecture. Designed to 'shape a new interdependent and integrated global economy through stability and growth' this new framework promised 'prosperity and opportunity for all' whilst eradicating '"boom-and-bust" on a global scale'.[67] This new global architecture, Brown argued, was to be underpinned by four elements: (1) macroeconomic stability; (2) 'sound' monetary and fiscal policies emphasising credibility and transparency; (3) a series of internationally agreed disciplines and codes to support these policies; and (4) increased surveillance and accountability.[68] These elements, developed from New Labour's domestic political economy, would be assimilated to form the 'new' conditionality that would apply to countries seeking to secure debt relief.

In establishing the credibility of New Labour's political economy, Gordon Brown had handed over control of monetary policy to the Monetary Policy Committee at the Bank of England. For Brown, this was a deliberate strategy of depoliticisation, designed to reassure the market that the setting of interest rates was free from any political influence and based upon 'good long-term economics' rather than 'bad short-term politics'.[69] Abroad, the credibility of this new global architecture rested upon the handing over of greater powers to the IMF. Brown believed that acting as a 'politically neutral' *de facto* central bank, the Fund could provide the credibility that his new global architecture required by institutionalising and locking in stability and 'market-reinforcing' policies.[70]

To this end, the IMF was to have two clearly defined but interrelated roles. The first was to maintain and promote stability; a role that it had been afforded since its creation at Bretton Woods in 1944. In a global economy now dominated by interdependent, instantaneous and often volatile capital markets, however, such stability was increasingly difficult to maintain.[71] While it was neither desirable nor indeed possible to restrict these flows of capital, maintaining stability became a prerequisite for successful economic policymaking. Brown believed that the IMF could and should be reformed to take into account the complexities of the new economic system. Taken at face value, the Chancellor's proposals might have appealed to those constituencies who had long since called for just that. However, while many groups – including within the Labour Party itself – had expressed the need for a change in the ideological direction of the Fund, and a greater representation from the global South, what Brown meant was 'an enhanced role for the IMF monitoring and reporting on the operation of codes and standards'.[72]

According to Brown, however, reform of the IFIs was needed, not because of any ideological failings but because the IMF and the World Bank were presently ill-equipped to carry out the surveillance necessary to support the development of emerging countries' financial systems.[73] Keeping these countries 'on track' would require tightening the grip of the IMF and granting the Fund greater powers to control and restrict, where it deemed necessary, the monetary and fiscal policies of developing countries. As for those countries seeking debt relief, Brown argued that they could not be allowed to 'pick and mix which good and bad policies they wanted to pursue'. Despite the urgent need for debt relief – a point continually made by the Chancellor – this would only be made available if countries accepted 'regular surveillance of how they are meeting the codes'.[74]

By forcing developing countries to open up their economies, Brown's mantra of 'stability through surveillance' carefully shifted any blame for the continued indebtedness and underdevelopment away from asymmetric global power relations and towards the HIPCs themselves. For the Chancellor, secrecy, corruption and the lack of agreed rules of the game were preventing developing countries from attracting the foreign investment necessary to become successful economies in their own right. The answer, according to Brown, lay in developing countries publishing 'figures about what is happening to their reserves, what is happening to their fiscal policy' in an era of globalisation.[75] For 'globalisation to work for the poor' – the title, of course, of DFID's second White Paper – Brown maintained that developing countries in particular must be open to the global economy and pursue transparent, corruption-free policies for stability and the attraction of private investment.[76]

Sensing the importance of information to market actors, Brown pressed to increase the availability of this information within a credible framework to promote a much higher level of investor confidence.[77] Within the wider context of the 'economics of information' of the 'post-Washington Consensus', these procedures would give the policy decisions reached by national governments credibility with the markets, and market actors the confidence to make more informed investment decisions. Again therefore, these processes were designed not primarily to create a more accountable form of poverty-focused policymaking, but rather to orientate economic policies towards the expectations of market actors.

As this new architecture was being carefully crafted within the walls of HM Treasury, Gordon Brown was quickly establishing himself within the constellation of IFIs located in Washington. His growing reputation as the finance minister *par excellence* earned Brown the chairmanship of the International Monetary and Financial Committee (IMFC). This not only helped institutionalise New Labour's own model of political economy within these structures of global economic governance but also gave the Chancellor considerable clout within the Fund itself. Perhaps unsurprisingly, but crucially nonetheless, Brown's proposals received fulsome praise from the IMFC for 'promoting greater financial stability and stronger global growth'.[78] Critically, this new global architecture was applauded for its capacity 'to help countries strengthen policy frameworks and prevent crises, and improve the framework for assessing debt *sustainability*'.[79] Rather than challenge or problematise debt sustainability, the Chancellor's blueprint actually worked *within* the existing framework of the HIPC Initiative whilst strengthening the hand of creditors in the process.

Yet Brown's own attempt to increase the surveillance by the IMF of debtor countries actually undermined one of its more progressive claims, namely the increased country 'ownership' supported under the terms of the Enhanced HIPC Initiative and the 'post-Washington' PRSP process. By ceding power to a *non*-elected body of external economic elites merely for the sake of market credibility whilst increasing the severity of demands placed upon debtor countries, it begged the question, who really did 'own' the development of these indebted countries? Certainly, it said a great deal about the character of the Chancellor's new global architecture that it was the HIPCs who found themselves restricted in the policies that they were able to implement by the same IFIs whose remit for surveillance and control Brown had increased.

During this period, and against the backdrop of Brown's new architecture, New Labour claimed credit for the role it played in securing the Enhanced HIPC Initiative at the G7 summit in Cologne, with a series of measures that provided 'faster, broader and deeper debt relief'.[80] For its part, the Enhanced HIPC Initiative committed the IMF to 'deeper debt relief through lower debt sustainability targets, lower qualifying thresholds, and calculations based on earlier actual data rather than projections' and 'faster debt relief, including through the earlier provision of front-loaded assistance to free up resources for poverty-reducing spending, such as on health and education'.[81] Yet, embedded within this new financial architecture, despite promoting the goals of poverty reduction and sustainable development, the new initiative also reinforced the need for developing countries to reform 'appropriately'.

For those who had gathered in Birmingham the previous year to call for increased levels of debt relief, this new initiative may have represented a significant step forward. In the light of Gordon Brown's new global architecture, however, these headline announcements masked what amounted to a tightening of the grip maintained by the IFIs. In return for this 'deeper' and 'faster' debt relief, poverty reduction programmes would have to be reconfigured to reflect the demands of this new architecture. Debtor countries would have to ensure that these outlays in social expenditure were consistent with the imperatives of 'macroeconomic stability and faster sustained growth'. Moreover, national governments would have to accept greater levels of surveillance through the 'good governance' agenda including 'full transparency and . . . monitoring of government budgets'.[82]

Therefore, while Brown and his counterparts in Whitehall, Washington and the rest of the G7 spoke of 'poverty reduction' as the outcome, it was clear from the conditions attached that this was secondary to the principle focus of building institutions for markets, and maximising the accountability and transparency to market constituencies. In accordance with the orthodoxy of the 'post-Washington Consensus', the main responsibility of the state was to make markets work: to open up their books, and to design tax regimes, investment rules and economic policies all responsive to the needs of increasingly globalised markets, the net result of which was to leave entirely intact the neoliberal prescriptions of global integration in macroeconomic policymaking.

Whilst undoubtedly appealing in its two-fold commitment to tackling corruption *and* poverty, Brown's approach remained problematic in its failure to consider, let alone address, those structured fault-lines that entrenched underdevelopment in the global South. Of these, debt continues to be arguably the most damaging since it locks in a deeply skewed power relationship between the (Southern) debtor and (Northern) creditor, whilst at the same time draining away public resources that might otherwise be used to address this poverty. Rarely, however, did these concerns appear in Brown's frequently made calls for a 'new global architecture'. There was instead a continued commitment to debt *sustainability* and an assumption that the servicing of these debt repayments would continue whilst the HIPCs reprioritised and reordered their national economies to work with the grain of these financial systems and the demands of international investors.

At one level, this outcome dovetailed neatly into the Chancellor's belief that the 'right' kind of government was a precondition of market growth.[83] However, making countries work for globalisation through 'good', 'credible' policymaking served only to oversimplify the often complex structural contexts upon which transnational economic relations take place. Nevertheless, such was the Chancellor's zeal in proselytising this message that he, inadvertently or otherwise, simply erased the agency and undermined the economic sovereignty of these low-income countries. In its place, Brown prioritised the concerns of investors who, he feared, might not make the long-term commitments on the scale necessary for jobs, growth and social progress, if these clear and transparent frameworks were not in place.[84]

If countries were to secure both the investment and the day-to-day confidence of global market actors, then national governments must pursue consistent and credible policies that would guarantee the required stability.[85] For developing countries, however, it was expected that their economic policies would be orientated towards meeting the expectations of these self-same market investors. Crucially, since these measures were an intrinsic part of the 'sound' policy reforms that developing countries were expected to pursue in order to receive debt relief, these HIPCs would find themselves allocating much of their limited resources and capacity to creating 'the right investment climate' and persuading market actors of the credibility of their policies. Despite the scale of emergency and the more acute problems of poverty faced by their own people, the availability of debt relief as a financial resource to address these issues would have to wait.

The road to Gleneagles and beyond: the Multilateral Debt Relief Initiative

Having convinced the international financial community of his proposals for his 'new global architecture', the Chancellor's attention turned – or rather was turned – to the constituencies within civil society who had continued to press for a fairer and more comprehensive resolution to the debt crisis. During this phase of New Labour's debt strategy, ministers continued to meet with both the larger NGOs in the British Overseas Aid Group (BOAG) and the smaller NGOs that made up BOND, the British Overseas NGOs for Development, to discuss progress over debt relief. Both the Treasury and DFID held a series of meetings with representatives of the UK faith groups and continued to receive many letters and postcards from members of the public pressing for more debt forgiveness. However, the relationship between the government and these constituencies was rarely a straightforward one. As I have already mentioned in this chapter, while there were times when New Labour officials were fulsome in their praise for the work of these groups, there were other times when these campaigners appeared to get under the skin of government ministers with a series of demands that Whitehall officials deemed to be too unrealistic.

New Labour's ambivalence towards debt relief was reflected in its 'enthusiasm for debt relief' but rejection that 'all debt should always be written off'.[86] Like her counterparts in the World Bank and IMF, Clare Short made it clear that 'poor countries need to be able to borrow and repay responsibly, so that they have a good track record and can secure foreign investment and enable their economies to grow'.[87] The government's objective was therefore 'not to achieve debt relief at any price', but rather 'to lever policy so that it would bring real benefit to the poor, in terms of both better economic growth and better social policy'.[88] While for the government, debt relief was but one instrument to achieve its commitment to poverty reduction, for these faith groups, NGOs and other parts of civil society, debt relief was far more significant than that. In strictly development terms, poverty could not be eradicated whilst the governments of the HIPCs continued to spend much of their budgets servicing debts that had been accrued decades before. Although, as this next phase would reveal, New Labour ministers accepted these arguments, they continued to view debt, not as an issue of systemic inequality and global injustice, but as principally the result of irresponsible and short-sighted policy decisions. For government officials, this was the *real* cause of poverty. If these issues were to be tackled and poverty reduced, then the 'correct' policy framework of the new global architecture would need to be implemented.

Gordon Brown's chairmanship of the IMFC (discussed in the previous chapter) enabled the Chancellor to set about persuading his counterparts and other economic elites of not only the need but also the viability – and indeed, the *credibility* – of his new global financial architecture. Hard-wiring his proposals into the 'post-Washington Consensus', Brown appeared to know instinctively what language to use in order to discursively construct a global macroeconomic framework that would appeal to these particular audiences. The Chancellor spoke extensively of the importance of maintaining 'stability' and 'monetary and fiscal policy discipline', creating the 'right conditions for investment', 'opening up' and orientating national economies towards 'the global economy', and supporting these reforms through increased 'surveillance'.

To convince NGOs and faith groups of New Labour's commitment to debt relief and poverty reduction, however, Gordon Brown drew upon a set of language and themes distinct from any other policy narrative offered by his colleagues in Whitehall. In these speeches, the Chancellor did not simply speak about the moral element of debt relief, but instead made explicit reference to the Scriptures held to by the different faith groups represented in the civil society coalition. These Scriptures were used to complement and square with Brown's own social liberalism, the philosophy of which underpinned the Chancellor's work in this area.

These references were designed to send a signal to civil society that the economic dimension to New Labour's commitment to reducing the debt burden of developing countries was complementary to, rather than in conflict with, the moral appeal made by these constituencies. New Labour's strategy in this third phase was therefore to focus upon the similarities, rather than the differences, that existed between the government and those demands made by civil society. It was hoped that this would in turn build support for the new Multilateral Debt Relief Initiative proposed by Tony Blair, Gordon Brown and Clare Short's successor at DFID, Hilary Benn, initially to the Commission for Africa in 2005, before its formal launch at the G8 summit, hosted by Britain later that summer in Gleneagles. This new MDRI would not replace the Enhanced HIPC Initiative but would cancel 100 per cent of the debts owed to the IMF, the IDA and the African Development Fund by countries that had reached 'completion point' under the Enhanced HIPC Initiative.

For its part, civil society was being galvanised by the emergence of a new coalition of NGOs, faith groups, trade unions, celebrities and members of the general public. Part of the Global Call to Action Against Poverty campaign, the Make Poverty History movement sought to raise awareness of global poverty, and in particular issues relating to trade, debt and aid. To this end, it had three core messages for national governments in the global North: 'trade justice'; 'drop the debt'; and 'more and better aid'.[89] As with other recent anti-poverty and debt campaigns and demonstrations, the target of the Make Poverty History movement was to be the G8. The question that confronted New Labour therefore was not whether there was sufficient public support for its proposals – it was abundantly clear that there was – but whether the government could persuade civil society that its own proposals concerning debt relief were sufficient to meet these demands. Therefore, in the same way that New Labour had sought credibility for its proposals from amongst financial and economic constituencies, it now sought credibility from civil society. Given just how different these two sets of expectations were, however, Gordon Brown in particular faced a real test in securing an outcome that would not renege on the commitments that he had made to the two respective constituencies. How Brown would solve this problem would reveal the true character of his debt relief policies, and the depth of his commitment to the more normative claims that he had made concerning debt as a moral issue.

Developing the analysis of the previous phase, this particular phase demonstrates that while Gordon Brown actively sought to engage with civil society – for example, by regularly meeting representatives from the coalition, and borrowing the language and the discourse of faith groups and NGOs – the narratives that appeared in these conversations were used only selectively to justify the New Labour government's position in relation to debt relief and the IFIs, rather than to directly meet the expectations of civil society. This enabled Brown in particular to talk to certain audiences about the government's moral commitment to debt relief whilst continuing to embed its actual policy within the neoliberal ideas of the global financial architecture. For Brown, the only response to the moral challenge that developing world debt posed to Western governments and other lenders was the creation of a distinctly market-orientated framework, one that would oversee the integration of heavily indebted countries into the global market economy.

The idea of debt forgiveness was derived from the biblical commandment of Jubilee that appears in the Book of Leviticus (25: 8–54). Every forty-nine years, those who found themselves enslaved were to be set free and allowed to return to their families in readiness for the fiftieth year, which would then be marked as a year of Jubilee or celebration. This precept was to act as the referent point for church leaders and their various congregations as they called upon government leaders to celebrate the year 2000 and the turn of the millennium by freeing those countries enslaved by debt. Publicly at least, Gordon Brown was fulsome in his praise of churches and faith groups:

> Churches and faith groups . . . have, across the world, done more than any others – by precept and by example – to make us aware of the sheer scale of human suffering – and our duty to end it. Indeed, when the history of the crusade against global poverty is written, one of its first and finest chapters will detail the commitment of the churches in Britain to help the world's poor.[90]

Brown's impulse of Christian socialism prompted the Chancellor to declare that 'the burden of unpayable debt was morally wrong'.[91] Although his own faith remained a private affair, Brown nevertheless made it a priority to meet with church leaders and other faith groups. Brown frequently referred to 'a network of mutuality' that he believed bound 'together, all of us – citizens and nations, rich and poor – in one moral universe'.[92] This philosophy enabled Brown to place his personal commitment to debt relief in terms not simply of hard economics but of his own faith and understanding of morality. For Brown, debt relief had a profoundly moral and spiritual significance. Winning 'the economic argument' mapped out in his 'new global architecture' would require sharing communion with and making disciples of New Labour's non-economic constituencies.

In reaching out to these audiences, the Chancellor set about showcasing the full wealth of his knowledge of the Bible. It was here that growing up as a 'son of the manse' enabled Brown to quote – quite literally, chapter and verse – scriptural references in support of his arguments. The Chancellor drew upon verses from the prophet Isaiah which spoke of undoing 'the heavy burdens . . .

to let the oppressed go free' (58: 6) and the allegory in the Book of Revelation (21: 1–27) of a 'new Jerusalem', symbolising a new world, free from debt.[93] These narratives provided Brown with a distinctly ecclesiastical and moral purpose to debt relief. Indeed, in an address to the development NGO, CAFOD, the Chancellor actually agreed that debts should be 'wiped out . . . because people weighed down by the burden of debts imposed by the last genera-tion on this cannot even begin to build for the next generation'.[94] To insist on the payment of these debts, the Chancellor added, 'offends human dignity and is therefore unjust. *What is morally wrong cannot be economically right.*'[95] Drawing upon an array of spiritual teachings and philosophies, Brown invoked the gospels of Matthew (7: 12) and Luke (6: 31), the Jewish Shabbat (31a), and the Buddhist teachings of Udana-Varga (5: 18) alongside the liberal social thought of Gertrude Himmelfarb, Abraham Lincoln, Michael Winstanley, Adam Smith and James Q. Wilson.

Like his Chancellor, Tony Blair also praised the work of the Jubilee 2000 movement and, in a lecture to the Christian Social-ist Movement (CSM), the prime minister took the opportunity to spell out the achievements of his neighbour in Downing Street. Since the end of the millennium year, Blair told the audience, no profit had been taken from the HIPCs, and the British govern-ment had already agreed to cancel their debts, or to place these repayments in a Trust Fund for when this money could be used to tackle poverty.[96] Although this was just three months after the end of this momentous year, the prime minister was clearly keen to demonstrate that, like Brown, he too understood (at least in part) the Jubilee principal that many in his audience supported. Just as the passage in Leviticus (25: 17) spoke of not taking advantage of each other or lending money at interest (25: 37), so Blair sought to reassure the CSM that his government would not take advantage of indebted countries by charging excessive interest on the debts that were owed to Britain.

Of course, both Blair and Brown do deserve some praise for these commitments. However, it was insufficient merely to invoke the principal of Jubilee. In Mosaic Law, the underlying reason for Jubilee was to restore liberty and equality to a land torn apart by inequity and economic servitude. Therefore, although the New Labour government would no longer profit from its debtors and put on hold the repayments owed to it by the HIPCs, its continued commitment to the neoliberal orthodoxy failed to recognise, let alone address, the structural inequalities of the wider global economy. Furthermore, although there was an acknowledgement that 'debt "relief" merely relieves the creditor of a balance sheet fantasy',[97] the actual process towards debt reduction would still be contingent upon HIPCs pursuing 'sound' policies and promoting the growth necessary to reduce poverty. The bonds of debt therefore would be replaced only with the shackles of conditionality of Brown's financial architecture. Rather than freeing these countries, as the Jubilee precept demanded, heavily indebted states would instead be subjugated through all manner of surveillance measures – standards, codes and increased transparency – to ensure that they orientated their economies to the exigencies of the global market.

The force of these moral arguments was certainly compelling. However, what was almost as striking was the complete absence of these same arguments when Brown spoke to financial (i.e. 'non-civil society') constituencies. Any references to the 'moral sense' that the Chancellor had spoken about at such great length and with such apparent conviction on the eve of Britain's presidency of the G8 in December 2004 had disappeared by the time Brown made his statement to his colleagues at the IMFC in Washington just a few months later. On this occasion, the Chancellor preferred instead to address issues relating to enhancing 'the authority and credibility of surveillance, particularly of debt sustainability'.[98] Two months later, the 'moral' rhetoric returned and a virtually identical copy of Brown's speech on 'the moral sense' was delivered at UNICEF's annual lecture in June. Although inflecting less the 'faith' aspect of debt relief, the Chancellor nevertheless spoke of how this 'moral sense' underpinned New Labour's commitment to debt relief as a means of empowering individuals.[99] True to form, however, no mention was made of the moral imperative of debt relief, neither in the statement made by Brown to the IMFC later that September, nor to his counterparts at the conclusion of the G7 finance ministers meeting in London at the close of the year.[100] Despite viewing debt relief as both a moral and an economic issue and one that required a solution that was moral and therefore economically right, these ended up being two very distinct messages for two very different audiences.

Keen to talk about the 'moral' and faith-driven aspects of debt relief to sympathetic audiences, Brown reverted to playing the 'Iron

Chancellor' when it came to discussing debt in the corridors and meeting rooms of the IFIs. It would appear that not even Brown was prepared to reconcile the two imperatives, calling into question the depth of his commitment to the moral dimension of debt relief. Although New Labour sought to engage with civil society and faith groups in particular, these were audiences that did not need convincing of the need for more extensive debt forgiveness. The general message to this type of audience was that the government had seen some success and was looking to improve in those areas where progress had been slow. Interestingly, where this was the case, it was never the fault of New Labour. The recalcitrance of fellow creditors, the lack of reform on the part of indebted countries, and even the unrealistic demands of civil society were all at one stage or another frequently cited as being roadblocks to debt relief; it was never due to the shortcomings of the British government.

Under Brown's watch, however, New Labour *did* fall short and it failed frequently to meet its responsibilities to the developing world through an inability and unwillingness to voice the same sort of moral commitment in the conference halls and meeting rooms of the IFIs as it had when speaking to civil society. Although Brown spoke often about the need to build international support for faster and deeper levels of debt relief, when it came to flexing his muscle within these institutions, the Chancellor appeared not to have the stomach for a political fight in Washington. The moral dimension that Brown claimed would be so crucial as to make any debt relief policy 'economically right' was overlooked in favour of a policy agreement that would support the expectations of market actors instead.

Conclusions

Developing world debt was symbolic in that it was the first of New Labour's many forays into the realm of international development, but crucially it provided Gordon Brown with the perfect opportunity to showcase his own carefully crafted model of political economy on the global stage. In many respects then, this chapter is about much more than simply New Labour's attitude towards debt relief. Its response to indebtedness in the global

South went beyond simply freeing up the much-needed financial resources for development. Instead, Brown offered an ostensibly 'new global financial architecture' which would incorporate and reform (or 'enhance') the pre-existing HIPC Initiative, underpin the MDRI and set heavily indebted poor countries on the road to not simply debt sustainability but long-term economic growth and development. Both the HIPC Initiative and MDRI provide an insight as to how New Labour worked, firstly within the established structures of global economic governance, and secondly, through the reforms that it offered as a means of meeting its own objectives in government.

Based upon the measures that Gordon Brown himself had introduced at home, this new architecture was designed in a similar way to maintain macroeconomic stability, strengthen economic governance, and provide confidence to investors by increasing the visibility of market information. The design of this new architecture was striking, since these principles reflected the thinking of the 'post-Washington Consensus' subscribed to by the *nébuleuse* of IFIs located in Washington, just as much as it did the policy ideas of Brown and other senior officials in the Treasury. This new architecture was predicated upon a commitment by indebted countries in particular to 'sound policies'. Macroeconomic stability, market liberalism, economic growth, fiscal discipline and anti-inflationary policies were the touchstones of this architecture; all of which in turn enabled it to bear the considerable imprint of the 'post-Washington Consensus'. Within this framework, HIPCs were to be locked in to a series of internationally agreed standards and codes at the national level, and monitored closely by institutions such as the IMF, whose remit to maintain stability would be strengthened under the terms of this new architecture.

The language used by Gordon Brown to describe these policies, and indeed this new architecture, was certainly interesting. Although they appeared to be neoliberal in character, Brown described these policies as being 'pro-poor'. Without these policies in place, the Chancellor argued that the investment necessary for growth-led development would not be forthcoming and would preclude the governments of HIPCs from making the necessary investments in healthcare, education, infrastructure and job creation. This understanding of development dovetailed with that of the Washington-based IFIs, and the IMF and the World Bank in particular, who viewed development in largely economic terms. Labelling these policies as being 'pro-poor', however, was strategically useful when speaking to constituencies who viewed themselves as being outside of this orthodoxy, and who narrated the debt crisis in terms of morality and social justice, rather than simply a matter of economic expediency. According to these groups, governments and banking institutions in the global North had, for far too long, been guilty of extracting usury from the poorest and most vulnerable countries and people on the planet. The issue was not about debt sustainability and keeping these countries locked in a two-speed economic system, but about debt justice, forgiveness and the removal of this millstone from around the necks of the world's poorest countries. Only then could these countries begin to develop and see their own standards of living increase.

These constituencies certainly loomed large over New Labour's strategy in this area, and to his credit, Gordon Brown did not shy away from engaging with them. Indeed, the issue of debt and the church-based make-up of this movement gave Brown the opportunity to talk openly about his own faith and the influence that it had upon his politics. The speeches made to these audiences were infused with the moral imperative of debt justice. However, while these were no doubt warmly received, it was surely disappointing for these constituencies that such support and the moral weight of such arguments never seemed to materialise when it *really* mattered. Through his role as chair of the IMFC, Brown held a uniquely influential position within Washington as well as Whitehall. To these altogether more market-minded audiences, however, the Chancellor's moral argument for increased debt relief never appeared. Instead, the debate continued to be framed in altogether more 'credible' economic terms: stability, growth and the right conditions for investment.

Despite a clear engagement with civil society, Gordon Brown's drawing of New Labour's debt relief strategy demonstrated a continued orientation towards the expectations of these 'economic' constituencies. This said a great deal about the character of New Labour and the political economy of Brown himself. Firstly, rather than representing any real break from the neoliberal orthodoxy of the 'post-Washington Consensus', Brown framed New Labour's response to the debt crisis in virtually the same terms as these Washington institutions, consolidating and in some instances, actually deepening these neoliberal reforms. Secondly, and perhaps even more significantly, while the Chancellor was at least aware of and acknowledged the moral imperative of debt forgiveness, he appeared to lack the conviction to carry this moral argument right to the heart of where it was needed most; namely, the institutions of global finance where his New Labour government could have brought about very real change to the lives of millions across the developing world.

Notes

1. Gill, *Power and Resistance in the New World Order*, 2003.
2. Pettifor, *Debt, the Most Potent Form of Slavery*, 1996.
3. IMF, 'Debt Relief under the Heavily Indebted Poor Countries (HIPC) Initiative', 2011.
4. Gondwe, 'The hazards of debt cancellation point to benefit in Africa finding its own sustainable growth path', 1998.
5. Ibid.
6. Wolfensohn, remarks made at the Multilateral Development Banks Meeting on the HIPC Initiative, 2000.
7. Krueger, 'Stability, Growth, and Prosperity', 2006.
8. Thirkell-White, *The IMF and the Politics of Financial Globalization*, 2005, p. 74.
9. The IMF's Extended Credit Facility issues loans to low-income countries at subsidised rates.
10. IMF, 'IMF Extended Credit Facility', 2011; IDA, *IDA Eligibility, Terms and Graduation Policies*, 2001, p. 1.
11. IDA, *IDA Eligibility, Terms and Graduation Policies*, 2001, p. 5.
12. IMF, 'IMF Extended Credit Facility', 2011.
13. Köhler, 'Promoting Stability and Prosperity in a Globalized World', 2001.
14. Krueger, 'Pursuing the Achievable', 2004.
15. Krueger, 'Stability, Growth, and Prosperity', 2006.
16. IMF, 'Sound policies, support can help Africa ride crisis', 2009.
17. IMF, 'Financial System Soundness', 2011.
18. Burnside and Dollar, 'Aid spurs growth', 1997, p. 4.
19. Ibid. p. 5.
20. Ibid. p. 5.
21. Gould, *The New Conditionality*, 2005.
22. IMF, 'Debt Relief under the Heavily Indebted Poor Countries (HIPC) Initiative', 2011.

23. Soederberg, *The Politics of the New Financial Aid Architecture*, 2004, p. 174.
24. Thirkell-White, 'The international financial architecture and the limits to neoliberal hegemony', 2007, p. 23.
25. World Bank Group, *Economic Growth in the 1990s*, 2005, p. 100.
26. UNDP, *Beyond the Midpoint*, 2010, p. 85.
27. Labour Party, *New Labour*, 1997, p. 39.
28. Brown, speech delivered at the Lord Mayor's Banquet, 1997.
29. Ibid.
30. Williams, *British Foreign Policy under New Labour, 1997–2005*, 2005, p. 152.
31. DFID, *A Challenge for the 21st Century*, 1997, p. 71.
32. Short, 'Global Free Trade', 1997.
33. Brown, 'The Central Economic Objectives of the New Government', 1997.
34. Brown, 'Debt 2000', 1997.
35. Brown, 'The Central Economic Objectives of the New Government', 1997.
36. Liddell, 'Heavily Indebted Countries', 1998.
37. Short, 'Heavily Indebted Poor Countries Initiative', 1998.
38. Oxfam, *Debt Relief and Poverty Reduction*, 1998, p. 2.
39. South Centre, 'Foot-dragging on foreign debt', 2001.
40. Jubilee Debt Campaign, 'Heavily Indebted Poor Countries Initiative', 2006.
41. World Vision, 'Debt Cancellation', 2006.
42. Blair, 'Denver Summit', 1997.
43. Short, 'International Development', 1997.
44. Brown, 'Financial Statement', 1998.
45. HM Treasury, *Modern Public Services for Britain*, 1998.
46. Jubilee 2000 Coalition, 'Memorandum from Jubilee 2000 Coalition', 1998.
47. HM Treasury, *The Code for Fiscal Stability*, 1998.
48. Short, 'International Monetary Fund–World Bank Meeting', 1998.
49. Brown, 'Third World Debt', 1998.
50. Liddell, 'Mauritius Mandate', 1998.
51. G8, *The Birmingham Summit Communiqué*, 1998.
52. Ibid.
53. Blair, 'G8 Summit', 1998.
54. Short, 'Debt Reduction', 1998.
55. Liddell, 'Debt Relief', 1998.
56. Short, 'Debt Relief', 1998.
57. Short, 'Central America (Hurricane Mitch)', 1998.
58. Ibid.

59. Ibid.
60. Brown, 'New Global Structures for the New Global Age', 1998.
61. See DFID, *Making Globalisation Work for the Poor*, 2000, pp. 89–91.
62. DFID, *A Challenge for the 21st Century*, 1997, p. 71.
63. Short, 'Central America (Hurricane Mitch)', 1998.
64. Brown, statement made at the International Monetary and Financial Committee, 2003.
65. Brown, 'State and market', 2003.
66. Brown, 'The Central Economic Objectives of the New Government', 1997.
67. Brown, 'Comprehensive Spending Review', 1998; Brown, speech delivered at the News International Conference, 1998.
68. Brown, 'The conditions for high and stable growth and employment', 2001.
69. Brown, 'Exploiting the British Genius', 1997.
70. Brown, speech delivered at the 'Financing Sustainable Development, Poverty Reduction and the Private Sector' conference, 2003.
71. Brown, 'Q. 254', 1998.
72. Brown, speech delivered at the International Action Against Child Poverty conference, 2001.
73. Brown, 'Q. 254', 1998.
74. Ibid.
75. Brown, 'Financial Statement', 1999.
76. Brown, 'Budget Statement', 2001.
77. Brown, 'World Economic Situation and Prospects', 2002.
78. IMFC, 'Communiqué of the International Monetary and Financial Committee of the Board of Governors of the International Monetary Fund', 2002.
79. Ibid., emphasis added.
80. G7, 'The Cologne Debt Initiative', 1999.
81. IMF, 'Transforming the Enhanced Structural Adjustment Facility (ESAF) and the Debt Initiative for the Heavily Indebted Poor Countries (HIPCs)', 2000.
82. Ibid.
83. Brown, The Gilbert Murray Memorial Lecture, 2000.
84. Brown, speech delivered at the Smith Institute, 1999.
85. Ibid.
86. Short, 'Debt Relief', 2000.
87. Ibid.
88. Ibid.
89. Make Poverty History, 'What Do We Want?', 2007.
90. Brown, 'Poverty and Globalisation', 2004.

91. Brown, speech delivered at the British-American Chamber of Commerce, 2000.
92. Ibid.; Brown, 'Making Globalisation Work for All', 2004; Brown, 'Financial Statement', 2004.
93. Brown, 'Poverty and Globalisation', 2004.
94. Ibid.
95. Ibid., emphasis added.
96. Blair, speech delivered to the Christian Socialist Movement, 2001.
97. Commission for Africa, *Our Common Interest*, 2005, p. 108.
98. Brown, 'International Development in 2005', 2005.
99. Brown, 'A Comprehensive Plan for HIV/AIDS', 2005.
100. Brown, 'International Finance Facility', 2005; Brown, 'Financial Statement', 2005.

6   Morals and Medicines

In 2004, at the midpoint of New Labour's time in office, the global AIDS epidemic was at its height. UNAIDS, the United Nations body tasked with addressing the crisis, estimated at the time that since the early 1980s the disease had claimed the lives of some 20 million people, with between 34.6 and 42.3 million people worldwide living with HIV, the virus that causes AIDS.[1] As it remains today, sub-Saharan Africa was the worst affected region, with many of its countries decimated by a disease responsible for the deaths of more people than any other illness. As infection rates and mortality rates peaked, the New Labour government set about tackling this crisis. Sandwiched in between its efforts to raise finance for development through increased debt relief and overseas aid, government ministers – again led by Gordon Brown – unveiled a strategy to increase the availability of the antiretroviral drugs with a specific focus upon developing countries. While these medicines would not cure those living with the disease, improving their accessibility would help promote greater adherence to appropriate treatment regimes and prolong the lives of those living with HIV.

Again, to its credit, New Labour took the initiative, and as this chapter will show, set about addressing the shortfall of both the amount of and access to antiretroviral drugs in some of the poorest parts of the world. Central to this commitment was again Gordon Brown. In both his role as Chancellor and then prime minister, Brown was ever-present, co-ordinating New Labour's response and bringing to bear his moral call to arms against this deadly global disease through a high-level partnership with Britain's powerful pharmaceutical industry. On the face of it, this appeared to be a sound enough strategy: several of the world's biggest and wealthiest drug companies, many of which were based in Britain, redoubling their efforts to address this global catastrophe. Yet it was a partnership that often appeared contradictory and riven with tensions. This conflict Brown himself appeared to embody. For whilst Brown led a number of New Labour officials who agreed that the price of these drugs remained prohibitively high, he was also instrumental in introducing a number of market-based measures to incentivise rather than regulate the industry into meeting its wider obligations towards HIV and AIDS.

Crucially, therefore, much like with his personal commitment to debt relief, Brown found himself struggling to make the trade-off between the 'economic' and 'moral' imperative. Having exalted the pharmaceutical firms at home – placing them at the heart of Britain's own so-called 'knowledge economy' – Gordon Brown and New Labour came under increasing pressure from groups within a civil society demanding greater and far quicker action over the access to and cost of antiretroviral drugs abroad. This enclave of civil society pointed to inappropriate and expensive pricing structures; a chronic lack of research and development (R&D); and continued intransigence over intellectual property (IP) and patent rules as being the main reasons why rates of new HIV infections continued to outstrip the provision of medicines, and why millions already living with the disease across the developing world were still without lifesaving medicines.[2] According to these groups, British and other Western pharmaceutical firms were concerned more about their own profitability and their shareholders than they were about their moral responsibilities as global health providers.

For the main part, Brown agreed with this analysis – but he was also sympathetic to the arguments put forward by the pharmaceutical industry that its continued profitability was of vital importance if it was to continue to invest in drug innovations. Accepting that the industry did in fact have 'a moral responsibility to make its products accessible to poor people', British-based firms like GlaxoSmithKline argued that they needed the protection offered by international IP laws to prevent their drug innovations from being copied and sold on by smaller pharmaceutical firms in low-cost, emerging economies such as India and South Africa.[3] The real barrier to access was not the IP rules – as claimed by civil society – but the severely underfunded healthcare systems found in developing countries affected by HIV and AIDS.[4]

As New Labour's strategy unfolded, Brown and his colleagues found it difficult to square the financial concerns of these firms and the appeals for increased access made by civil society. On the one hand, there was a very clear commitment to address global health concerns and roll back the spread of HIV in the global South. On the other hand, however, ministers did not want to risk alienating the very same set of British-based firms whose own reticence to invest in life-prolonging antiretrovirals was costing the lives of millions in the worst affected parts of the world. Ultimately, New Labour chose to prioritise the interests of an industry that it had identified as being one of the jewels in the crown of Britain's 'knowledge economy'. Overseeing this policy from his position in the Treasury and Downing Street, and working closely with colleagues across Whitehall, Gordon Brown could have pressed ahead with a strategy that prioritised global public health, and one that demanded far greater responsibility on the part of the pharmaceutical industry to increase access to the availability of antiretroviral medicines in the developing world. From this position of power, however, Brown chose not to disrupt this relationship, and pursued instead a set of policy measures orientated more towards meeting the preferences of the industry itself.

Having already explored in Chapter 3 the importance attached to the 'knowledge economy' by New Labour and the pharmaceutical industry's significant role within it, this particular chapter opens by addressing the government's carefully cultivated relationship with the industry and the moral obligation that the drug companies in this sector had as providers of (global) healthcare. With this relationship in mind, my attention turns to the ways in which New Labour's stated aim to increase access to these antiretroviral drugs in the developing world unfolded during its time in office. As its efforts underwent several phases of policy, this chapter demonstrates how New Labour constrained its international commitment by making its chief priority the ongoing competitiveness and profitability of Britain's pharmaceutical industry. Despite an awareness of, and some limited appeals for, the moral case for action, officials, led by Gordon Brown, continued to orientate their response to the crisis towards the pharmaceutical industry. This chapter concludes with a brief assessment of the implications for those living with HIV and AIDS in the developing world of this particular aspect of New Labour's political economy.

Moral obligations and market realities: revisiting New Labour's relationship with Britain's pharmaceutical industry

Unlike most other businesses, pharmaceutical firms are not, or perhaps should not be, concerned only with the sale of goods and services, profit maximisation and satisfying shareholder expectations. They have unique and intrinsic duties as health providers, and an acutely ethical commitment to make available affordable, effective medicines to all those who need them. This is not simply a normative claim; Richard Barker, the then director of the Association of the British Pharmaceutical Industry (the trade association for more than seventy-five companies in the UK producing prescription medicines), acknowledged as much: 'As a global industry whose aim is to improve health, it is a clear responsibility of the pharmaceutical sector to do its part in addressing this [global] need.'[5] Therefore, while other businesses might have duties that fall under the broader umbrella of corporate social responsibility, pharmaceutical firms have a much more specific ethical and moral obligation in the products they provide; one that extends far beyond their self-regulating, corporate behaviour, and which actually forms the very basis for their existence. For firms such as GlaxoSmithKline, for example, 'increasing access to medicines is important . . . for ethical, reputational and commercial reasons *because it is morally the right thing to do* and is valued by our shareholders, employees and other stakeholders'.[6] That this moral commitment was understood to be vital for both commercial and strategic reasons of course reflects a large degree of self-interest. Nevertheless, there was a clear acknowledgement from pharmaceutical firms themselves that they have a distinct ethical obligation to meet the global shortfall in essential medicines.

Indeed, other pharmaceutical firms did not shy away talking about the 'big role' that they had to play in addressing 'the interlinking issues of poverty and health'.[7] It was perhaps with this role in mind that the New Labour government noted that pharmaceutical firms can – and do – make a difference in public health outcomes.[8] In the midst of these warm words, however, there remained a distinct ambiguity in just how this obligation and role might be fulfilled. For a number of senior New Labour ministers, it was clear that, despite this moral commitment, the transformation of these health outcomes would depend upon the developing countries themselves. This emphasis upon the health systems would end up abrogating any responsibility on the part of the pharmaceutical firms, and shift the burden of care away from these multi-billion-pound corporations and onto the shoulders of what, in many instances, were heavily indebted governments with only limited, and in some instances diminishing, resources.

No minister articulated this approach more than Clare Short, New Labour's first secretary of state for international development. Her tenure from 1997 to 2003 saw DFID focus specifically upon these market conditions, and prioritise the strengthening of basic healthcare systems so as to improve the capacity of states to manage the crisis themselves.[9] Short was adamant that 'even if the drugs were free, most poor people would not get them, because they have no access to healthcare'.[10] Even at greatly reduced prices, she maintained, these drugs would remain unaffordable for many people in the developing world.[11] Moreover, Short pointed out that many low-income countries did not have the capacity to cope with the huge influx of medicines demanded by civil society, let alone to administer and monitor the complex drug combinations required by patients living with HIV. It was far more important, Short argued, that there was a much bigger commitment from African heads of state in order that faster progress could be made.[12]

Elsewhere, Short even appeared dismissive of the place of antiretrovirals in fighting the disease, going as far as to say that she hoped 'that no one will pretend that antiretrovirals are the answer, *because they are not*'.[13] Lambasting the calls made by civil society for a fairer deal for AIDS-affected countries as 'not helpful',[14] Short remained critical of 'the whole Western, European obsession with antiretroviral drugs'.[15] Accepting her evidence, the Commons Select Committee for International Development duly noted the need to focus on basic healthcare systems. 'Antiretrovirals', it argued, 'must not be seen as a magic bullet; the crisis in southern Africa is primarily one caused by poverty and vulnerability, rather than by lack of access to medicines.'[16]

This thinking persisted in a DFID-led report designed to map out 'best practice' in the pharmaceutical industry. Skimming over the moral obligations that firms might otherwise have, the government's *Framework for Good Practice in the Pharmaceutical Industry* noted that responsibility for improving access to these medicines was not limited to the pharmaceutical industry but rather extended to the whole international community.[17] Moreover, according to the report, it was not the fault of the industry that there was a lack of access to cheap generics and investment in R&D but rather 'poor quality health systems and a lack of financing to purchase medicines'.[18]

There was, of course, some merit in such assessments. However, these responses ignored the wider crisis of poverty faced by many countries in the global South, namely the underdevelopment exacerbated by the Structural Adjustment Programmes that had been rolled out during the 1980s and 1990s. These policies, introduced by the International Monetary Fund and World Bank in the wake of the debt crisis of the 1970s, and supported by countries including the UK, had imposed austerity measures upon many of the countries now worst affected by HIV and AIDS. With many public services privatised, and access to healthcare and education narrowed, the money that governments might have spent providing these services free of charge was instead eaten up in debt repayments. For those countries now in the grip of the AIDS epidemic, chronically underfunded healthcare systems, combined with a shrinking domestic tax base, a decimated workforce and a declining level of overseas aid, meant that it was virtually impossible for these countries to cope with the financial cost of the crisis, let alone put in place the highly developed healthcare systems demanded by Short.

According to the secretary of state, however, only the right market conditions would persuade pharmaceutical firms to invest in these lifesaving drugs. Indeed, the government viewed 'the prospect of affordable antiretroviral drugs as *an additional incentive* for strengthening health systems'.[19] Once these health markets were properly in place, then pharmaceutical firms would be far more prepared to invest and provide the drugs that were needed. There was, however, very little evidence of the moral purpose that the industry had continued to claim. According to Short, their motive was to 'get some return on their investment, particularly their massive research budgets',[20] and this was evident by the less than impressive research track records of these firms:

> Over 95 per cent of global investments in drug development [were] targeted to the medical needs of the richest 20 per cent of the world's population. By contrast, only *1 per cent* of the drugs developed over the previous 25 years were for tropical diseases and tuberculosis, diseases that together accounted for over 11 per cent of the global disease burden.[21]

With national governments unable to afford to rebuild their health-care programmes and pharmaceutical firms sitting on 'massive' research budgets only prepared to invest in profitable markets, it meant that those living with HIV in some of the world's poorest countries effectively faced a death sentence.

Despite its unwillingness to invest in the so-called 'diseases of poverty', other senior government figures also remained firmly in support of the pharmaceutical industry. Prime Minister Tony Blair and Hazel Blears, then a junior health minister, both maintained the importance of safeguarding the research budgets of the pharmaceutical firms. Also dismissing the appeals by civil society to relax the rules set by the WTO surrounding the trade-related aspects of intellectual property rights (TRIPS) designed to protect these firms, Blair argued that intellectual property was the 'life-blood' of the industry and any legislation designed to safeguard this should be *more* tightly enforced – not less.[22] Repeating this policy in a speech to the Association of the British Pharmaceutical Industry, Blears reaffirmed that 'intellectual property rights are the lifeblood of the innovative pharmaceutical industry' and were 'essential to investment in R&D'. The junior minister pledged that her government would 'uphold that position in the face of those who claim that getting rid of patents would somehow solve the problem'.[23] Offering a slightly different but no less pro-business perspective, Baroness Valerie Amos, who would later replace Short as secretary of state, went further and suggested that it was actually *in the interests* of those countries affected by HIV and AIDS to support the TRIPS legislation. Speaking in the House of Lords, Amos argued that 'developing countries *need* intellectual property protection as a way of encouraging more investment, research and innovation, from which they should benefit'.[24]

By prioritising business interests over those living with HIV and AIDS, all these statements did was simply excuse those firms that were willing only to invest and distribute drugs in well-established markets. In these predominately Western markets, there was no such problem of a lack of cheap generics, nor was there any problem for firms to fund high-quality, highly productive research programmes. By contrast, owing to the risks to profitability and shareholder value, the industry was simply unwilling to invest in and supply the necessary medicines to those poorer countries where there were weak and underdeveloped healthcare systems. For their part, many senior New Labour ministers appeared unwilling to apply pressure upon the pharmaceutical firms to help boost this capacity themselves and invest in drug formulations suitable for use in developing countries.

Despite her own reservations over the availability of antiretrovirals as a solution to the unfolding crisis, Clare Short still accepted the chair of a High Level Working Group on Access to Medicines set up by Tony Blair. Strikingly and surprisingly, this group called upon pharmaceutical firms to keep 'prices close to the cost of manufacture' and increase 'R&D into diseases of poor people in the developing world'.[25] Indeed, Short's position was muddied further when her own department announced a significant contribution to the multilateral Global Fund in order 'to improve provision of [the] drugs and commodities to treat those diseases'.[26] Interestingly, both these initiatives had distinct supply-side objectives – increased funding for drug research and availability of medicines – that contradicted the secretary of state's personal argument that it was purely the demand side that needed to be addressed.

Given Short's antagonism towards the benefits of antiretrovirals in tackling the AIDS epidemic, it was certainly remarkable that she could agree with a remit of the group to scale up the levels of access to these same drugs, or spend 'US$200 million . . . over five years' on an initiative which she clearly had some reservations over.[27] Crucially, the stance taken by Clare Short put her at odds with not only the aims of her own working group but also the measures that were being designed by Gordon Brown at the Treasury. Here, Brown introduced a fiscal policy based upon increased spending and tax relief measures *specifically* to increase the availability of antiretrovirals suitable for dispensation in developing countries. It is to these measures and Brown's central role in capturing this area of development policy that this chapter now turns its attention.

Enter Gordon Brown and the Treasury's supply-side policy measures

Unlike Clare Short, Gordon Brown and his team at the Treasury did believe that the pharmaceutical industry had an altogether more prominent role to play and a far greater responsibility in the fight against HIV and AIDS in the developing world. Rather than focusing upon the demand-side issues identified by DFID as being the biggest barrier to tackling AIDS, the Treasury was far bolder in probing the pharmaceutical industry over what it was doing to combat the spread of the disease in the developing world. The Treasury did not criticise the stance taken by Clare Short's DFID, nor did it suggest that the pharmaceutical industry on its own could tackle the crisis. The Treasury did believe, however, that the pharmaceutical industry *should* step up and meet its obligations over the provision of antiretroviral medicines.

Drawing upon the government–industry links that Tony Blair and other senior New Labour officials had been keen to develop at home, staff at the Treasury, led by Gordon Brown, designed a series of proposals in order to address the problem of chronic underinvestment in the health sector within the developing world. As part of these supply-side measures, the Treasury announced plans for a tax credit to incentivise pharmaceutical firms into spending more on R&D into vaccines suitable for developing countries. In the 2000 pre-Budget Report, the Treasury argued that the underlying problem of access to drugs in the developing world was because:

> Only a tiny fraction of new patents address diseases in developing countries. This is mainly because those who might be able to develop vaccines fear they would not be able to recoup the significant research expenditures that will be needed.[28]

To address this problem, Brown proposed a new tax incentive to encourage firms to 'develop, cut the costs for and ensure the supply of anti-tuberculosis, anti-malaria and anti-AIDS drugs'.[29] This tax credit would be part of an overall package of policy measures designed to tackle the diseases of poverty by stimulating increased investment into R&D.[30] The Chancellor announced plans to encourage

> commitments by the industry . . . to make donations on a more con-
> sistent basis, in support of developing countries' own health strate-
> gies, and launch a new global purchase fund, both to encourage the
> development and delivery of effective and affordable treatments that
> do not yet exist, and for the treatments already available.[31]

The sweetener in this deal was that the Treasury would look to remove the 'constraints in the tax system on donations of drugs and vaccines'.[32]

In the 2001 pre-Budget Report, the Treasury continued its com-
mitment to increasing access to essential medicines by rewarding R&D into drugs and vaccines to treat diseases threatening lives in the least developed countries.[33] While DFID had (correctly) identified AIDS as a disease of poverty, the Treasury offered an altogether more acute diagnosis. The underlying problem was that only 18 per cent of the world's pharmaceutical market was in developing countries – yet these developing countries made up 80 per cent of the world's population. This meant that the poorest within these countries were faced with a double burden: spending a high proportion of their low incomes on unsuitable treatments.

For the Treasury, the current R&D pipeline for effective drugs and vaccines that would address this problem was 'negligible'. To boost the levels of research, the Treasury pledged to provide an extra 50 per cent relief on qualifying expenditure for companies undertaking research into specified diseases. Alongside these tax measures, the Treasury also looked into options for increasing the incentives for pharmaceutical companies to donate drugs, vaccines and suitable equipment in support of developing countries' health strategies. Crucially, therefore, Brown's Treasury afforded the pharmaceutical industry a far greater role than that implied by DFID in supporting the demand side and sustaining the healthcare systems of developing countries.

Underpinning the Treasury's supply-side strategies was 'a capacity to help and a moral duty to act' that Brown argued the phar-
maceutical firms and developed countries had to those parts of the world experiencing high levels of HIV and AIDS.[34] Brown maintained that it was vital that governments 'urge the pharmaceutical

companies to do more by supporting research and development and making drugs available to the poorest countries at affordable prices'.[35] Addressing a Special Session of the United Nations General Assembly, Brown further stepped up the pressure on the industry by urging it to match the commitment demonstrated by the developed countries in the creation of the new Global Fund with a commitment of its own 'to create new drugs and vaccines in ways that truly help the poor and sick'.[36] The Chancellor called on pharmaceutical firms 'to step up to their responsibility, to recognise the scale of the challenge we face and to respond on an equal scale'.[37]

Although admirable, what was striking about these speeches and statements was that – much like Brown's apparent support for 'faster and deeper debt relief' assessed in the previous chapter – this moral appeal was made only to 'non-industry' audiences. Again, therefore, these policy commitments flattered to deceive. Whilst emphasising to these 'pro-development' constituencies the moral obligation of pharmaceutical firms, there was a distinct lack of any similar rhetoric in the government's partnership and policy dialogue with the industry. While the Chancellor spoke of the pharmaceutical firms' and rich countries' 'capacity to help' and 'moral duty' to act, his government's own framework with the industry spoke only about providing market-based solutions as a means of addressing what Brown's financial secretary, Paul Boateng, called 'a specific case of market failure'.[38]

Treating the issue as one of 'market failure', however, raised questions as to the suitability of promoting a 'market-based solution' as a means of correcting this failure.[39] If, as the working group had already noted, pharmaceutical companies were 'run for profit' and 'the poor of the world cannot generate a market',[40] Brown's tax relief initiative would act only as a 'carrot' rather than a 'stick' in order to prompt the industry to take seriously its moral obligations. It did not address the fundamental inequality running throughout the global healthcare system, nor encourage the redistribution of resources and drug technology from the wealthiest to the poorest parts of the world. Instead, Brown's colleagues in the Treasury remained steadfast in their belief in the market to deliver if they created the right fiscal conditions.[41]

The High Level Working Group provided the platform for dialogue between government and industry officials, and it was during these meetings that the pharmaceutical firms outlined two telling concerns that, according to Paul Boateng, firms had about New Labour's antiretroviral policy:

> First, they have shareholders whom they must satisfy and to whom they have certain fiduciary responsibilities. Secondly, they see themselves, as health providers, as having a moral purpose and a degree of corporate responsibility. They recognise that they have skills and an infrastructure for research and development, but – they are very upfront about it – there is no market because the developing world does not have the resource base available to it either to put in place the infrastructure or to fund the research and to buy its product.[42]

Despite identifying two clear commitments – economic or 'fiduciary responsibilities' to their shareholders, and moral obligations as health providers – there was a distinct prioritisation of these two imperatives. While admitting that they had the skills and the infrastructure to increase levels of research into HIV and AIDS, the pharmaceutical firms were unwilling to invest this capital themselves *because there was no market incentive to do so*. This was particularly problematic because many developing countries did not have the resources or the infrastructure necessary to facilitate these types of investments. In the midst of this impasse, while it would be the moral, and indeed 'the right thing to do' in terms of fulfilling their duties as health providers, for pharmaceutical firms to invest in research and products solely for use in these 'non-markets' would be, in the eyes of their shareholders, financially irresponsible.

As his position grew within New Labour's AIDS strategy, Brown attempted square this problem by assimilating these two elements; talking about increasing access in distinctly moral terms but embedding the response of the Treasury firmly within the strictures of the market. The Chancellor clearly felt that if he was to be more successful in persuading the pharmaceutical industry to scale up access to medicines, any policy measures would need to accept these economic realities. Only by accommodating the overriding economic expectations held by the pharmaceutical industry could Brown's own moral commitments be met. As the government stepped up its dialogue with the pharmaceutical industry into the second half of its time in office, New Labour also started to take even more seriously its own commitment to those living with HIV and AIDS in the developing world. The next phase of this policy would be underpinned by the government's 'Taking Action' strategy, a series of key measures designed explicitly to increase access to essential medicines. It is to this strategy that I now turn my attention.

Increased policy coherence and ambition . . . but business as usual?

Throughout this particular phase of policy, DFID produced a proliferation in policy literature to reveal its ambition to increase access to essential medicines in the developing world. This message became undoubtedly *the* focal point of New Labour's efforts to halt and reverse the spread of HIV in the developing world. The 'Call for Action' launched in December 2003 demanded better funding, stronger political direction, better donor co-ordination, and better HIV and AIDS programmes.[43] This was to prove to be the catalyst for the UK's own 'Taking Action' strategy the following July, which outlined how Britain would respond to these challenges. This report was flanked by two further specific reports, one revealing the UK's policy and plans for increasing access to essential medicines in the developing world,[44] and the other detailing the government's HIV and AIDS treatment and care policy.[45] Arguably the most important document that New Labour published during this period, however, was its *Framework for Good Practice in the Pharmaceutical Industry*.[46] This outlined the partnership between the government and the pharmaceutical industry and formed the second part of New Labour's commitment to 'Increasing People's Access to Essential Medicines in Developing Countries'. Taken together, these policies would provide the template for the government's presidency of the G8 in Gleneagles in 2005, where tackling HIV and AIDS would be high on the agenda.

New Labour's renewed strategy in 2003 coincided with a change in key personnel within DFID. Clare Short's resignation following Britain's invasion of Iraq led to the temporary appointment of the junior Foreign Office minister, Baroness Valerie Amos, and then the promotion of the junior development minister, Hilary Benn, to the position of secretary of state for international development. It would be under Benn and his parliamentary under secretary of state, Gareth Thomas, that DFID's HIV and AIDS strategy would move into a policy phase away from the demand management of the Short years to a policy position that took on board the supply-side measures introduced by the Treasury. For Thomas, it was crucial that the government tried:

> to increase the affordability of key pharmaceuticals [and] step up efforts to encourage the research and development of specific global public goods such as new knowledge, new drugs, diagnostic treatments and vaccines, which are all necessary to meet current and future challenges.[47]

To do this, Benn argued that it was important to 'engage the pharmaceutical companies because of the contribution that they can make to bring down the price of the medicines' and because of their capacity to undertake 'more research on the diseases to which we paid less attention in the past but that matter enormously to developing countries'.[48]

At the heart of this renewed strategy was an increased dialogue between the government and the pharmaceutical industry. The head of DFID's HIV/AIDS team, Robin Gornal, noted how 'massive pressure' had already been brought to bear upon 'pharmaceutical companies from people living with HIV and AIDS and from developing country governments about the inequity of the lack of access for people living in poor countries'.[49] This had resulted in a number of pharmaceutical firms taking 'very brave steps forward to reduce prices', and the introduction of 'differential prices for poor countries and rich countries'.[50] Whether or not it was right to describe what these firms had done as particularly 'brave' is obviously a moot point, but it certainly represented a step forward. Moreover, 'a DFID voice saying, "make these drugs cheaper"'[51] certainly marked a change from Clare Short's argument that less-expensive medicines would not solve the problem. Nevertheless, like their counterparts in the Treasury, DFID ministers remained reluctant to impose any formal regulations upon the industry. In fact, officials were content to adopt a broadly light-touch approach when it came to framing the research agenda of the pharmaceutical industry.

Despite this progress, tensions between the economic and ethical imperatives underpinning New Labour's strategy remained unresolved with the clear moral case for action offset by the belief that 'business knows best'. Government ministers and civil servants were only too aware of the issue of profitability that loomed large over the decisions taken by industry officials. In a memorandum to the House of Commons Health Select Committee, the Department of Health stated quite clearly that:

> The government believes that the current model – whereby medicines are developed by the private sector in response to what *they perceive to be the demand of healthcare systems* – is more effective and efficient than alternatives that could be considered (such as nationalising the drug industry, or by government directing the research that the industry should undertake).[52]

The director of the DTI's Bioscience Unit, Monica Darnbrough, further reinforced this view. Seemingly content to let the industry decide which treatments and areas of the world to invest in, Darnbrough stated that 'it is very much a question for the companies themselves what lines of research and development they choose to go down. Obviously, they go down roads where they think there is a real market for their products.'[53]

Affirming this view, the National Institute for Clinical Excellence noted in its evidence to the Health Select Committee that the aim of a pharmaceutical firm 'ultimately, is to ensure a market for their products and a return for their shareholders'.[54] These shareholder obligations impact upon commercial decisions: how research funding is allocated, which drugs are developed, what markets are ventured into, and crucially, its moral duties as a healthcare provider. As the Health Select Committee remarked, the industry's 'commitment to provide its shareholders with a good return on investment' could inhibit the 'development of new and improved treatments in the areas of greatest medical need'.[55] The imperative of profitability and meeting shareholder demands mean that drug innovation would tend 'to be targeted at diseases of affluence rather than priority health needs'.[56] For illnesses such as HIV and AIDS, there was little commercial benefit for pharmaceutical firms to invest. This meant that it was highly problematic for the government to make a commitment to increase access to medicines that could treat these types of illnesses, leaving the industry to regulate itself. Without a more robust regulatory framework in place to influence the research direction of firms, the industry would continue to focus its efforts upon the 'diseases of affluence' and neglect the illnesses found in the developing world.

Treasury officials had of course already recognised this behaviour within the industry, and this formed the basis of Gordon Brown's earlier supply-side proposals. Under Hilary Benn, DFID too began to meet with pharmaceutical companies to discuss 'issues such as the affordability of existing medicines and other health technologies, and the need for increased research and development into new technologies – including vaccines – for diseases disproportionately affecting developing countries'.[57] For Benn's under secretary of state, Gareth Thomas, it was important that New Labour continued 'to work with the many pharmaceutical companies that have offered their support to the governments of affected countries by, among other things, reducing the prices of antiretroviral drugs'.[58] Balancing supply-side concerns with management of the demand side, Thomas reaffirmed DFID's commitment to 'press for lower prices for those drugs' and 'meet the challenge of getting antiretroviral drugs out to the communities that need them'.[59]

Despite a greater degree of consistency and convergence in the respective policy approaches of DFID and the Treasury, this strategy of increased engagement with the pharmaceutical industry took place in the same 'light-touch' regulatory framework that New Labour had established domestically to attract and retain investment from the pharmaceutical industry. There would be no compulsion upon the industry to act. Instead, as the secretary of state for health, John Hutton, and the health minister, Lord Warner, remarked, the government's focus would be on 'incentivising policies' such as tax relief measures and advance purchase agreements,[60] 'to create the right financial incentives for pharmaceutical companies to invest in research'.[61] As the Treasury had sought to do through its supply-side proposals, these industry sweeteners would enable New Labour to maintain the ongoing competitiveness of the British pharmaceutical industry, yet appear to appeal to the moral commitment of increasing access to medicines in those parts of the world least able to afford them.

Like each of the three case studies explored here, New Labour's plans to combat HIV and AIDS formed part of Gordon Brown's 'global New Deal' or 'modern Marshall Plan'. To tackle the disease, DFID and the Treasury set about drawing together these 'demand' and supply-side policies to form 'a comprehensive strategy from funding work on the first preventative vaccine to treatment and care to developing health systems and anti-poverty programmes'.[62] This plan is outlined in Box 6.1.

Box 6.1 The Chancellor's 'Comprehensive Plan for HIV and AIDS'.

- A global HIV and AIDS research platform and increased funding for research
- A global advance purchasing scheme for HIV and AIDS vaccines
- Treatment for all those who need it and the development of effective healthcare systems
- More finance for drugs like antiretrovirals and for other treatments
- Increased funding in support of plans to build up healthcare, education and infrastructure systems
- Technical assistance to help countries to scale up their AIDS measures effectively
- Investment in HIV and AIDS research and the development of vaccines, microbicides, and new and better diagnostics and drugs

---

To deal with the funding issue, Brown outlined his proposals for an International Finance Facility (IFF), which, as I shall explain in more detail in the following chapter, would provide a long-term, predictable source of finance. This set of proposals would address the demand-side concerns by providing funding for health systems that required continued investment, and give practitioners and patients confidence that the supply of drugs they depended on would be maintained. The IFF would also tackle issues on the supply side by encouraging private sector operators into the market and raising incentives for increased R&D.[63] Therefore, although as Chapter 7 explains, the IFF was designed to 'frontload' resources – to double aid in order to halve poverty – it also served to finance the right market conditions into which the pharmaceutical industry could invest and secure its core economic goals.

The way in which the IFF was used as a response to HIV and AIDS, and New Labour's commitment to increase access to antiretrovirals, reveals a great deal about the character of New Labour's political economy. Quite simply, the Chancellor defined the role of the state as one that provided the conditions necessary for firms to invest. It was the state whose responsibility it was to undertake the spadework – bulk-buying drugs; building up healthcare sanitation and education systems – alongside the fiscal incentives such as tax relief credits, all of which were necessary before firms would be willing to set up laboratories and trial sites for testing treatments and develop effective vaccines to make them affordable.[64] To meet the moral commitment that New Labour officials had signalled was important, government officials considered there to be no alternative but to prioritise the market-led expectations of firms.

The disinclination, however, amongst pharmaceutical firms to invest in treatments for poor-country diseases such as HIV and AIDS meant that in 2005, 'only £400 million [was] being spent on researching and developing an AIDS vaccine every year'.[65] Despite the severity and the prevalence of the disease, this amounted to 'less than 10 pence a year per citizen'.[66] To put these figures into context, in 2009, GlaxoSmithKline posted pre-tax profits of £7.8 *billion*.[67] For Brown, the challenge required:

> At least a doubling of money for AIDS research . . . over the next 5 to 10 years [which] could bring forward the discovery of an AIDS vaccine by three years . . . save six million lives that would otherwise be lost [and reduce] future HIV/AIDS treatment costs . . . by US$2 billion a year – money that could then be spent on education, water supplies and other critical needs.[68]

In encouraging the pharmaceutical firms to meet the challenge, Brown used 'carrots' of extra funding, tax relief and market guarantees rather than the 'sticks' of increased regulation and a more redistributive tax system. Indeed, in these advance purchase schemes, the onus remained upon *the donors* of finance rather than the suppliers of medicines. For:

> if donors committed to buying the first 300 million vaccine courses at US$20 dollars per course of vaccinations; this would translate into a US$6 billion dollar guarantee – large enough to induce much stronger interest from both large and small pharmaceutical firms.[69]

The offer of these 'carrots' to the industry signalled the thinness of the Chancellor's previous appeals concerning the pharmaceutical industry in the first phase of policy. To these 'non-industry' audiences, Brown had demanded that the pharmaceutical industry do far more and take greater responsibility for increasing access to drugs. To industry audiences, however, Brown spoke in altogether more conciliatory terms of the role that the pharmaceutical industry *could*, rather than *should*, play in scaling up access to medicines. This message was matched by the language of partnership that was used by DFID officials when drawing up the principles behind the *Framework for Good Practice in the Pharmaceutical Industry*. Here, Gareth Thomas sought 'to recognise the good work of the many companies in the industry',[70] while 'the spirit' of the Framework itself was one of 'building upon the best work being done by the industry'.[71]

Clearly, however, there were areas in which pharmaceutical industry practice was far from impressive. The Chancellor had already raised the issue of underinvestment in research for diseases affecting developing countries, but as one Labour backbencher pointed out, there was also the issue of young children in the developing world living with HIV. As the Wrexham MP, Ian Lucas, noted, 'drug companies do not manufacture dedicated drugs for young children and as a result there is some over and underprescribing of drugs'.[72] Like the issue of underfunded research, this was clearly yet another instance whereby market-driven imperatives overtook moral obligations. There was little in the way of a market incentive in developing paediatric drug formulations, which led to the industry neglecting the illnesses that children living in the developing world were vulnerable to. Therefore, while this partnership framework took as its point of departure 'the good work' that the industry was doing, for it to be truly effective then it would need to go beyond the existing economic expectations of the pharmaceutical industry. Although well intentioned then, this partnership framework remained firmly geared towards safeguarding profitability and continued shareholder value.

This framework (summarised in Box 6.2) set about addressing the demand-side issues since 'without effective health systems, or the money to buy medicines, many patients will [still] be denied access to even the cheapest medicines'.[73] It represented a major step forwards from Clare Short's position as it argued that the industry had a 'significant role to play'.[74] Given that the actions of the pharmaceutical industry had in the past actually served to deepen the AIDS crisis by restricting access to vitally needed antiretrovirals, any strategy which now actively engaged the industry and urged it to address the pressing issues surrounding access and increased research should be welcomed. This new strategy looked far more like what a partnership should look like with responsibilities at least being apportioned more equitably.

Box 6.2 Joint government and pharmaceutical industry policy framework. (Source: DFID, *Increasing Access to Essential Medicines in the Developing World: UK Government Policy and Plans*, London: DFID, 2004, pp. 34–42; DFID, *Increasing People's Access to Essential Medicines in Developing Countries: A Framework for Good Practice in the Pharmaceutical Industry*, London: DFID, 2005, p. 16.)

The Government 'will':	<ul><li>Increase its overseas aid budget to £6.5 billion a year by 2007/08</li><li>Commit to spend £1.5 billion to tackle AIDS over the next three years, including support for ARV therapy and treatment for opportunistic infections</li><li>Work to increase the amount of international development finance available by reaching the UN target to spend 0.7 per cent of GDP on overseas aid by 2013; promoting the IFF, and supporting increased debt relief for developing countries</li></ul>
Pharmaceutical firms 'encouraged' to:	<ul><li>Engage in widespread differential pricing of essential medicines in developing countries, especially the world's poorest, to support the development of viable markets</li><li>Increase R&D investment for diseases affecting developing countries, including engagement in public-private partnerships</li><li>Work to support broader health and development goals in developing countries, including by considering voluntary licences</li><li>Report on activities designed to increase access to essential medicines</li></ul>

This new-found recognition of the responsibilities that the pharmaceutical industry had in delivering essential medicines was, however, skewed by the commitment that New Labour said it *would* make, and the measures that the industry was *encouraged* to take. To its credit, through this framework, the New Labour government did establish a series of measurable benchmarks through its 'Taking Action' strategy, such as closing the funding gap, which could be used to assess performance.[75]

While these funding commitments demonstrated New Labour's willingness to financially underwrite its response to the crisis, any similar sort of measurability was missing on the pharmaceutical industry's side of the partnership. The strategies, such as differential pricing, were far less precisely defined and problematic in their application. Other questions remained: by how much should R&D investment increase? What auditing mechanisms would be in place to report this increase in research activity? Put simply, there was no concrete obligation upon the firms to undertake any of these measures. It was rather strange then that although 'the Framework's development was influenced by a request from some companies for a clearer articulation of what the UK government would like to see companies do in this area',[76] the Framework document provided no regulation and no compulsion for the pharmaceutical industry to act in any of these areas. As a result, there was little genuine accountability from the pharmaceutical industry. Therefore, despite New Labour's call for the 'ethical case', it was not afforded the same priority as the set of economic expectations held by the pharmaceutical firms to which New Labour entrusted a crucial role in increasing access to antiretrovirals. In these terms then, the Framework therefore remained a broadly blunt instrument.

Rather than the Framework reorienting the pharmaceutical industry towards recognising its unique and moral duty as a provider of healthcare, it set up the response to this crisis in terms of corporate social responsibility.[77] Perhaps this was deemed sufficient to appease the calls from developing countries, civil society and, in more muted tones, Whitehall officials, but the sheer size and scale of the AIDS crisis meant that a response was required that went far beyond the corporate social responsibility activities of firms. What it did reveal was that any desire that might have existed on the part of the industry to tackle this human tragedy was subordinate to the profitability of the firms.

For its part, in developing the Framework, New Labour sought to make its response as 'industry-friendly' as possible by focusing upon the 'business case' for action. Government officials claimed that 'ethical arguments about what should be done have developed into arguments about the business case for action'.[78] Rather than the moral crisis facing the developing world, it was the 'perceived threats to business interests and long-term profitability' that animated policymakers and industry representatives.[79] Yet the continued prioritisation of corporate interests over any moral commitment should not be entirely unexpected when one considers the division of labour in the Framework. Twenty-five representatives from the pharmaceutical industry and other business groups were consulted during the development of DFID's *Framework for Good Practice*, compared with just eight NGOs.[80]

New Labour's intent to safeguard the profitability of the pharmaceutical industry occurred in two key ways in the Framework. Firstly, the government argued that if pharmaceutical firms could scale up access to essential medicines, these firms would 'enhance their [own] reputation', 'protect the credibility of the intellectual property system', and leave themselves 'better able to maintain a market share in developing countries'.[81] Essentially, pharmaceutical firms could manipulate their response to the AIDS crisis as a means of protecting their competitive advantage. In the face of the 'international pressures' brought about by 'changes in the global environment', this would of course stand to benefit the firms concerned. In altogether less ethical terms, this suggests that pharmaceutical firms could actually use the suffering of the crisis as leverage to increase their competitiveness and global market share still further.

The second means by which New Labour matched the expectations of industry was derived from the set of proposals that emerged out of the UK Working Group formed in the first phase of the government's strategy. Here, the group recommended 'differential pricing' as an 'economically and commercially viable' means of achieving the aim of increasing access to essential medicines.[82] Differential pricing enables firms to sell medicines at lower prices in developing country markets, and at higher prices in richer countries. It was deemed viable because the variable costs comprise around 15 per cent of the total costs of producing drugs.[83] As pharmaceutical firms could decide with some flexibility upon the geographic market in which they might recover non-variable costs, pricing would remain close to the cost of manufacture, enabling firms to retain a profit. As developing country markets offered very little in the way of overall profitability – in 2004, Africa for example constituted just 1.1 per cent of the global pharmaceutical market by value[84] – differential pricing provided a 'rational way for global companies to maximise profits in both low and high-income countries'.[85]

Although this appeared to be a step in the right direction, this strategy was again problematic. Despite its commercial appeal, if such a strategy was undertaken on a voluntary basis, as the government proposed, then the WHO warned that it was likely to have only a modest impact on people's access to care and leave developing countries with little control over the availability, channels of distribution and the volume of medicines available.[86] Paradoxically then, given DFID's previous commitment to this end, this strategy would do little to address the weaknesses of health infrastructures in AIDS-affected countries, and undermine broader attempts made by the government to ensure a regular, predictable and sustainable supply of antiretrovirals in these areas.

In pressing the 'business case' over more moral grounds for action by pharmaceutical firms, the Framework added little to the Treasury's earlier policy initiatives designed to address the persistent problem of chronic underinvestment in the research of diseases that disproportionately affect the poor in 'low-profit'/low-income country markets. Despite these countries remaining hugely unattractive to the pharmaceutical firms, government officials continued to keep the industry onside by offering incentives on a purely voluntary basis. In spite of the urgent and profoundly moral challenge presented by the AIDS crisis, there was to be no regulation of corporate research agendas; simply a proposal that firms consider increasing their levels of R&D for the 'diseases of poverty' and participate in a series of PPPs, which by spreading the outlay on research investment, would minimise the exposure of risk to the firms themselves.

As one of the world's leading finance ministers, Gordon Brown was instrumental in transposing the imprint of the Framework into the multilateral policy arena. This was achieved in two ways: firstly, through the work of the Commission for Africa, and secondly, through the agreement reached at the 2005 G8 summit.

Like the Framework mapped out by Brown and his colleagues in Whitehall, the reports presented by both the Commission and the G8 offered a combination of demand- and supply-side measures designed to 'revive Africa's health services',[87] and achieve 'an AIDS-free generation'.[88] Crucially, however, both these sets of commitments continued to protect and prioritise the profitability of the pharmaceutical industry. Moreover, it quickly became clear that whatever problems there were with this strategy at the domestic level, these would only be intensified internationally.

On the demand side, both the Commission and the G8 spoke of the importance of healthcare infrastructures being strengthened, African governments increasing their healthcare budgets, and recruiting and retaining more staff, and donors supporting this with increasing amounts of financial assistance. Although clearly important, these solutions raised a number of issues that neither the Commission nor the G8 leaders addressed. Firstly, there was, for instance, the continuing legacy of structural adjustment and the slow progress over debt relief that continued to hang over the healthcare budgets of many African governments, making the scaling-up of expenditure in this area not quite as straightforward as these two reports made out. Secondly, the scale and the nature of the AIDS epidemic across Africa brought its own unique pressures, which again the Commission and the G8 appeared not to fully appreciate. As an epidemic, AIDS demands that governments increase their health and education budgets in order to halt its spread. Governments in these areas, however, have found their response put under pressure by dwindling economic growth and a decimated tax base; pressures not helped by an already weakened health system and the continued migration of many skilled health professionals overseas.

On the supply side, there was a marked difference in the language of both the Commission and the G8 from the earlier appeals made by Gordon Brown to these 'non-industry' international audiences. The Chancellor's earlier appeal for the pharmaceutical industry to take more seriously its responsibilities as provider of global healthcare was not reflected either in the report of the Commission or in the G8 communiqué. For example, even though both these sets of actors recognised that the paediatric formulations and microbicides, which protect women from HIV infection, were not being made available or receiving the priority they deserved by the pharmaceutical industry, these firms were in effect let off the hook. Instead, the burden of responsibility was placed upon donors. Following Gordon Brown's lead, both the Commission and the G8 leaders called upon governments to incentivise these knowledge- and resource-laden companies into investigating the diseases that affect Africa, and to make legally binding commitments to buy these drugs so that firms are induced into putting these new medicines and vaccines into production.[89]

Given the extent to which New Labour bought into, and indeed Gordon Brown himself extolled, the virtues of globalisation, there was a certain irony to this particular phase of government policy, and its relationship with the pharmaceutical industry in particular. At home, the New Labour government had been desperately keen to retain these firms since they would place Britain at the forefront of the high-skilled, high-tech 'knowledge economy' and enable it to compete with low-cost, emerging countries. However, once these industries were mobilised in the global economy – the same global economy that made this 'knowledge economy' so crucial – the technology, the skills and the innovation that these firms had at their disposal were left untapped and underdeployed. The activities of these companies were not truly 'global' since in reality they served only to benefit those wealthy and affluent parts of the world: a fraction of the world's population.

All this meant that although New Labour's ambitions to tackle the AIDS crisis were laudable, its strategy of prioritising the profitability and competitiveness of the industry above all else did little to address the gross inequalities in access to and quality of healthcare that existed between developed and underdeveloped countries. If this inequality was to be addressed and the spread of the AIDS epidemic reversed, the government would need to re-evaluate and reconfigure its assessment of the role that private firms had to play in the delivery of public goods.

Placing people before profits? Change and continuity in New Labour's strategy

Given its significance to Gordon Brown as Chancellor, unsurprisingly, the fight against HIV and AIDS continued to be a priority during his time at Number 10. In 2008, the Brown government embarked upon another policy strategy to achieve universal access to comprehensive HIV prevention programmes, treatment, care and support. Although curtailed by New Labour's General Election defeat in May 2010, this third phase of government policy was altogether more nuanced than the previous two phases as it sought to introduce a new 'social' imperative, one designed to address the needs of people living with HIV in the developing world. To this end, Brown's new secretary of state for international development, Douglas Alexander, promised a strategy that would place 'people at the heart of the response'.[90] This section explores the depth of this new commitment and where this left the pharmaceutical industry as a key interlocutor of policy. This phase reveals that while this shift in emphasis appeared to represent a welcome break from the continued prioritisation of the industry's competitiveness over global health concerns, the concerns of Britain's pharmaceutical firms nevertheless continued to be a key driver behind government thinking in this area of policy.

As well as this change in the leadership of New Labour, and the subsequent cabinet reshuffle, this latest phase of policy took place against a backdrop of economic turmoil and global uncertainty. None of these factors, however, appeared to dampen the government's commitment to tackling HIV and AIDS. If anything, they strengthened Brown's resolve to eradicate these and other diseases, and 'the first financial crisis of the global era' underlined the importance of international co-operation and dialogue.[91] Insofar as New Labour's own fight against AIDS was concerned, it published a comprehensive policy paper, *Achieving Universal Access*,[92] and then, a year later, a fourth White Paper in just twelve years, *Building Our Common Future*.[93]

Little mention was made in these documents of the role that the pharmaceutical industry had to play in scaling up access to antiretrovirals but there was a slight change in the language of both the policy paper and the White Paper. There was to be a fresh focus upon three key areas: (1) supporting the claims of the developing countries by responding to the needs and protecting the rights of those most affected;[94] (2) supporting more effective and integrated service delivery;[95] and (3) making money work harder through effective partnerships.[96] The first area was designed to support the 'people-centred' response that the new secretary of state sought to put at the heart of this new commitment. The second and third areas, however, re-emphasised the demand- and supply-side policies developed from the government's previous 'Taking Action' strategy, now designed to secure universal, rather than simply increased, access to essential medicines.

On the demand side, DFID committed to contribute a further £1 billion to the Global Fund,[97] and to spend £6 billion on health systems and services by 2015 and over £200 million on developing and supporting social protection programmes. In addition to this financial support, the government promised to work with international partners to support countries with health-worker shortages so that there would be at least 2.3 doctors, nurses and midwives per 1,000 people.[98] With this infrastructure in place, the supply side was boosted by a central research budget to stimulate innovation by the pharmaceutical industry.[99] As Chancellor, Gordon Brown had called upon the industry to increase its investment into the research of treatments for diseases affecting the developing world. However, despite the huge research budgets that these firms had at their disposal, and the tax incentives now offered by the Treasury to fund this type of research, levels of investment remained stubbornly low.

Indeed, despite the 22.4 million people living with HIV and AIDS in sub-Saharan Africa alone, the government could only point to 3 million actually having access to antiretroviral treatment in 2009.[100] Despite repeated claims of 'a moral obligation' on the part of the pharmaceutical industry, this represented a clear failure of government policy. It did, however, underline the need for the government to create its own research fund to finance the necessary investments in the required medicines if this access was to be scaled up and these drugs made available to all those who needed them.

Despite these shortcomings, Brown's government remained of the view that the pharmaceutical did have a role in improving access to medicines. As a follow-up to the Framework developed in the earlier phase of New Labour's policies, the Industry Government Forum on Access to Medicines (IGFAM) was set up to facilitate better and sustainable access to medicines in developing countries.[101] The purpose of this new forum, however, was decidedly unclear since it neither offered any sort of recommendations, nor did it include any participation from development agencies. Instead, the membership of the IGFAM reflected far more the Western 'business' concerns of the industry rather than the experience and expertise of NGOs and other 'non-business' health organisations, let alone any real voice from those countries most affected by HIV and AIDS.[102] The intent and the interests of the group were clear from the make-up of the IGFAM. Jon Pender, vice-president of intellectual property and access at GlaxoSmith-Kline, was appointed, along with Sam Walker, a senior policy adviser at DFID, as joint chair of the forum. Pender and Walker met with pharmaceutical industry representatives from the UK, the United States and Japan, as well as the government's own Intellectual Property Office. The remit of the IGFAM was to maintain the competitiveness of an industry dominated by firms based in the global North, and ensure that industry priorities were protected in any commitment to increase the availability of antiretrovirals in poorer parts of the world.

Much like the Framework that preceded it, there was an implicit understanding – even amongst firms – that there was an ethical imperative at play here. However, in similar terms to the Framework, GlaxoSmithKline also argued, 'it is good for GSK's image and reputation; and there is a sound business rationale'.[103] Remarkably, the company no longer viewed emerging markets as 'peripheral' but as representing a major market opportunity currently constrained by a lack of purchasing power.[104] Such a frank and astonishing argument made the government's own commitment 'to place people at the heart of the response' look foolish and naïve. GlaxoSmithKline appeared to understand the issue only in terms of projecting the right corporate image and capitalising upon new market opportunities that HIV and other deadly illnesses in the global South now represented.

Again like the Framework, the IGFAM also lacked any real representation from those areas most affected by HIV and AIDS, and the generic firms based in low- and middle-income countries. If Brown's government was really serious about tackling the issue of essential access in the developing world – as opposed to simply maintaining the competitive advantage of these large multinationals in the global economy – then one might have expected it to invite to the debate representatives from the global South. The generic firms based these countries, particularly India and South Africa, for example, had a very different set of priorities from the large, supposedly 'research-led' firms which had dominated the dialogue between the British government and those firms that appeared to be concerned only with recouping the investment that they had made during the initial R&D stage. As the case of the major US pharmaceutical firm Gilead illustrated, these larger firms were willing to invest only in those areas in which they could secure this return more quickly. Holding the marketing rights to the antiretroviral, Tenofovir, in 2006 Gilead voluntarily licensed the drug to more than ten generic firms, each of which paid a 5 per cent royalty back to Gilead. Three years later, however, Gilead itself was still selling Tenofovir at US$365 (US$200 to governments), while the generic licensees were selling the drug for US$100, mainly to developing countries.[105]

These weaknesses in the strategy pursued by the Brown government demonstrated why it was simply inadequate to continue relying upon the corporate goodwill or the research agendas of the larger multinational firms. While the secretary of state was correct to diagnose the AIDS crisis as, above all, a human crisis, it continues to be one that cannot be addressed by protecting the profitability of a narrow corporate elite. Strikingly, Gordon Brown, in his final conference speech as prime minister and leader of the Labour Party admitted as much. 'Markets need what they cannot generate themselves. They need what people alone can bring to them ... markets need morals.'[106] Although reflecting a shift in broader ideological direction under Brown's premiership, or an acknowledgement that the financial crisis was beginning to recalibrate the Labour Party away from a strictly market-orientated model of political economy, on reflection, this statement might well have also served as a useful lesson for Gordon Brown himself as he grappled with the exigencies of increasing access to essential antiretrovirals in the developing world.

Conclusions

Chapter 2 demonstrated the ways in which New Labour's understanding of globalisation placed considerable constraints upon the domestic policy options available to Whitehall officials in accommodating the expectations of business and capital. This particular chapter, however, has revealed the grave effects of internalising such logic. At home, senior New Labour officials stressed the importance of the 'knowledge economy' as the *only* means by which Britain could compete in this ostensibly new global economy, and set about accommodating the expectations of key sectors like the pharmaceutical industry in order to retain the inward investment that these firms provided. Abroad, however, Whitehall ministers, led by Gordon Brown, were faced with the challenge of a lack of access to the antiretrovirals in the developing world that these firms were *supposed* to be producing. This presented New Labour with a dilemma: whether to continue to support and champion the interests of its pharmaceutical industry in the face of an unfolding global tragedy, or to challenge and demand firms to take seriously their obligations as producers of global public goods. Over the course of New Labour's time in office, government ministers, including Brown himself, proceeded to send out a series of different and often seemingly contradictory messages concerning the importance or otherwise of these industries and their treatments in the developing world.

New Labour's early forays into the area of policy saw some senior government figures including Tony Blair, Hazel Blears and Valerie Amos defend the commercial interests of Britain's pharmaceutical firms, while others such as Clare Short went as far as to deflect any responsibility the industry might have had onto the resource-stretched economies in the global South. This resulted in Short's own department promoting a series of measures designed to boost the demand side. For his part, Gordon Brown did not reject these assessments outright but did direct his energies towards creating a set of supply-side proposals designed to incentivise the industry into stepping up the amount of research into antiretroviral treatments suitable for prescription in the developing world. In the midst of these different appeals, however, there was a common thread that ran through Whitehall. Each respective department prioritised the profitability and continued competitiveness of the industry over any real moral imperative to tackle the crisis.

There was a tacit understanding, certainly insofar as Brown himself was concerned, that there was indeed an increasingly moral case for pharmaceutical firms to redouble their efforts into researching and developing treatments for people living with HIV in the developing world. This was perhaps most evident in the more joined-up strategy between the Treasury and DFID where the Chancellor's proposals to incentivise the industry through a series of tax relief measures were met with a commitment from DFID to increase the financing and capacity of healthcare systems in the developing world. By and large, however, the crisis was visualised through the eyes of the industry, rather than those living with the disease and the developing countries that were struggling to cope with the impact of the epidemic. Although clearly well intentioned, both the 'Taking Action' strategy and the Framework between the New Labour government and the pharmaceutical industry viewed the crisis as one of market failure. The government therefore attempted to respond to this crisis in largely market-based terms, preferring to listen to and keep onside the concerns of the pharmaceutical industry – rather than those who were calling for firms to act in altogether more moral terms.

Against a background of political change within the Labour Party, and economic turmoil both at home and abroad, the direction of policy during Brown's time as prime minister appeared to finally recognise the human tragedy of AIDS, and the need to respond to it by meeting the needs of people. Despite this shift in emphasis, however, the Brown government continued to give what appeared to be special dispensation to the pharmaceutical industry. This was particularly striking since many of the larger firms were blocking access to antiretrovirals by keeping the prices of these drugs high. Where access had increased, it was due largely to the efforts of the smaller generic firms which, having secured a patent licence from the large multinationals, were able to sell copies of these drugs at a fraction of the price. Although these generic firms were at the forefront of increasing access – and therefore far more likely to meet New Labour's commitment in this respect – remarkably, Brown's government did not engage with them. It chose instead to continue to protect the interests and the profitability of the larger, more research-led firms domiciled in Britain.

New Labour's strategy to meet its commitment concerning the access and availability of lifesaving antiretroviral drugs reflected a model of political economy orientated towards protecting the profits of a small but transnational business elite. That shareholder value was prioritised over the urgent needs of the global poor undermined any moral imperative that may have been present. Had the commitment of Gordon Brown and New Labour to those living with HIV and AIDS in the developing world gone beyond meeting these 'pro-business' expectations, then one might have expected it to have engaged in more dialogue with, and demonstrated greater support for, those constituencies and those parts of the pharmaceutical industry that *were* attempting to address the crisis and make universal access to these drugs a reality. Although these constituencies did not wield the structural power that New Labour's understanding of globalisation had granted to the pharmaceutical industry, they would have nevertheless enabled the government to meet far more effectively its commitment to increasing access to these essential medicines.

Notes

1. UNAIDS, *2004 Report on the Global AIDS Epidemic*, 2004, p. 13.
2. Third World Network, 'Patent Rights vs. Patient Rights', 2000.
3. GlaxoSmithKline, *Our Responsibility*, 2008, p. 19.
4. GlaxoSmithKline, *Global Public Policy Issues*, 2011.
5. Barker, 'Introduction', 2007.
6. GlaxoSmithKline, *Our Responsibility*, 2008, p. 53, emphasis added.
7. ABPI, *Global Health and the Pharmaceutical Industry*, 2007, p. 18; see also AstraZeneca, 'Millennium Development Goals', 2011; GlaxoSmithKline, *Making a Difference Every Day*, 2004, pp. 10–13.
8. DFID, *Increasing People's Access to Essential Medicines in Developing Countries*, 2005, p. 1.
9. Short, 'Medicines (Access)', 2001.
10. Short, 'Medicines (Patents and Pricing)', 2001.
11. Short, 'HIV/AIDS Drugs (Africa)', 2001.
12. Short, 'Medicines (Patents and Pricing)', 2001.
13. Short, 'HIV/AIDS', 2001, emphasis added.
14. Ibid.
15. Short, 'Q. 168', 2003.
16. Ibid.
17. DFID, *Increasing People's Access to Essential Medicines in Developing Countries*, 2005, p. 18.
18. Ibid. p. 21.
19. House of Commons Select Committee for International Development, *The Humanitarian Crisis in Southern Africa*, 2003, p. 21, emphasis added.
20. Short, 'HIV/AIDS', 2001.
21. World Health Organization, *WHO Medicines Strategy*, 2004, p. 36, emphasis added.
22. Blair, 'Blair sides with drug giants', 2001.

23. Blears, 'Minister says govt backs UK pharma industry, highlights activities of PICTF', 2002.
24. Amos, 'Southern Africa', 2001, emphasis added.
25. Short, *UK Working Group on Increasing Access to Essential Medicines in the Developing World*, 2002, pp. 5, 7.
26. Short, 'Disease Prevention', 2002.
27. Ibid.
28. HM Treasury, *Building Long-Term Prosperity for All*, 2000, p. 116.
29. Brown, statement on the Pre-Budget Report, 2000.
30. DFID et al., *Forging a New Commitment*, 2001.
31. HM Treasury, 'Call to action on global child poverty to meet 2015 development targets', 2001.
32. Ibid.
33. HM Treasury, *Building a Stronger, Fairer Britain in an Uncertain World*, 2001, p. 98.
34. Brown, speech delivered at the annual European Bank for Reconstruction and Development conference, 2001.
35. Ibid.
36. Brown, 'Financing a World Fit for Children', 2002.
37. Ibid.
38. Boateng, 'Finance Bill', 2002.
39. Ibid.
40. Short, 'Medicines (Patents and Pricing)', 2001.
41. Boateng, 'Finance Bill', 2002.
42. Ibid.
43. DFID, *Taking Action*, 2004, pp. 11–12.
44. DFID, *Increasing Access to Essential Medicines in the Developing World*, 2004.
45. DFID, *HIV and AIDS Treatment and Care Policy*, 2004.
46. DFID, *Increasing People's Access to Essential Medicines in Developing Countries*, 2005.
47. Thomas, 'Action on the Three Major Communicable Diseases', 2003.
48. Benn, 'AIDS', 2003.
49. Gornal, 'Q. 26', 2004.
50. Ibid.
51. Allan, 'Q. 30', 2004.
52. Department of Health, 'Memorandum (P 11)', 2005, emphasis added.
53. Darnbrough, 'Q. 26', 2004.
54. National Institute of Clinical Excellence, 'Memorandum (P 32)', 2005.

55. House of Commons Select Health Committee, *The Influence of the Pharmaceutical Industry*, 2005, p. 45.
56. Ibid. p. 45.
57. Benn, 'Development Financing', 2004.
58. Thomas, 'HIV/AIDS (Developing World)', 2004.
59. Ibid.
60. The government guaranteed 'under such schemes . . . to buy vaccines for developing country markets, at a fixed price, from any firm that could develop an effective new product, thus providing the private sector with the financial incentive that is presently missing'. DFID, *Making Globalisation Work for the Poor*, 2000, p. 44.
61. Hutton, 'Written Ministerial Statement', 2004.
62. Brown, 'A comprehensive plan for HIV/AIDS', 2005.
63. Ibid.
64. Ibid.
65. Ibid.
66. Ibid.
67. GlaxoSmithKline, *GSK Annual Report 2009*, 2010, p. 94.
68. Brown, 'A comprehensive plan for HIV/AIDS', 2005.
69. Ibid.
70. Thomas, 'HIV Treatment', 2005.
71. DFID, *Increasing People's Access to Essential Medicines in Developing Countries*, 2005, p. 7.
72. Lucas, 'International AIDS Day', 2005.
73. DFID, *Increasing People's Access to Essential Medicines in Developing Countries*, 2005, p. 6.
74. Ibid. p. 16.
75. DFID, *Taking Action*, 2004, pp. 16–23.
76. DFID, *Increasing People's Access to Essential Medicines in Developing Countries*, 2005, p. 6.
77. DFID, *Increasing Access to Essential Medicines in the Developing World*, 2004, p. 36.
78. DFID, *Increasing People's Access to Essential Medicines in Developing Countries*, 2005, p. 28.
79. Ibid. p. 28.
80. Ibid. p. 36.
81. Ibid. p. 28.
82. Short, *UK Working Group on Increasing Access to Essential Medicines in the Developing World*, 2002, p. 4.
83. DFID, *Increasing People's Access to Essential Medicines in Developing Countries*, 2005, p. 31.
84. DFID, *Increasing Access to Essential Medicines in the Developing World*, 2004, p. 13.

85. DFID, *Increasing People's Access to Essential Medicines in Developing Countries*, 2005, p. 32.

86. World Health Organization, *The World Medicines Situation*, 2004, p. 71.

87. Commission for Africa, *Our Common Interest*, 2005, pp. 65–8.

88. G8, *The Gleneagles Communiqué*, 2005, p. 22.

89. Commission for Africa, *Our Common Interest*, 2005, p. 67; G8, *The Gleneagles Communiqué*, 2005, p. 22.

90. Alexander, 'Foreword by the Secretary of State', 2008, p. ii.

91. Brown, 'A Culture of Peace', 2008.

92. DFID, *Achieving Universal Access*, 2008.

93. DFID, *Building Our Common Future*, 2009.

94. DFID, *Achieving Universal Access*, 2008, pp. 22–9.

95. Ibid. pp. 30–41.

96. Ibid. pp. 42–56.

97. Lewis, 'HIV/AIDS', 2009.

98. DFID, *Achieving Universal Access*, 2008, p. 64.

99. Ibid. p. 65.

100. DFID, *Building Our Common Future*, 2009, p. 94.

101. Ibid. p. 94.

102. DFID, 'Industry Government Forum on Access to Medicines', 2009.

103. IGFAM, *Summary Report of the Industry Government Forum on Access to Medicines*, 2009, p. 8.

104. Ibid. p. 8.

105. Ibid. p. 14.

106. Brown, speech delivered at the Labour Party conference, 2009.

7 Coming to the Aid of Africa

This final case study chapter returns to the theme of finance for development explored in Chapter 5. Alongside debt relief, overseas aid was viewed as an important instrument in raising the money necessary to finance poverty reduction. Despite sharing this common objective, however, Gordon Brown separated the management of aid and debt relief along policy lines demarcated at home. While the Chancellor embedded the issue of debt relief within New Labour's macroeconomic strategy, Brown transposed into the international realm the Treasury's 'golden rule' for borrowing and spending, and the manner in which government had framed the welfare state at home.

Gordon Brown's influence here was unmistakeable and these domestic principles would underpin his own proposals for a 'global New Deal' or 'Marshall Plan for Africa'. The centrepiece of this development pact was the International Finance Facility (IFF).[1] In both political and personal terms, so significant was the IFF that one biographer called it Brown's 'single most important political priority' aside from reaching Number 10 itself.[2] Brown viewed it as enabling Britain to finally meet the United Nations target set in 1970 for 0.7 per cent of its GDP to be allocated to foreign aid. Although a broadly symbolic target, it remains to this day one that provides a gauge as to the significance (or lack thereof) that a government attaches to international development. Therefore, although New Labour might have claimed that overseas development was 'not just about aid',[3] so emblematic was this target that if Brown and his New Labour government *were* genuinely committed to improving the lives of millions across the developing world – irrespective of their other endeavours in this field – they would have to make meeting this longstanding goal a clear priority for Britain and the rest of the international donor community.

The IFF would enable this target to be met by drawing upon two distinct themes that appeared in New Labour's domestic political economy. The first developed the Treasury's commitment to a credible and prudent fiscal policy, and its 'golden rule' of 'borrowing to invest'. At home, Gordon Brown had promised to borrow only as a means of financing long-term capital investment rather than current or ongoing public expenditure, which would be funded by the taxpayer. Despite tight spending controls, particularly in the first few years in office, Brown had overseen an increase in the level of long-term public investment by using a combination of PFIs and PPPs.

These arrangements enabled the government to fund large-scale investment projects at home, but to do so in a way that would ease the current burden upon the public purse. These spending strategies found their way into Brown's proposals for the IFF. The IFF would not detract from Britain's ongoing commitment to spend 0.7 per cent of its GDP on overseas aid – its current spending – but in order to fill the US$50 billion funding gap that existed in the global level of development finance, Brown suggested borrowing from international capital markets to lock in and 'frontload' the future aid commitments of donor countries. Without this money, it was felt that many developing countries would be left unable to reach the UN's Millennium Development Goals (MDGs) before 2015. It was upon this basis that the Chancellor was prompted into launching his 'global New Deal' and IFF initiative.

The second theme of the IFF drew upon New Labour's 'New Deal' – a policy that again Brown had been instrumental in rolling out. Here Treasury ministers drew up plans designed to lift people out of unemployment and include them in training schemes and an increasingly global world of work. Central to this 'New Deal' was the maxim of 'rights and responsibilities' and upon similar terms, Brown's 'global New Deal' – to which the IFF was central – was geared towards equipping developing countries with the political, economic and social investment necessary to participate in the global economy.

For New Labour ministers including Gordon Brown, claimants under both these schemes held rights to support from the UK government. However, in claiming these rights, they also had responsibilities to use this support appropriately. Like Britain's own welfare system under New Labour, this assistance was not to be an end in and of itself, but rather a 'springboard' for inclusion into the workplace and the global economy. Similarly, just as welfare claimants at home had to comply with a specific set of obligations in order to become eligible for this finance, so too were conditions laid down that developing countries were required to meet if they were to receive this aid money.

The overarching message articulated by Gordon Brown was that economic and social exclusion lay at the root of poverty. This signalled a clear shift away from traditional Labour and social democratic concerns regarding 'equality' towards a set of policies that placed much greater emphasis upon 'inclusion' and 'participation' in the global economy. For Brown, it was from globalisation that opportunity, wealth and prosperity could be derived. To take advantage of these benefits, however, individuals and countries alike needed to work with the grain of globalisation for poverty reduction to take place. Citizens and states were therefore obliged to include themselves within the global economy, requiring the recipient to actively take up a series of responsibilities and duties to this end. As I have already demonstrated in Chapter 3, this had far-reaching implications for the framing of New Labour's welfare policies at home. As this chapter will show, it would also have repercussions for the delivery of development aid overseas.

From these two themes, there were two key dimensions to the IFF that this chapter explores. The first examines the design of the IFF itself, and the feasibility of using finance raised, or to use the Chancellor's term, 'frontloaded' from global capital markets as a means of increasing the amount of aid available for redistribution in the developing world. The case for the IFF was made principally on the basis that transnational and instantaneous markets – almost as emblems of globalisation itself – could be used to redistribute wealth from the global North to the global South, and so meet New Labour's overarching commitment to 'make globalisation work for the poor'.[4] The IFF would work on the basis of Britain and other donor countries initially committing to an increase in aid resources up to 2015. These legally binding commitments, together with the credit-worthiness of donor governments, would act as collateral against bonds raised on international capital markets. These bonds would enable the proposed additional flows of US$15–20 billion per year suggested by the Treasury to be leveraged up to US$50 billion per year, which could then be used straightaway to finance poverty reduction programmes across the developing world.

The second dimension assesses the political economy of the IFF and how Gordon Brown sought to manage these expectations through the conditions imposed by the IFF, upon the recipients of its finance. This particular dimension reveals a clear internationalisation of policy from the way welfare was viewed at home to the disbursement of aid overseas. Both at home and abroad, Brown treated individuals and developing countries alike as 'global citizens', each with a set of obligations to participate fully in the global economy. At home, welfare recipients had a clear duty to fulfil these responsibilities. Abroad, developing countries had, in similar terms, a distinct set of conditions linked to the 'new economic architecture' discussed in Chapter 5, which they needed to meet in order to receive this aid. New Labour's welfare system at home and its international aid programme were both imputed with the same principles of 'rights and responsibilities' that government officials had articulated at home. This meant that any redistribution of wealth, both in Britain and across the developing world, would only occur upon the fulfilment of a particular set of obligations rather than the immediate needs of the poorer and excluded members of society. These conditions were hugely significant for two reasons. Firstly, given that the very character of these 'obligations' was market-orientated (despite its 'pro-poor' rhetoric), they prioritised the expectations of market constituencies over the needs of recipients. Secondly, the framing of aid in the contractual terms of 'rights and responsibilities' would serve only to shift the burden of responsibility away from wealthy donors and onto the poorest and most vulnerable people on the planet instead.

This chapter takes as its point of departure the challenge that New Labour faced in raising a sufficient amount of finance required to meet the MDGs. A failure by the largest industrialised economies to meet the 0.7 per cent/GDP aid target had left a shortfall of US$50 billion per year. This chapter looks at three interlinked policies that Treasury officials argued could fill this gap. I examine each one in turn, drawing out the domestic lineages of these proposals and assessing the likelihood of their success. The first proposal I examine is the International Development Trust Fund; however, my main focus is upon its successor, the IFF, since this would be central to Gordon Brown's 'global New Deal'. This was predicated upon the rule of 'borrowing to invest' and the principle of 'rights and responsibilities'. The final phase explores the International Finance Facility for Immunisation (IFFIm). Based upon the same principles of the IFF, rather than raising money purely for aid, this mechanism sought to raise money on international bond markets to purchase vaccines for the diseases and illnesses such as malaria and tuberculosis that disproportionately affect the poorest people in the world. Throughout each of these phases I demonstrate how, despite the change in the content of the policy, Brown continued to prioritise market expectations over those his policies were purportedly designed to help.

The challenge of increasing aid for international development

Ever since the UN set the 0.7 per cent/GDP target in 1970,[5] only a handful of countries have met, let alone exceeded, this commitment. Despite the overall increase in aid seen under the New Labour government, a comparison between Britain's record on aid and that of other similar countries in the Organisation for Economic Co-operation and Development/Development Assistance Committee (OECD/DAC) makes for mixed reading. Certainly none in the G7 group had met the 0.7 per cent/GDP target during the forty-year period between 1970 and 2010. Whilst Brown held the government's purse strings, however, Britain did at least lead the way amongst this group of nations towards meeting this goal, giving around twice as much from its GDP than Italy, Japan and the United States. Despite its position as the G7's leading donor, Britain was still outperformed by the Benelux countries and the major Scandinavian countries. The Netherlands, Denmark, Norway and Sweden had all met the 0.7 per cent/GDP target within ten years of it being set, while Luxembourg met this target in 2000. Indeed, it was only in 2013, under the Conservative–Liberal Democrat coalition government, that Britain finally met this target.

Table 7.1 OECD/DAC countries, overseas development aid as a percentage of GDP, 1970–2010. (Source: OECD, 'DAC1 Official and Private Flows', 2011, <http://stats.oecd.org/Index.aspx?DatasetCode=TABLE1>, last accessed 23 August 2011.)

	1970	1975	1980	1985	1990	1995	2000	2005	2010
Australia	0.62	0.65	0.48	0.48	0.34	0.34	0.27	0.25	0.32
Austria	0.07	0.21	0.23	0.38	0.11	0.27	0.23	0.52	0.32
Belgium	0.46	0.60	0.50	0.55	0.46	0.38	0.36	0.53	0.64
Canada	0.41	0.54	0.43	0.49	0.44	0.38	0.25	0.34	0.33
Denmark	0.37	0.55	0.74	0.80	0.94	0.96	1.06	0.81	0.90
Finland	0.06	0.17	0.22	0.40	0.65	0.31	0.31	0.46	0.55
France	0.52	0.44	0.44	0.61	0.60	0.55	0.30	0.47	0.50
Germany	0.32	0.40	0.44	0.47	0.42	0.31	0.27	0.36	0.38
Italy	0.15	0.10	0.15	0.26	0.31	0.15	0.13	0.29	0.15
Japan	0.23	0.23	0.32	0.29	0.31	0.27	0.28	0.28	0.20
Netherlands	0.62	0.74	0.97	0.91	0.92	0.81	0.84	0.82	0.81
New Zealand	0.22	0.52	0.33	0.25	0.23	0.23	0.25	0.27	0.26
Norway	0.33	0.65	0.87	1.01	1.17	0.86	0.76	0.94	1.10
Sweden	0.35	0.78	0.78	0.86	0.91	0.77	0.80	0.94	0.97
Switzerland	0.14	0.18	0.24	0.31	0.32	0.34	0.34	0.43	0.41
United Kingdom	**0.39**	**0.38**	**0.35**	**0.33**	**0.27**	**0.29**	**0.32**	**0.47**	**0.56**
United States	0.32	0.27	0.27	0.24	0.21	0.10	0.10	0.23	0.21

The continued failure of much of the international donor community to meet the 0.7 per cent/GDP target resulted in a huge gap emerging in the aid resources available to the developing world. Despite the increasing levels of prosperity across the global North, the existing level of bilateral aid given from the DAC countries remained insufficient if the MDGs were to be met by 2015:

> The MDGs will not be achieved without additional resources for low-income countries. In addition to increasing domestic revenue and external investment, a substantial increase in both aid and debt relief is needed. This needs to be secure, predictable, and sustained up to 2015 and beyond.[6]

Indeed, as Gordon Brown would later remark, if current trends persisted, it was more likely that they would be met 'in 2150, 135 years [too] late'.[7] In order to reach the MDGs, Brown's financial secretary in the Treasury, Stephen Timms, argued that 'an additional US$50 billion of aid was needed immediately'.[8] This huge scaling-up of finance for development would require a completely new approach to aid.

The first signs of this new approach to aid emerged late in 2001, when Gordon Brown, again taking his cue from another US aid intervention, proposed his own 'Marshall Plan' for the developing world. This recovery programme would help finance the fourth 'building block' of the Chancellor's 'global New Deal' through the 'substantial transfer of additional resources from the richest to the poorest countries in the form of investment for development'.[9] For Brown, this form of wealth redistribution at a global level would signal a shift away from 'providing short term aid just to compensate for poverty, to a higher and more sustainable purpose'.[10]

Gordon Brown argued that aid should be viewed as 'a long-term investment to tackle the causes of poverty by promoting growth, prosperity and participation in the world economy'.[11] This change in emphasis is important since it meant that aid would no longer be seen just as 'charity' or as a 'hand-out', but rather as a means by which rich countries in the global North could 'invest' in the global South. For Brown, increased spending on areas such as welfare and overseas aid would not automatically increase social justice. It was more important to create the *opportunities* that would enable developing countries to participate and compete in the global economy.

Significantly, this emphasis upon 'participation' and 'inclusion' in the global economy would replace traditional Labourite concerns regarding 'equality' and 'social justice'. As in its welfare policies at home, the fundamental issue of equality was conspicuous by its absence in the speeches and policy documents that set out New Labour's ambitions for international development. Clearly, both at home and abroad, Gordon Brown in particular remained firmly in support of redistribution and, where prudence allowed, increased spending too. However, this was a new kind of redistribution: one of *opportunity* rather than simply a redistribution of wealth. The pursuit of equality – that is, correcting the imbalances between the poor and the well-off – was replaced with 'making work pay'. Since the role of the state was to be one of 'enabler' rather than 'provider', of 'hand-ups' rather than simply 'hand-outs', any assistance it might provide meant creating the *opportunities* that recipients needed to participate in the workplace and the global economy. Once the state had created these opportunities, it became the responsibility of individuals and countries alike to make the most of these opportunities themselves.

The International Development Trust Fund

The IFF started life as the International Development Trust Fund (IDTF), a mechanism that, according to Gordon Brown, would involve 'the richest countries making a substantial additional commitment of resources beyond 2015'.[12] Although light on detail, there was, typically, a domestic antecedent to the IDTF since Brown's proposals mirrored that of the 'asset-based welfare' policies that were being rolled out in Britain, most notably through the Child Trust Fund (CTF). At home, the CTF was designed to create a 'savings habit' and improve financial awareness, which Treasury ministers argued would give the recipient households in particular a greater sense of financial empowerment and independence. Abroad, the IDTF was a means for rich countries to invest in the future of developing countries and combat global poverty. For these countries to be lifted out of poverty, it was important that their national governments became more financially independent (and less reliant upon overseas assistance) and more integrated into the global economy where they could make the most of the opportunities presented by globalisation.

New Labour's logic of welfare-as-aid in an era of globalisation suggested that once integrated in the global economy, developing countries could gain greater financial independence. No longer would they have to rely upon continued assistance from wealthy donors in the global North. Instead, these countries would be transformed into self-capitalising subjects, with greater autonomy and self-reliance to make the most of the opportunities presented to them. Like the CTF, and indeed New Labour's welfare strategy at home, this was to be realised through a contractual, 'something-for-something' arrangement. Monies raised through these trust funds would only be forthcoming if recipient countries fulfilled strict conditions concerning their economic and trade policies.

Therefore, despite this commitment to move low-income countries from a continuing, passive dependency upon aid to an altogether more active culture of financial empowerment, this logic relied upon a series of 'responsibilities' that government ministers demanded be fulfilled. According to Gordon Brown, the responsibilities to which the IDTF was beholden were based upon 'the existing achievements of the World Bank, the IMF and the Regional Development Banks'.[13] This was significant because, despite a commitment to social justice that such a large spending pledge might suggest, in reality the IDTF was embedded within the neoliberal conventional wisdom espoused by these IFIs and global market investors. As Brown argued:

> Developing countries must pursue corruption-free policies for stability, for opening up trade and for creating a favourable environment for investment. In return, we should be prepared to increase by 50 billion [dollars] a year in the years to 2015, vitally needed funds to achieve these agreed Millennium Development Goals.[14]

These conditions and responsibilities chimed with the expectations articulated by the IFIs, which maintained that poverty reduction was best achieved by embedding open and investor-friendly market reforms. As Brown prepared his IDTF, the president of the World Bank, James Wolfensohn, was remarking how important it was for developing countries to 'put in place good and strong governance, effective legal and judicial systems, and a robust financial system

. . . to attract [the] foreign and domestic private investment [that is] crucial as engines of growth and poverty reduction'.[15] Similarly, Horst Köhler, the managing director of the IMF, noted that across the developing world, 'steps to strengthen governance and fight corruption have often lagged behind other reforms, undermining credibility and investor confidence'.[16]

Senior officials, both in Washington and in Whitehall, were convinced that the failure to redistribute wealth at the global level and the lack of development finance available could be traced to the opaque decision-making processes of central government treasuries and other institutions of public finance in developing countries. This argument is explored in greater depth in Chapter 5, but essentially, this lack of transparency was deemed to be destabilising to both domestic and international markets. This instability created a sense of unease and uncertainty amongst investors all of which inevitably dampened the levels of much-needed investment in these poorer economies. For Köhler, 'only by getting access to investment capital from the rest of the world will the IMF's poorest member countries be able to make a real breakthrough in poverty reduction'.[17] For the international finance ministers, if there was to be the sustained flow of investment capital to enable poor countries to develop and lift individuals out of poverty, any development strategy must be geared towards meeting the market-based preferences of investors and, as an extension of this, the IFIs themselves.

This revealed something of an inconsistency in Treasury thinking. While officials would, as the following section shows, press for donor countries to dig deeper and give more aid, through its 'new' conditionality, the New Labour government would carefully restrict who it would give that money to.

The International Finance Facility

It was during the 2002 Spending Review that Gordon Brown announced a new US$50 billion International Financing Facility to spearhead a new alliance against poverty.[18] Replacing the IDTF, this new Facility was designed to address the huge financing challenge that the donor community faced for the MDGs to be met by

2015. The first really concrete proposals for this new IFF appeared in December 2002, promising to:

> Lock-in a clear and binding – but conditional – commitment over the longer term from donors to provide substantial additional resources to 2015 and beyond in order to meet the MDGs. The Facility would ... borrow funds in international capital markets, secured against these commitments ... by issuing bonds, and so raise additional financing. The finance raised would be distributed in the form of grants and concessional loans depending on country circumstance, and it would not contribute to a burden of unsustainable debt for the poorest countries.[19]

Moreover:

> Its provision would be conditional on developing countries following good governance and implementing sound policies. To minimise bureaucracy and avoid the costly duplication of existing structures, additional resources should be distributed in a balanced way through existing effective bilateral and multilateral mechanisms, supporting poverty reduction strategies in developing countries.[20]

The secretary of state for international development, Hilary Benn, illustrated the Chancellor's proposals in even simpler terms. The IFF was just like 'the rich world taking out a mortgage to help the poor world, so the people of that world can improve their lives'.[21] Rather than waiting for there to be enough money to tackle poverty, the IFF would borrow from international capital markets – just as a homebuyer would borrow from a mortgage lender – on the basis of future aid commitments. Indeed, just as a personal mortgage needs to be securitised, Benn later argued, so too would this 'global mortgage' lock in the political commitment of donors, provide a means of securitising borrowing, and provide the predictability and critical mass of aid needed for simultaneous and sustainable investment in developing countries.[22] This, Benn argued, would allow there to be faster progress in the fight against poverty.

The principles underpinning the IFF reflected Gordon Brown's own rules concerning domestic borrowing and spending, and the creation of a welfare regime orientated to meet the challenges presented by the global economy. The following sections explore how these principles were internationalised by Brown, and their implications for New Labour's overseas aid programme.

The IFF and the Treasury's 'Golden Rule' of Borrowing and Spending

Gordon Brown's initial freeze on spending in New Labour's first few years in office notwithstanding, the IFF reflected the Treasury's commitment to spend big both at home and overseas. Although significant, this increase in government expenditure was constrained by the self-imposed 'golden rule' of borrowing and spending set by the Treasury. Institutionalising the prudence that Brown had sought to bring to New Labour's fiscal policy, this rule permitted the Chancellor to spend only what his government could afford, and to borrow only as a means of financing investment that would be of benefit to future generations. Laying out its proposals for the IFF, the Treasury argued that the Facility would enable rich countries to borrow in order to invest in the developing world. Indeed, according to the Treasury, 'borrowing to invest' was a well-established domestic and development principle. All donor countries borrow to invest in future prosperity, while the World Bank is a longstanding borrower in the capital markets.[23] By enabling these rich countries to make an investment in the poorer parts of the world in the lead-up to 2015, the international donor community could finance a real change in the lives of not only those currently living in poverty but future generations who might otherwise be born into these same conditions of want. This money was therefore to act not 'as compensation for past failures but as investment for future success'.[24]

Securing investment for the developing world was a key part of the IFF proposals. This meant reconfiguring overseas aid as an instrument that went beyond simply a means of recompensing the poor. As Gordon Brown remarked, the Facility was not only 'designed specifically to help meet the internationally agreed Millennium Development Goals' but was 'an essential condition to allow the poorest countries to attract private investment and participate in the global economy'.[25] Indeed, the money that the IFF would raise and the means by which it would be disbursed was designed to 'ensure a domestic environment in which people and firms can produce goods and services efficiently and get them to international markets'.[26] Funds raised by the IFF would 'provide developing countries with the means to invest in schools and healthcare, roads and legal systems'.[27] This investment, Brown argued, would:

> Help create the environment businesses need to start-up, invest and grow, as well as create the conditions that will enable countries to participate in, and benefit from, global trade. And as families in those countries are lifted out of poverty, new and dynamic markets will be created.[28]

For Brown, securing health and education outcomes, building roads and infrastructure, and developing a domestic environment conducive to trade and inward investment were all part of a 'virtuous circle' necessary to lift poorer countries out of poverty. By injecting finance into developing countries through the frontloading of aid, the purpose of the IFF was to create and set this virtuous circle into motion. Acting almost as 'start-up capital', the IFF would trigger investment in these areas, which in turn would benefit future generations.

Given the tight spending rules that Gordon Brown had imposed upon himself at home, it was both politically and economically expedient for the Chancellor to borrow this capital rather than simply increase aid spending. In this respect, the IFF could be cast as an accounting device to allow for what would be a significant increase in aid expenditure whilst all the while maintaining the tight fiscal stance of the Treasury at home. This was obviously attractive to those within New Labour, such as Brown, who were keen to portray their international development credentials in a manner altogether more reassuring to market actors. Politically too, the IFF was an appealing proposition since the repayment of the IFF bonds was scheduled to take place long after the current crop of ministers had departed the scene. Freed from the future burden of fulfilling the pledges made through the IFF, New Labour could claim, quite plausibly, to be embarking upon a huge increase in ODA without placing undue strain upon the public purse now.

In addition to these benefits, Whitehall ministers were also keen to point out that the Facility would not signal the end of ODA in the medium to long term.[29] Gareth Thomas, the parliamentary under secretary of state at DFID, insisted that the IFF should be viewed as being *complementary* to, rather than a substitute for progress towards achieving the 0.7 per cent/GDP target.[30] Despite the large flows of finance that the IFF was forecast to provide, the UK remained committed to meeting this goal beyond 2015.[31] For Thomas, the IFF was only a short-term mechanism, and it remained important that this financial support was sustained beyond 2015 with donor countries increasing their development budgets accordingly.[32] I shall return to the significance of this point shortly, but this continued commitment to the 0.7 per cent/GDP target would enable there to be the 'safety-net' of a continuing flow of aid once the disbursement of IFF funds had stopped. As a joint Treasury–DFID report argued, 'finance ministers in developing countries will not be prepared to increase spending on the basis of short-term or unpredictable donor commitments'.[33]

In the midst of this clear transmission of the Treasury's 'golden rule' of borrowing and spending policies into the arena of international development, however, there was a rather striking tension between New Labour's commitment to market-led development on the one hand, and its delivery of more overseas aid promised on the other. In the first instance, Treasury and DFID officials were at pains to portray the IFF as a temporary mechanism for front-loading finance; one designed to frontload aid and enable recipient countries to invest in schools, healthcare and infrastructure. Both the Treasury in London and the IFIs in Washington claimed that investment in these areas, combined with an increased market liberalisation and openness to the global economy, would raise the levels of trade and attract the foreign flows of private finance that were necessary to integrate developing countries into the global economy and reduce poverty accordingly. Over time, this integration into the global economy would lessen the dependence of these countries upon foreign aid.

Just as New Labour had sought to do through its welfare-to-work schemes, most notably through Brown's 'New Deal' programme, the pursuit of this altogether more market-based form of aid would enable countries to reduce poverty more independently rather than simply continuing to rely upon the benevolence of foreign donors. At home, young people and the unemployed were urged not to rely upon the state for hand-outs, but to instead obtain the skills required to participate in the increasingly global labour market. The government would offer support through the 'New Deal', but once an individual had secured employment and financial independence this funding would stop. Similarly, and certainly insofar as the Treasury was concerned, by bringing forward the aid commitments of donor countries, the IFF could support the integration of the developing countries into the global economy. This would enable these countries to become economically independent, create their own wealth and reduce poverty upon these terms.

The temporality of the IFF was reflected in the Treasury's claim that the Facility would be 'a limited-life entity' with an estimated lifespan of around thirty years.[34] The initial surge in aid would be supported by the IFF bonds receiving a AAA credit rating, which would enable up to US$50 billion to be frontloaded and disbursed every single year leading up to 2015. With the subsequent US$500 billion that the Treasury forecast would be raised over the ten-year period between 2005 and 2015 having been invested into poverty reduction strategies and development programmes,[35] the amount of aid disbursed by the Facility would begin to diminish.[36] This would enable the recipient countries to stand more independently in the global economy and lessen their dependency upon foreign aid.

Like the Treasury's earlier proposals for the IDTF, the IFF reflected New Labour's belief that welfare should be a short-term measure – a means rather than an ongoing end in and of itself. The high level of government spending seen under New Labour was intended to move recipients – whether welfare claimants at home or developing countries overseas – off a 'culture of dependency' and into a position of financial independence; one that would enable individuals and countries to make the most of the opportunities presented to them. The projected disbursements of the IFF reflected this way of thinking. As a later draft of the Treasury's IFF proposals argued, 'while increased aid could increase aid dependency in the short to medium term, the experience of well-managed countries in receipt of large aid flows suggests that aid has helped them to grow fast enough to reduce aid dependence over time'.[37]

Despite the temporality of the IFF, government ministers also sought to provide assurances that Britain would meet the 0.7 per cent/GDP aid target both prior to and beyond the lifetime of the IFF. While this would remain the benchmark (a benchmark that would become legally binding once New Labour had left office), this suggested that officials were not completely convinced that the leveraged investment offered by the IFF alone would be enough to address world poverty. After all, this money only provided recipient countries with an opportunity to develop and become more integrated within the global economy. As with New Labour's welfare strategy at home, the IFF was to be underpinned by a series of clear conditions that would govern the terms upon which the money raised by the Facility would be disbursed. It would be up to the recipient countries to meet their responsibilities and pursue a series of market reforms so as to ensure the growth deemed to be crucial for development.

The overarching concept of conditionality enabled donors to set out the terms upon which money should be disbursed, and to withhold or stop this money altogether should a recipient renege upon these terms. An integral element in the disbursement of both bilateral and multilateral aid programmes, two main forms of conditionality have come to dominate the international aid system: *tied aid* and *policy-based conditionality*. Tied aid requires the recipients of aid to purchase the goods and services needed for development from the donor countries themselves. More often than not, tied aid prioritises the export markets and commercial interests of aid donors over the more immediate development needs of the recipient economies.

Policy-based conditionality, on the other hand, requires the implementation of a series of policy prescriptions, typically to restructure the economy of the recipient country towards a more market-based form of development. This particular form of conditionality was introduced as part of structural adjustment measures first implemented in the 1980s by the IFIs under the rubric of the 'Washington Consensus'. Again, these policies typically prioritised economic growth over equality, and market concerns over the more immediate social issues such as healthcare and education. Both these forms of conditionality had invoked widespread criticism from the NGO community and developing countries alike, who considered these demands to be excessive and indicative of the exploitative power relations between the rich countries and those living in poorer parts of the world.

Although there was therefore a clear line of transmission between New Labour's conceptualisation of welfare conditionality at home and the policy design of the IFF for consumption abroad, the issue of conditionality was a prickly one for government officials. Conditionality had, after all, been heavily criticised by large parts of civil society – including many within the Labour Party itself – for effectively imposing sanctions on developing countries and limiting their political autonomy. New Labour ministers appeared to be sympathetic to these concerns. In DFID's second White Paper, policy officials rejected tied aid as being 'grossly inefficient', and outlined their commitment to 'untying aid and promoting local procurement'.[38] A little while before succeeding Clare Short as secretary of state for international development, Valerie Amos promised that 'conditionality in the form of the "one-size-fits-all" prescriptions imposed on developing countries' had gone from the government's agenda.[39] Amos's successor at DFID, Hilary Benn, also attempted to put clear water between the policies of his department and those of the World Bank and IMF. 'In the days of the "Washington Consensus"', Benn noted, 'there was scant regard for the impact on poverty and social conditions of an inappropriate "one-size-fits-all" economic orthodoxy on poor countries.'[40]

Despite this rejection of the 'one-size-fits-all' orthodoxy, Gordon Brown remained adamant that conditionality was 'essential if we are to ensure the best use of overseas aid'.[41] There was still an acceptance of what Amos termed 'the international consensus on what works in development'.[42] Here, macroeconomic stability and economic growth trumped the more immediate social issues faced by poor countries, while a commitment to 'sound' pro-investment policies, open markets and trade liberalisation provided the necessary prerequisite for aid disbursement. For the government, these foundations would ensure aid and development assistance was used much more effectively.[43] The IFF would be instrumental in this too by delivering reform and an improved allocation of aid.[44] The reality of this approach to aid, however, was that the fight against global poverty remained predicated upon a universal 'consensus' amongst Western policymakers rather upon the specific and often highly differentiated needs of individual countries in the developing world.

The character of this 'international consensus' was reflected in the distinctly neoliberal, pro-market conditions that countries in receipt of IFF finance were required to adopt. Laying out Gordon Brown's proposals for the IFF, the Treasury spelled out three distinct elements to its own policy conditionality; elements that were linked heavily to the 'new international economic architecture' discussed in Chapter 5. Firstly, countries were required to pursue anti-corruption, pro-stability policies and the necessary transparency in economic and corporate policies. Secondly, there must be a commitment to a sequenced opening-up of markets to global trade. Thirdly, countries must improve their macroeconomic environment to encourage increased investment and private sector-led growth.[45]

These ambiguities over aid conditionality were perhaps best captured in the publication of *Rethinking Conditionality* in 2005. This document did not call for the end of aid conditionality, but rather sought to focus upon the issue of 'process conditionality', whereby standards of 'good governance' would be the benchmark for aid rather than any exacting policy conditions.[46] Despite this attempt to clarify the government's position, the lines of difference between the 'process conditionality' that New Labour officials claimed to support, and the 'policy conditionality' they claimed to have left behind were frequently blurred. As the case of the IFF demonstrated, the disbursement of aid would remain provisional upon recipient countries continuing to put in place the same set of 'sound' policies conducive to economic growth. It was a recurring theme in the policy speeches and statements of government ministers that the implementation of pro-trade, investment-friendly policies was not only a necessary prerequisite for poverty reduction but also represented 'good governance' on the part of developing countries.

Introducing his proposals, first to the House of Commons Select Committee for International Development and then in his pre-Budget Report, Gordon Brown set out these conditions as a partnership – a 'global compact' – between the developed and developing nations:

> In return for developing countries pursuing corruption-free, pro-stability, pro-investment and pro-trade policies, developed countries should substantially increase the development aid they are prepared to offer in the run-up to 2015.[47]

> In return for the developed countries insisting on corruption-free policies for stability, better conditions for trade . . . and a more conducive environment for investment, we should in return be prepared to put in the additional development aid.[48]

As he continued to build support for the IFF the following year, Brown again called for 'a commitment from developing countries to pursue policies for stability, growth and the opening up of trade and investment'.[49] In return for this commitment, the Chancellor went on to argue, 'the international community, particularly the richest countries, should be prepared to say that we will help to meet the millennium development targets: ensuring that poverty is halved by 2015'.[50] For Brown:

> The opening up of trade and of opportunities for investment . . ., combined with the programme for aid, will help the developing countries most . . . If the developing countries are prepared to open up to trade and to allow private investment to play its role in the development of their countries, we must in turn support them with rises in our aid budgets and with the new International Finance Facility.[51]

In the 2003 Budget, the Chancellor again returned to his 'global compact' between rich and poor nations. 'In return for action by developing countries to tackle corruption and establish stable conditions for equitable and sustainable economic growth', the Treasury promised that 'developed countries will increase aid from US$50bn a year today to US$100bn a year up to 2015.'[52] Similarly, 'in return for African countries tackling corruption, pursuing policies for stability and opening up to investment, we will provide the resources to enable them to tackle their problems'.[53] This meant that although the IFF could claim to produce distinctly social outcomes, it was understood that these could *only* be achieved through the pursuit of a 'pro-market' model of development. Put simply, for more children to attend school, for more teachers and nurses to be trained and be employed, for more lives of mothers and babies to be saved during childbirth, developing countries *must* open up their markets, increase investment opportunities and integrate themselves in the global economy.

The conditionality that was strongly evident in this particular phase of development policy overseas borrowed extensively from the concept of 'rights and responsibilities' that Brown's ministerial colleagues in Whitehall had used at home to underpin New Labour's strategy for lifting individuals out of welfare (for which read, aid) and into the world of work and global markets. Although there was a clear difference in the substantive content of the obligations that both these sets of recipients were required to adhere to, these conditions – or moreover, these responsibilities – shared a character which reflected the putative demands upon both the state and the individual that globalisation was understood to have invoked. As I argued in Chapter 2, both at home and abroad, government officials understood the changing strategic context of globalisation to have necessitated a qualitatively new way of approaching and responding to policy issues and challenges.

It was Hilary Benn who explicitly transposed New Labour's domestic rhetoric of 'rights and responsibilities' into the arena of international development. The secretary of state argued that 'development aid should be about a wider, longer term global interest' and this principle 'should govern the rights and responsibilities of states in this interdependent international community'.[54] In substantive terms, however, it was the conditionality evident in Gordon Brown's proposals for the IFF that demonstrated what these rights and in particular what these responsibilities looked like in practice. Indeed, Brown's 'global compact' between rich and poor countries was based upon this relationship between the rights and the responsibilities of developing countries as recipients of aid. The Chancellor deemed it essential for developing countries to pursue 'anti-corruption, pro-stability [policies] to enable them properly to participate in the world economy'.[55] Both at home and abroad, these policy narratives revealed the importance that New Labour placed upon recipient 'responsibility' as a means of encouraging increased integration into the global economy.

Strikingly – but perhaps not surprisingly – little mention was made in any of the numerous draft proposals of the IFF or the speeches made in support of the Facility of the responsibilities donors themselves had in this mechanism. Gordon Brown appealed for rich countries to increase the amount of aid they gave to the developing world, yet only a handful had so far demonstrated the necessary political will to do so. Since 1970, many donors had simply shirked their own responsibilities and pledge to meet the 0.7 per cent/GDP target, leaving the demands of the 'compact' between the global North and South resting far more heavily upon the shoulders of the latter. Rather than redressing this imbalance, Gordon Brown chose to frame the IFF in terms of 'global inclusion', and to prioritise this particular imperative over more pressing – and more traditionally Labourite – concerns such as inequality and social justice. Like his wider 'new international economic architecture' in which Brown's IFF would be animated, the Facility became a means of imposing a series of market-based responsibilities upon the recipients of this global welfare with the designated outcome of integrating individual citizens and developing countries alike into the global economy.

The conditionality of the IFF was therefore designed to address four key areas that Gordon Brown and his colleagues considered to be of crucial importance if the finance raised by the IFF was to be used effectively, and if support for the IFF was to be forthcoming beyond Whitehall. The first and most distinctive of these four areas addressed the need for recipient countries to 'meet their obligations to pursue stability and create the conditions for new investment'.[56] Although Brown promised not to make British aid designed 'for education, health and anti-poverty programmes conditional on either trade or commercial agreements', he did maintain that it was nevertheless necessary for African countries to open up their economies 'to trade and private investment' as a means of reducing poverty.[57] The character and the imprint of this particular brand of neoliberalism dominated Brown's proposals, embedding them firmly within the so-called 'international consensus' that now existed in the 'post-Washington' era.

The second issue concerned the need for developing countries to demonstrate 'good governance' and particularly, a commitment to tackle corruption. For Gordon Brown, this was necessary to ensure that the funds earmarked for developing countries were 'properly and effectively used'.[58] Indeed, if Britain and the rest of the donor community was 'to provide additional help . . . it must have a guarantee that the money will go not to corrupt elites, wasteful military expenditure and prestige projects by bureaucracies' but instead be spent on 'health, education and anti-poverty programmes'.[59] Clearly, such a move was to be welcomed. This narrative, however, enabled British government officials to depict their counterparts in the developing world in less than favourable terms. Here New Labour played up to the crude but popular caricature of developing world leaders as being despotic, corrupt and profligate. Reinforcing the purpose of the 'new economic architecture', Brown maintained that what was required was increased economic surveillance to discipline 'good' as well as 'bad' governments into following the neoliberal orthodoxy of the 'international consensus'.

224

To this end, and with the full backing of the New Labour government, the IMF set up two centres in order 'to advise on the proper preparations of fiscal and monetary policy'.[60] Yet this raised serious questions over the way in which political leaders and decision-makers in the global South were viewed by their Northern counterparts, and the autonomy (or lack thereof) that they would be afforded in formulating policies appropriate for their own national contexts. As Brown remarked, 'in return for providing additional aid . . . central banks and finance ministers *of those countries* should be prepared to be far more transparent by opening their books to show where money was really being spent'.[61]

These two aspects of conditionality could be linked into two further reasons why conditionality itself remained so important for Gordon Brown as he sought to build support for the IFF both at home and abroad. Again the depiction of corrupt, wasteful elites in the developing world came in handy for New Labour ministers like Benn, who noted the 'fiduciary responsibility' that donor governments had 'to their taxpayers to ensure that aid is spent on development'.[62] This was highlighted by DFID's policy paper on conditionality, which noted the 'particular responsibility' that donors have 'as part of their accountability to parliament and the public, to ensure that their development assistance is not used in ways that abuse human rights'.[63] The logic here was simple: any government commitment to increasing aid would not be supported by their electorate if this money was being spent lining the pockets of the leaders of developing countries, particularly those who were guilty of human rights abuses.

Taken at face value, this, of course, is a fair enough reason, and there might be much merit in this position. It was somewhat disingenuous, however, for several of those self-same UK government officials to take this line *now* whilst remaining complicit in the continuing sales of arms to countries with notorious human rights records.[64] This would also suggest that this line of policy was designed to appease domestic audiences that had traditionally been sceptical of aid, largely on the (often exaggerated) grounds that it had a tendency to be wasted by foreign governments or pocketed by corrupt officials. Crucially, however, this specific emphasis upon 'accountability' served to signal and reinforce the responsibility that New Labour officials believed developing countries had to conform to the demands of the international donor community.

As well as building support at home, New Labour's continued emphasis upon conditionality was important in the building of support amongst other constituencies from the donor community. Tony Blair even went as far as to suggest that without these conditions in place, the IFF would not work. While the prime minister believed that the IFF was 'a sound idea', he warned that Britain would not obtain the full support for increased development assistance unless it was in return for a partnership with those countries that were taking the necessary measures to improve their governance.[65] For government officials, it was clear that an initiative such as the IFF needed the safeguard of conditionality to persuade other donors to support the proposals. Without this accountability, donors would be unwilling to scale up their aid commitments to the amount that was required to meet the MDGs.

Two rather striking observations can be made, both from Blair's remarks and the way, in much broader terms, in which the IFF was framed. New Labour officials had frequently stated the urgent case for increasing aid as a means of meeting the MDGs. For both Brown and his colleagues in DFID, it was essential that the aid community took seriously this challenge in order to fund desperately needed poverty reduction strategies across the developing world. Such an appeal, however – much like the Treasury's own spending plans at home – was tempered with economic caution and constraint. Only if recipient countries in the developing world adopted 'appropriate' macroeconomic policies would the international donor community be under any obligation to deliver on its aid commitments. Despite the gravity of the situation faced by the poorest countries and people groups in the developing world, any redistribution of wealth was to take place on these economic terms, and these terms alone, rather than through any moral or humanitarian obligation on the part of the rich countries in the global North.

The priority that these economic concerns were afforded over the moral impulse that New Labour officials claimed elsewhere was reflected in the design of the IFF itself. Although its projected ability to raise US$50 billion in aid enabled Gordon Brown to talk about meeting 'the moral challenge' of poverty, the Facility was clearly hard-wired into addressing the 'economic' imperative of development. Like the IDTF before it, the IFF would not become a 'new' aid agency with a new set of criteria. Rather, it would continue to disburse money through 'existing development agencies' and 'effective bilateral and multilateral mechanisms'.[66] This was significant since it appealed directly to the pro-market sensibilities of these particular institutions, by assimilating their neoliberal ideas and practices into the design of the IFF. In an unambiguous endorsement of the current practice of aid disbursement, particularly by the IFIs, the financial secretary to the Treasury, Stephen Timms, justified the use of these arrangements as being 'tried, tested and shown to be effective'.[67]

This was a remarkable statement given the criticism that this particular approach to aid had attracted amongst large parts of civil society, senior Labour backbenchers as well as rank-and-file party members. In spite of such criticism, however, neither New Labour officials nor the proposals for the IFF conceived of the need or the possibility to reform these existing institutional arrangements. As John Healey, the economic secretary at the Treasury, remarked, 'the International Finance Facility would not impose new conditions on recipient countries'.[68] Instead, the finance raised and disbursed through the IFF would remain at the discretion of the donor with funds allocated 'by each donor to its choice of country and delivery channel'.[69] Despite many donors (including Britain) reneging on their own aid responsibilities in the past, the onus remained firmly upon the developing country to step up to the plate; to create 'a good policy environment' where this aid could be 'used most effectively'.[70]

The 'doubling of aid to halve poverty' and commitment to spend US$500 billion over the course of the next ten years were all headlines clearly designed to appeal to faith groups, NGOs and members of the Labour Party who had all pressed the New Labour government into taking greater action over global poverty and spending more on overseas aid. In the midst of these bold projections, however, the Treasury also sought to reassure the altogether more market-based audiences of the economic credibility of the IFF. When addressing the former, New Labour championed the Facility as an 'innovative' mechanism which could solve the chronic shortfall in overseas aid and finance the means by which developing countries could grow and lift themselves out of poverty.

At the same time, however, the IFF was a further means by which 'already shock-prone economies' could be disciplined and stabilised.[71] Clearly forgetting that many of these economies were 'shock-prone' precisely because of the policies rolled out by global institutions such as the IMF, Gordon Brown and his colleagues set up the IFF to accommodate the preferences of these institutions – namely, macroeconomic stability, trade liberalisation and 'the right conditions for foreign investment'. This suggested that any commitment to increase aid was not principally a moral concern, but rather a means to institutionalise market-led growth in the developing countries. Moreover, rather than tackling the structural causes of poverty experienced across the global South, Brown's vision only extended as far as treating the *effects* of this inequality and underdevelopment. That the IFF was driven by largely economic imperatives, rather than any distinctly ethical mandate, crucially undermined the moral leadership that Brown was otherwise keen to demonstrate over this issue.

The International Finance Facility for Immunisation

Despite extensive promotion by government ministers both at home and abroad, most notably in the report published by the Commission for Africa,[72] and in the lead-up to and during the 2005 G8 summit in Gleneagles, the IFF as a mechanism for delivering increased aid to the developing world was quietly dropped by Treasury officials shortly after. Given how hard Gordon Brown had pushed the IFF, it can only be assumed that a failure to convince Britain's key allies in the G8 of its viability left the Chancellor without the political and economic support he needed for its successful implementation. Unperturbed by this setback, Treasury officials instead set about exploring the possibility of extending the 'frontloading' principles of the IFF to more specific areas of development, such as water and sanitation,[73] climate change[74] and children's health. It was the latter – through became what known as the International Finance Facility for Immunisation (IFFIm) – that Brown set about convincing the international community as to the feasibility of the 'frontloading' principles as a means of financing the scaling-up of access to lifesaving vaccines, specifically for children living in the developing world.

The potential for an IFFIm had actually been suggested as early as 2004. Government officials noted that such an initiative could form part of the supply-side policies that the Treasury introduced to encourage pharmaceutical firms to invest in the unprofitable, so-called 'diseases of poverty' (see Chapter 6). The IFFIm could help persuade the manufacturers of vaccines to increase production and encourage new investments, as well as providing greater predictability and security of funds to countrywide immunisation systems.[75] Sticking closely to the Treasury's design for the original IFF, the IFFIm was to be operationalised by converting long-term aid commitments from donors into frontloaded resources for immunisation.[76] The first tranche of finance would be used to purchase vaccines and other essential medicines, and disbursed over a ten-year period.[77] DFID ministers claimed that these vaccinations could save an additional 5 million children's lives in the years to 2015,[78] and over time, enable over 500 million people to be vaccinated across the developing world.[79]

Like the original IFF, the IFFIm used the principle of 'borrowing to invest' alongside international capital markets to raise the finance necessary to buy in large quantities the lifesaving vaccinations, suitably modified for use in tropical regions. In keeping with Gordon Brown's own carefully cultivated model of political economy, these aspects of the IFFIm gave market actors a key role to play in the raising of this finance. Arguably the most important of these actors was the World Bank, which through its Concessional Finance and Global Partnerships (CFGP) division was appointed to act as the Treasury manager for the IFFIm.[80] The remit of the CFGP would include responsibility for the funding the IFFIm receives from capital markets, the management of risk, and donor co-ordination. The CFGP would also work closely with the credit-rating agencies to maintain the AAA rating that the IFFIm bonds needed to ensure the ongoing commercial attraction of these bonds to investors.

The CFGP designated the leading investment banks Deutsche Bank and Goldman Sachs to manage the first IFFIm bond issue in November 2006. Priced comparably to those of other sovereign and supranational issuers, the IFFIm bonds were subsequently purchased by central banks, fund managers and insurance companies,[81] raising US$1 billion.[82] Although this inaugural bond issue represented just a fraction of the US$50 billion that the Treasury hoped that the original IFF would raise on an annual basis, this money was nevertheless able to be used primarily by the GAVI Alliance (formerly known as the Global Alliance for Vaccines and Immunisation) to finance the purchasing of vaccines from pharmaceutical firms on behalf of poor countries, administer immunisation programmes and support healthcare systems in the developing world. This process would create the appropriate market conditions and incentivise the pharmaceutical firms to invest in the research of vaccine technology and to produce drugs suitable for use in tropical and ostensibly 'less-profitable' regions of the world.

By creating the right market conditions for investment by pharmaceutical firms, the IFFIm followed New Labour's broader commitment to increase access to medicines by incentivising these firms into developing paediatric formulations of vaccines to protect against diseases commonly found in developing areas. This reinforced both the demand- and supply-side strategies that government officials had come to recognise as being integral elements in the increase of access to vaccines and medicines in the developing world. As I have previously remarked, an overriding responsibility to the expectations of shareholder and a lack of profitability in poor country markets had tended to deter a lot of pharmaceutical firms from investing in the R&D of medicines needed in the developing world. Where medicines had been made available, countries in the poorer regions were often unable to afford such treatments and frequently lacked the infrastructure to administer medicines effectively.

In policy terms, the IFFIm revealed what the Treasury under New Labour actually meant when it spoke about 'borrowing to invest', particularly within the international arena. The IFFIm was a mechanism for long-term borrowing designed to be embedded within a matrix of global market actors. For the IFFIm to work as policy officials envisioned, the Facility needed to be calibrated in order to meet the expectations of these particular actors. For this to occur, however, New Labour officials clearly deemed it necessary to hand over all control of the Facility to IFIs and other economic actors that it deemed better placed to credibly deliver its own policy outcomes. The early performance and potential of the IFFIm (illustrated in Box 7.1) went a long way in vindicating this decision and enabled Treasury and DFID ministers to claim New Labour's continued commitment to global social justice.[83]

Box 7.1 The achievements and the potential of the IFFIm since 2006.

What the IFFIm has *already* achieved:
- The immunisation of more than 100 million children under the age of five against polio
- 194 million children in thirty-two developing countries immunised with a measles vaccine
- 14.5 million children vaccinated against hepatitis B
- 4.4 million children vaccinated against yellow fever

What the IFFIm *could* yet still achieve:
- The targeting of 26 million women living in developing countries with immunisation against maternal and neonatal tetanus
- The support of vaccine security and affordability, and the prevention of approximately 687,000 deaths up to the year 2050

The headline message of these achievements that New Labour ministers sought to get across was that 'specifically targeted aid' works. Allocated and disbursed through a private, carefully monitored mechanism such as GAVI, this type of aid *could* make a huge difference to the lives of millions across the developing world. Despite these successes, a question clearly remained over how much of a distinctly social democratic identity there was, in both New Labour's domestic and international development policies. Despite the initial success of the IFFIm, its moral basis was subsumed by the market-based preferences of a powerful set of international economic constituencies. The interests of patients in the developing world would continue to be secondary to meeting the expectations of these constituencies. Given this policy success, pragmatists might be forgiven for asking why this was such a problem. After all, as many at the modernising heart of the New Labour project had argued, 'what matters is what works'.

Such an assessment, however, would be to miss what really was at stake here. If it was indeed private markets and investors who were raising this finance, even for a policy objective as admirable as increasing the number of children receiving vaccinations and/ or scaling up access to essential medicines, the scheme remained hostage to the fortunes of these investors. Indeed, the ongoing funding of the project was contingent upon investors remaining confident that their money was being spent in the 'correct' way. Followed to its logical conclusion, it would be these market actors, rather than the developing countries themselves, who would determine how their money was to be spent and where in the world the purchased treatments were to be distributed.

The stark consequences of this market-based logic appear most acute during a period of financial uncertainty and economic recession. Such a scenario unfolded and overshadowed New Labour's final few years in office, making market actors – and, concomitantly, political actors – even more risk-averse in their behaviour. The main response to the financial difficulties that Gordon Brown, now as prime minister, faced during this time at home, was to increase public borrowing in order to stabilise the ailing banking sector and stimulate aggregate demand in the slowing British economy. Abroad, however, New Labour's response to the financial crisis had the effect of downgrading Britain's sovereign AAA rating that as Chancellor, Brown had argued was an important component of the IFF proposals. If the markets were to remain convinced of the long-term viability of the IFFIm, it was essential that Britain's own level of borrowing was kept in check and that the New Labour government pursued what the markets considered to be a credible set of spending plans.

Although Gordon Brown's government remained 'committed to fulfilling its pledge to dedicate 0.7 per cent of its gross national income to development by 2013', it argued that 'government spending on its own will not be enough'.[84] Instead, a much greater emphasis needed to be placed upon sources of private finance and entrepreneurship. This was significant since it reinforced the view held by New Labour officials that private finance and entrepreneurial activity in developing countries would not occur if recipient governments did not pursue the same sort of market-orientated policies that encouraged this type of economic activity in the first place. Therefore, although any reference to the conditionalities that underpinned the previous IFF proposals had all but disappeared from the speeches made by New Labour ministers during this phase of policy, the emphasis upon the private sector meant that these conditions remained implicit. Without these types of market reforms in place, the aid necessary to finance the development that Brown and his colleagues clearly remained in favour of would not be forthcoming. This shift in government policy suggested that if spending on development could no longer come from governments – particularly in an era of financial uncertainty and belt-tightening – it would be necessary to look to the private sector in order to fill this gap.

This particular move was also significant since it revealed New Labour's assessment of the role that the state should play in the delivery of forms of welfare both at home and abroad. Continuing the transmission of its welfare policies into the framework of the IFF, and in particular the responsibilities that recipients had in order to receive this assistance, New Labour understood the state to be an enabler rather than a direct provider of services. This stood in stark contrast to 'old' Labour, which had been concerned with what it provided as a government; its *outcomes* – for instance, a universal health service, extensive welfare provision and expansion of public services. For New Labour, the focus was upon the *means*, and the effectiveness of these in meeting the party's overarching commitment to social justice. As in other parts of its political economy, both at home and abroad, government officials argued that what was more important was the effectiveness of policies and how services were delivered. More often than not, this was understood to be best achieved through the innovation, entrepreneurialism and cost-effectiveness putatively found in the private sector. Insofar as overseas development aid was concerned, DFID emphasised the importance of private sector funding in its fourth White Paper. It set out an objective to:

> Use innovative ways of working with the private sector to help meet financing gaps and to secure better performance, value for money and investment. A good example is our support to innovative financing in health . . . through an expanded International Finance Facility for Immunisation.[85]

Under Gordon Brown's watch – both as Chancellor and then as prime minister – New Labour was clearly committed to the principle of global healthcare and increased aid in the developing world. In achieving this particular set of policy objectives, however, Brown's colleagues in Whitehall considered it necessary to underpin the government's development aid programme through a series of market arrangements. Although identified by Brown himself as the most efficient means of raising finance, this strategy nevertheless orientated policy towards the expectations of market investors rather than those living in developing countries. Periods of recession and market uncertainty tend to reinforce this shift in expectations since they draw the emphasis and the focus of these policies away from the policy outcome itself towards the means by which these policies are achieved. The same is true of forms of direct government spending. Where there is pressure over government spending increases, policies become less about the outcome and more about meeting the demands of 'austerity', 'cost reduction' and maintaining 'sound' public finances. Indeed, as the secretary of state for international development, Douglas Alexander, noted:

> The British people would expect efficiency savings in a department that received such a generous increase of resources in the Comprehensive Spending Review. They have the right to know that their money is being well spent on their behalf, and the nature of DFID's work does not, and should not, exempt us from such scrutiny.[86]

Alexander was 'determined that the government's aid, whether bilateral or multilateral, should aim to deliver maximum impact and represent value for money'.[87] As Brown's decision to recapitalise the banks loomed large over virtually every area of policy, the imperatives of 'cost-cutting' and 'cost-effectiveness' became the principal focus of New Labour's aid programme. Although officials continued to talk about the importance of aid in poverty reduction strategies, they continued to exercise restraint in how this money should be spent and the channels through which it should be raised. For both private and public forms of aid, the issue therefore became less about *what* New Labour was spending aid money on, but whether it was cost-effective or indeed worthwhile to do so in the first place.

The initial, and indeed impressive, set of results delivered by the IFFIm do certainly suggest a discernible shift towards social outcomes and the accommodation of calls made by public health advocates to scale up investment in healthcare in the global South. The design and the fundamental principles of the IFFIm, however, meant that the mechanism was – somewhat ironically, given Gordon Brown's emphasis upon maintaining macroeconomic stability – particularly vulnerable to financial uncertainty in the British and the wider global economy. If private market actors and other investors were at any stage unconvinced by the long-term viability of the mechanism, or whether or not the bonds would in fact be repaid, the policy outcomes of increased immunisation programmes across the developing world promised by the IFFIm would remain under threat.

Post-New Labour, the IFFIm is no longer part of DFID's development agenda. Jettisoned by the Conservative–Liberal Democrat coalition government, it now forms the basis of a public-private partnership between the GAVI Alliance and the World Bank. The moral thrust of what Gordon Brown and New Labour tried to achieve through the IFFIm cannot be disputed. The means of achieving this, however – prioritising and reinforcing the 'pro-market' preferences of private financial actors and institutions in the global North over the health and the well-being of those living in the developing world – means that for this reason alone, the IFFIm cannot be judged to be a complete success.

Conclusions

The purpose of this chapter has been to assess Gordon Brown's personal ambition to increase the level of Britain's overseas development aid through three closely interrelated aid mechanisms: the IDTF, the IFF and the IFFIm. Throughout each of these three stages of policy, Brown took various strands from New Labour's domestic political economy to meet this challenge. From his own proposals for a CTF, his 'golden rule' concerning borrowing and spending, to New Labour's broader reconfiguration of the welfare state, Brown's carefully crafted policies were transposed into this particular aspect of the government's international development commitment.

The internationalisation of these various domestic policy ideas, chiefly by Gordon Brown into Britain's aid programme, reveals a great deal about Brown's assessment of the terms upon which redistribution should take place in an era of globalisation, the role of the state in an increasingly global economy, and the extent to which development policy should be led by, and orientated towards, the preferences of market actors. The language of 'rights and responsibility' articulated by Brown and other ministers was a dominant theme of New Labour's welfare policies at home. To this end, inclusion in the global economy was prioritised over more traditionally social democratic concerns such as equality, and this shift in emphasis was evident both at home and abroad. Just as at home recipients of welfare were disciplined into taking up a series of duties that would prepare them for the demands of the global economy, the aid that the IFF promised to deliver would also be conditional upon developing countries opening up and orientating their economies to meet the challenges of globalisation. Officials both in Whitehall and Washington argued that increased market openness, trade liberalisation and investor-friendly policies would enable these developing countries not only to meet the challenges of globalisation but to take what was 'the only' route out of poverty.

To his credit, Gordon Brown was instrumental in ensuring that New Labour continued to retain a distinct commitment to the redistribution of wealth. However, these duties and obligations were underpinned by a significant change in emphasis. Wealth redistribution would no longer be based upon the immediate needs of the poor, but the extent to which recipients of this welfare were prepared to participate and become integrated within an increasingly global society. In practice, this new approach tended to overlook the historical failures of the international donor community and focus instead upon the perceived shortcomings of the developing countries, arguing for greater emphasis to be placed upon 'good governance', 'macroeconomic stability' and the creation of a liberal trade and investment regime.

Within this strategic context of globalisation, New Labour viewed the role of the state as one of 'enabler' rather than 'provider'. Again, this was reflected initially at home through the Treasury's CTF and those welfare policies that were designed as tools to equip individuals with the finance and the skills to participate in the global economy. This discourse of 'enablement', however, also framed the way in which policy was formulated. The state should 'enable', rather than simply 'provide' the best possible delivery of policy outcomes by putting in place the most cost-effective structures. For both the IFF and the IFFIm, market structures were deemed to provide the most efficient way of raising the finance that was urgently required to scale up levels of aid and to fund vaccination programmes in the developing world. The initial achievements of the IFFIm were certainly commendable. However, there was a clear sense from the policy statements and speeches of ministers that these achievements simply served to justify the means by which they were delivered, and that the real priority of the Brown government spending in this area was cost-effectiveness and a fiduciary responsibility to the British taxpayer. These reasons, however, undermined any real moral commitment that Brown and his colleagues might have claimed for their continued pledge to increase overseas aid spending. Instead, these financial and electoral concerns were afforded a far higher priority than the more immediate and pressing health needs of those living in the developing world.

Notes

1. Brown, 'International Development in 2005', 2005.
2. Peston, *Brown's Britain*, 2005, p. 293.
3. DFID, *A Challenge for the 21st Century*, 1997, pp. 16, 20.
4. DFID, *Making Globalisation Work for the Poor*, 2000.
5. Initially, this target was set in relation to the gross national income of a country. More recent accounts, however, use gross domestic product, or GDP, as the means of measuring this target.
6. HM Government, *The UK's Contribution to Achieving the Millennium Development Goals*, 2005, p. 58.
7. Brown, 'International Finance Facility', 2005.
8. Timms, 'Millennium Development Goals', 2005.
9. Brown, speech delivered at the Federal Reserve, 2001.
10. Ibid.
11. Ibid.
12. Ibid.
13. Ibid.
14. Brown, 'Globalisation', 2001.
15. Wolfensohn, 'The Challenges of Globalisation', 2001.
16. Köhler, 'Promoting Stability and Prosperity in a Globalized World', 2001.
17. Ibid.
18. Brown, 'Spending Review', 2002.
19. HM Treasury, *The International Finance Facility*, 2002, p. 5.
20. Ibid. p. 5.
21. Benn, speech delivered at the annual conference of the Jubilee movement, 2004.
22. Benn, 'Development Financing', 2004.

23. Ibid. p. 6.
24. Ibid. p. 2.
25. Brown, speech delivered at the 'Financing Sustainable Development, Poverty Reduction and the Private Sector' conference, 2003.
26. HM Treasury, *The International Finance Facility*, 2004, p. 2.
27. Brown, speech delivered at the 'Financing Sustainable Development, Poverty Reduction and the Private Sector' conference, 2003.
28. Ibid.
29. HM Treasury, *The International Finance Facility*, 2004, p. 7.
30. Thomas, *EU Contribution to Achieving the UN Millennium Development Goals*, 2005.
31. HM Treasury, *The International Finance Facility*, 2004, p. 7.
32. Thomas, *EU Contribution to Achieving the UN Millennium Development Goals*, 2005.
33. DFID with HM Treasury, *From Commitment to Action*, 2005, p. 3.
34. HM Treasury, *The International Finance Facility*, 2003, pp. 2, 8.
35. Ibid. p. 7.
36. Ibid. p. 8.
37. HM Treasury, *The International Finance Facility*, 2004, p. 6.
38. DFID, *Making Globalisation Work for the Poor*, 2000, p. 94.
39. Amos, 'Southern Africa', 2003.
40. Benn, 'Making Globalisation Work for All', 2004.
41. Brown, 'Third World Poverty', 2004.
42. Amos, 'Southern Africa', 2003.
43. DFID, *Making Globalisation Work for the Poor*, 2000, pp. 84ff.
44. HM Treasury, *The International Finance Facility*, 2002, p. 1.
45. Ibid. p. 2.
46. DFID, *Partnerships for Poverty Reduction*, 2005.
47. House of Commons Select Committee for International Development, *Financing for Development*, 2002, p. 9.
48. Brown, 'Pre-Budget Report', 2002.
49. Brown, 'International Monetary Fund', 2003.
50. Ibid.
51. Brown, 'Development Aid', 2003.
52. HM Treasury, *Building a Britain of Economic Strength and Social Justice*, 2003, p. 108.
53. Brown, 'World Debt', 2003.
54. Benn, 'Making Globalisation Work for All', 2004.
55. Brown, 'World Debt', 2003.
56. Brown, 'Q. 99', 2002.
57. Brown, 'International Finance', 2003.
58. Brown, 'Q. 99', 2002.
59. Brown, 'International Debt Relief', 2003.

60. Brown, 'Third World Poverty', 2004.
61. Ibid., emphasis added.
62. Benn, 'Making Globalisation Work for All', 2004.
63. DFID, *Partnerships for Poverty Reduction*, 2005, p. 8.
64. Kettell, *Dirty Politics?*, 2006, p. 36.
65. Blair, 'Commonwealth Heads of Government Meeting', 2003.
66. HM Treasury, *The International Finance Facility*, 2003, p. 2.
67. Timms, 'International Finance Facility', 2004.
68. Healey, 'International Finance Facility', 2003.
69. HM Treasury, *The International Finance Facility*, 2003, p. 2.
70. Short, 'Good Governance', 2002.
71. HM Treasury, *The International Finance Facility*, 2004, p. 7.
72. Commission for Africa, *Our Common Interest*, 2005, p. 110.
73. Benn, 'Water: Meeting our Promises', 2006.
74. Brown, 'The Global Economy', 2009; Vadera, 'Q. 182', 2008.
75. DFID, *Increasing Access to Essential Medicines in the Developing World*, 2004, p. 33.
76. Balls, 'International Finance Facility for Immunisation', 2006.
77. Thomas, 'Developing World', 2005.
78. Lewis, 'International Finance Facility for Immunisation', 2005.
79. Foster, 'Developing Countries: Vaccination', 2009.
80. World Bank Group, 'Corporate Responsibility Program', 2010.
81. IFFIm, 'Bond Issuances', 2010.
82. Ibid.
83. Malik, 'Developing Countries: Health Services', 2007; DFID, 'IFFIm raises money for immunisation', 2008; Merron, 'International Finance Facility for Immunisation Bonds', 2008; Kennedy, 'International Finance Facility for Immunisation', 2008; Foster, 'Developing Countries: Vaccination', 2009.
84. DFID, *Building Our Common Future*, 2009, p. 137.
85. Ibid. p. 137.
86. Alexander, 'International Development', 2007.
87. Ibid.

8 Saving the World?

One of the most powerful figures in British post-war politics, Gordon Brown was at the heart of a remarkable period for both the Labour Party and the country as a whole. Although his political destiny was bound up with Tony Blair, Brown's fiercest rival and predecessor as prime minister, Brown remained a personality within the New Labour machine in his own right. While it was Blair who embodied the modernisation of the Labour Party, Brown was the ever-present, and indeed, as this book has demonstrated, *the* principal figure of the New Labour project. Not only was New Labour based upon Brown's carefully designed model of political economy, so institutionalised was his model that its very arrangements allowed the Chancellor to gradually accumulate the power that could be exercised across Whitehall and into the world.

Although his premiership – the job he prized above all others – quickly unravelled, Gordon Brown was nevertheless a Chancellor distinct from any other. He was, of course, concerned principally with the management of the British economy, and the way in which monetary and fiscal policy was set. Yet whereas many, if not all, of his predecessors had at some stage or another felt restricted by the role, Brown revolutionised it. For Brown, the chancellorship became the means by which his strong moral instinct could address the economic and social injustice and inequality that he saw before him, both at home and abroad in some of the world's poorest nations. While it would be unfair to dismiss Brown's predecessors as dead-eyed economists and number crunchers concerned only with making the finances of the country add up, it quickly became clear that Brown sought to achieve far more than this in his own stewardship of the UK economy. For Brown, both his chancellorship and his premiership represented a challenge as well as an opportunity to not simply navigate Britain through the choppy waters of the global economy, but to apply the principles of his personal politics and economic philosophy in the fight against world poverty.

This book has told the story of how Gordon Brown attempted to reconcile these two previously distinct spheres of policy and governance. His diligent commitment to offer meaningful solutions to the most urgent and pressing matters of global poverty ensures that this 'son of the manse' takes his position as one of the all-time greats in the pantheon of the British Labour Party. Brown was a remarkable Chancellor of the Exchequer. The strong sense of social justice with which he had been imbued from a very young age remained with him and, even out of office, continues to this day.

Brown's profound moral purpose, combined with his intellectual gravitas, enabled him to become a true global statesman. Having been thwarted, initially at least, in his ambition to become prime minister, Brown's political career might have plateaued. Yet it did not and, in becoming Britain's longest-serving Chancellor of the modern era, it is testament to the resolve of Brown that he did not spend this time, as others have claimed, festering with resentment. Rather, the Brown chancellorship was one that, as this book has revealed, was dedicated to addressing the poverty in which millions around the world found themselves immiserated. Using a model of political economy carefully crafted by Brown himself, as both Chancellor and then, finally, prime minister, Brown remained steadfast in his mission to save the world.

However, although there can be no doubt about the sincerity and the ambitions of Gordon Brown in this regard, far greater questions remain over the very types of solutions that Brown proposed concerning global poverty. In answering these crucial questions, it is important to keep in mind the manner in which Brown set about addressing this issue. Since Brown's response to matters of international development was based explicitly upon a set of policies designed originally for consumption at home, any assessment of his and, of course, New Labour's track record with regards tackling global poverty must be judged in the light of his domestic as well as international political economy.

Operating in an ostensibly open, global economy, the political and economic framework designed and implemented by Gordon Brown was instrumental in New Labour's bid to be taken seriously as a 'credible' government. The economic credibility that this framework offered was hugely important, not simply in electoral terms, but in the building of a relationship with business that would enable the New Labour government to fulfil its altogether more social objectives. For Brown, at a personal level, whether or not he wanted to be viewed as a 'credible socialist', he certainly wanted to offer a 'credible' vision of social and economic justice. To achieve this particular aim, it was deemed necessary for Brown to demonstrate sufficient economic discipline so as to successfully manage the economy and, concomitantly, realise a set of social goals both at home and abroad.

This, however, proved a difficult balancing act. Gordon Brown's 'new global architecture', designed to stabilise those economies disrupted by investor uncertainty and putatively 'bad' policy choices made by national governments, ended up conforming to rather than reforming the economic orthodoxy and institutional structures of international finance. Preaching the same virtues of market liberalisation and private investment, Brown prized the credibility of his mission over a far deeper commitment to matters of global poverty. His economic blueprint as a result remained firmly within the doctrine and conventional wisdom of the so-called 'post-Washington Consensus' rather than outside it. Indeed, by proposing a more robust series of surveillance measures, Brown's architecture actually strengthened the hand of these institutions of international finance – when the clarion call from civil society and many national governments was to improve the autonomy and economic sovereignty of states. An inability or lack of willingness on Brown's part to democratise global finance, let alone offer more in the way of debt forgiveness, revealed the limits of his architecture and what the Chancellor considered politically or economically possible. Despite the stature and statesmanship that Brown enjoyed as the figurehead of New Labour's political economy, a glorious opportunity was passed up to radically transform economic relations between the global North and South.

A further set of tensions emerged at home, where New Labour's much-vaunted claim to be 'the new party of business' meant that it, as a government, inevitably prioritised the interests of firms and their shareholders. Gordon Brown, of course, more than played his part in this, frequently engaging in dialogue with business leaders and industry representatives, not least because it was again crucial to the 'credibility' and trust he sought to instil amongst market actors. When it came to international development, and in particular the response of the New Labour government to the issue of HIV and AIDS in the global South, Brown – unlike some other cabinet colleagues – recognised explicitly the role that the pharmaceutical industry had to play in this. Nevertheless, a further opportunity was missed to press British-based firms in particular to do more over the key issue of research into the less-profitable but vitally important tropical and paediatric formulations of these lifesaving drugs. Rather than forcing them to take greater action, Brown offered a series of tax incentives that he hoped would prompt the firms to scale up their research programmes, whilst – of course – protecting their profits. It was, unequivocally, the industry and its shareholders that called the shots, and, fatally, they simply did not share the same moral commitment as Brown did to the research and delivery of these medicines.

The creation of his very own International Finance Facility revealed another set of tensions in Gordon Brown's development strategy. In many respects Brown's flagship project for addressing poverty overseas, and vociferously championed as such by both the Chancellor and Treasury ministers at every opportunity, this mechanism nevertheless remained wedded to a set of distinctly parsimonious economic rules devised back home. It was still expected that countries receiving IFF money would continue to conform to the free market demands placed upon them by donor countries and institutions. Despite, then, Brown's appeal for a new 'global compact' between the rich and poor, the obligations demanded of the least well-off were far more exacting than they were for the wealthiest of these countries. Even an altogether more 'social' initiative such as the IFFIm, which did bear considerable success, appeared to prioritise the demands of private firms and, politically, was framed within the language of 'cost-effectiveness' and 'belt-tightening'. Rather than address the chronic structural inequalities that persisted with regards local health provision across the world, Brown's IFFIm focused solely upon the end result. Although at first glance these headline figures made for impressive reading, they nevertheless remained contingent upon the continued flows of (largely private) finance through the same sharply neoliberal disbursement mechanisms that in the past had done so much to stymie the prospects of development in the global South.

Many of the policy measures designed and introduced by Gordon Brown offered 'new ways of delivering old values', and for the majority of these it was simply accepted that market efficiency was the best way to deliver social and economic equality. Envisaging development in principally market terms, however, squeezed the space afforded to those constituencies who viewed global poverty as essentially a 'social' or even moral issue. This left a deficit in the response of Gordon Brown and New Labour to the questions of who development is for, and what purpose it should have. While for each of these areas there were clear moral imperatives at play, which even Brown himself acknowledged, these were always subordinate to the objective of securing credibility with market actors. Yet crucially, if only market constraints are accommodated in the development process, then only market outcomes will be delivered.

This draws me to my final point, and one that lies at the heart of Gordon Brown's political economy: the role of the market in the delivery of public goods. Despite Brown's claim that markets should serve people, the economic and financial architecture he proposed, his commitment to business, and the way he attempted to reconfigure the welfare state were all attuned to meet primarily the expectations of the market. Similarly, the provision of public goods abroad within the sphere of international development, whether debt relief, antiretrovirals or aid, all relied upon a series of arrangements that either depended upon market mechanisms for their delivery, or were derived from a specifically neoliberal understanding of the global economy.

However, the increased marketisation of publicly provided services leaves societies and individuals far more exposed to the excesses and inherent instability of global capitalism. While Gordon Brown, of course, recognised this and sought to institutionalise a new, more globally orientated model of political economy, the arrangements that he proposed merely consolidated the 'virtuous state': a particular neoliberal framework that strengthened the hand of the market and enabled it to flourish. That Brown was unable to envisage a model of political economy *outside* of this market orthodoxy did not just simply mean that those he sought to help were exposed to the deleterious effects of these self-same market processes, but would ensure that they were locked in to an economic system that had been the principle cause for much of the underdevelopment and inequality experienced across much of the global South. Gordon Brown's model of political economy, as I have described it here, ultimately failed to properly address the structural and systemic inequalities that continue to lie at the root of global poverty. Rather than saving the world, Brown's was a development strategy that, despite its moral vision, frequently fell short in empowering and improving the lives of those most vulnerable to the contradictions and crises of global capitalism.

Bibliography

ABPI, *Global Health and the Pharmaceutical Industry* (London: ABPI, 2007).

Abrahamsen, R. and P. D. Williams, 'Ethics and foreign policy: the antinomies of New Labour's "Third Way" in sub-Saharan Africa', *Political Studies*, 49(2), 2001, pp. 249–64.

Ainsworth, R., 'Departments: Lisbon Agenda', *Official Report (Commons Hansard)*, vol. 465, c. 1352W, 30 October 2007.

Alexander, D., 'Foreword by the Secretary of State', in DFID, *Achieving Universal Access: The UK's Strategy for Halting and Reversing the Spread of HIV in the Developing World* (London: DFID, 2008), pp. i–ii.

Alexander, D., 'Global Poverty', *Official Report (Commons Hansard)*, vol. 463, c. 778, 24 July 2007.

Alexander, D., 'International Development', *Official Report (Commons Hansard)*, vol. 467, c. 870, 15 November 2007.

Allan, R., 'Q. 30', in House of Commons Select Committee for International Development, 'Department for International Development: Responding to HIV/AIDS', Fourteenth Report of Session 2004–05, HC 443 (incorporating HC 807-i, session 2003–04), 2004.

Amos, V., 'Southern Africa', *Official Report (Lords Hansard)*, vol. 623, c. 272, 7 March 2001.

Amos, V., 'Southern Africa', *Official Report (Lords Hansard)*, vol. 644, c. 1203, 19 February 2003.

Anderson, P. and N. Mann, *Safety First: The Making of New Labour* (London: Granta, 1997).

Annesley, C. and A. Gamble, 'Economic and welfare policy', in S. Ludlam and M. J. Smith (eds), *Governing as New Labour: Policy and Politics under Blair* (Basingstoke: Palgrave, 2004), pp. 144–60.

Arestis, P. and M. Sawyer, 'New Labour, new monetarism', *Soundings*, 9, 1998, pp. 24–41.

AstraZeneca, 'Memorandum Appendix 54', in House of Commons Science and Technology Committee, 'The Use of Science in UK International

Development Policy', Thirteenth Report of Session 2003–04, Volume II, Oral and Written Evidence, HC 133-II, 2004.

AstraZeneca, 'Millennium Development Goals', <http://www.astrazeneca.com/Responsibility/Access-to-healthcare/Millennium-development-goals> (last accessed 11 December 2011).

Atkins, J., 'Assessing the impact of the Third Way', in S. Griffiths and K. Hickson (eds), *British Party Politics and Ideology after New Labour* (Basingstoke: Palgrave, 2010), pp. 39–52.

Atkins, J., *Justifying New Labour Policy* (Basingstoke: Palgrave, 2011).

Baker, A., '*Nébuleuse* and the "internationalization of the state" in the UK? The case of HM Treasury and the Bank of England', *Review of International Political Economy*, 6(1), 1999, pp. 79–100.

Balls, E., 'Delivering Economic Stability', Oxford Business Alumni annual lecture, London, 12 June 2001, <http://www.hm-treasury.gov.uk/press_65_01.htm> (last accessed 1 September 2010).

Balls, E., *Euro-Monetarism: Why Britain Was Ensnared and How It Should Escape*, Fabian Society Discussion Paper No. 14 (London: Fabian Society, 1992).

Balls, E., 'International Finance Facility for Immunisation', *Official Report (Commons Hansard)*, vol. 454, c. 1424W, 14 December 2006.

Balls, E., 'Key principles for policy making in an open economy', in E. Balls and G. O'Donnell (eds), *Reforming Britain's Economic and Financial Policy: Towards Greater Economic Stability* (Basingstoke: Palgrave, [1997] 2002), pp. 27–43.

Balls, E., 'Open macroeconomics in an open economy', *Scottish Journal of Political Economy*, 45(2), 1998, pp. 113–32.

Balls, E., 'Preventing Financial Crises: The Case for Independent IMF Surveillance', speech delivered at the Institute for International Economics, Washington DC, 6 March 2003, <http://www.hm-treasury.gov.uk/speech_cea_060303.htm> (last accessed 1 September 2010).

Balls, E., speech delivered at the Commonwealth, Middle East and North Africa Business Forum, 'Strategic Alliances, Financial Flows and Islamic Banking', London, 30 October 2006, <http://www.hm-treasury.gov.uk/speech_est_301006.htm> (last accessed 1 September 2010).

Balls, E., 'Stability, Growth and UK Fiscal Policy', speech delivered at the inaugural Ken Dixon Lecture, University of York, 23 January 2004, <http://www.hm-treasury.gov.uk/speech_cea_230104.htm> (last accessed 2 April 2009).

Balls, E. and G. O'Donnell (eds), *Reforming Britain's Economic and Financial Policy* (Basingstoke: Palgrave, 2002).

Balls, E., G. O'Donnell and J. Grice (eds), *Microeconomic Reform in Britain* (Basingstoke: Palgrave, 2004).

Barker, A. 'Introduction', in ABPI, *Global Health and the Pharmaceutical Industry* (London: ABPI, 2007), p. 3.

Barratt Brown, M. and K. Coates, *The Blair Revelation: Deliverance for Whom?* (London: Spokesman, 1996).

Beckett, F., *Gordon Brown: Past, Present and Future* (London: Haus Book, 2007).

Benn, H., 'AIDS', *Official Report (Commons Hansard)*, vol. 413, c. 272–3, 12 November 2003.

Benn, H., 'Development Financing', *Official Report (Commons Hansard)*, vol. 421, c. 365W–366W, 12 May 2004.

Benn, H., 'Engagements', *Official Report (Commons Hansard)*, vol. 361, c. 302, 31 January 2001.

Benn, H., 'Making Globalisation Work for All' speech, 16 February 2004, <http://www.dfid.gov.uk/Media-Room/Speeches-and-articles/2004-to-do/Making-globalisation-work-for-all/> (last accessed 25 January 2010).

Benn, H., speech delivered at the annual conference of the Jubilee movement, 27 March 2004, <http://www.dfid.gov.uk/Media-Room/Speeches-and-articles/2004-to-do/Jubilee-Movement-Annual-Conference/> (last accessed 25 January 2010).

Benn, H., 'Water: Meeting Our Promises' speech delivered to the Water Forum, London, 7 February 2006, <http://www.dfid.gov.uk/Media-Room/Speeches-and-articles/2006-to-do/Water-meeting-our-promises/> (last accessed 25 January 2010).

Bevir, M., *New Labour: A Critique* (London: Routledge, 2005).

Bevir, M., 'New Labour: a study in ideology', *British Journal of Politics and International Relations*, 2(3), 2000, pp. 277–301.

Biccum, P., 'Marketing development, Live 8 and the production of the global citizen', *Development and Change*, 38(6), 2007, pp. 1111–26.

Blair, T., 'Blair sides with drug giants', *The Guardian*, 31 March 2001.

Blair, T., 'Commonwealth Heads of Government Meeting', *Official Report (Commons Hansard)*, vol. 415, c. 925, 9 December 2003.

Blair, T., 'Denver Summit', *Official Report (Commons Hansard)*, vol. 296, c. 680, 24 June 1997.

Blair, T., 'Doctrine of the International Community' speech, Chicago, 24 April 1999, <http://www.number10.gov.uk/Page1297> (last accessed 1 September 2010).

Blair, T., 'Foreword by the Prime Minister', in PICTF, *Pharmaceutical Industry Competitiveness Task Force: Final Report* (London: PICTF, 2001), p. 1.

Blair, T., 'G8 Summit', *Official Report (Commons Hansard)*, vol. 312, c. 959, 20 May 1998.

Blair, T., 'Global Alliance for Global Values' speech, Canberra, 27 March 2006, <http://www.number10.gov.uk/Page9245> (last accessed 1 September 2010).

Blair, T., 'Helping People through Change' speech, Birmingham, 2 February 2001, <http://www.number10.gov.uk/Page1578> (last accessed 1 September 2010).

Blair, T., 'The Knowledge Economy: Access for All' speech, London, 7 March 2000, <http://www.dti.gov.uk/knowledge2000/blair.htm> (last accessed 21 January 2010).

Blair, T., 'The Modernisation of the Civil Service' speech, London, 24 February 2004, <http://www.number10.gov.uk/Page5399> (last accessed 1 September 2010).

Blair, T., 'New Britain in the Modern World' speech, Tokyo, 9 January 1998, <http://www.number10.gov.uk/Page1148> (last accessed 1 September 2010).

Blair, T., 'Our Nation's Future – Science' speech, Oxford, 3 November 2006, <http://www.number10.gov.uk/Page10342> (last accessed 23 January 2010).

Blair, T., speech delivered at the annual CBI conference, Birmingham, 5 November 2001, <http://www.number10.gov.uk/Page1642> (last accessed 26 March 2009).

Blair, T., speech delivered at the British Chamber of Commerce, Hong Kong, 24 July 2003, <http://www.number10.gov.uk/Page4258> (last accessed 1 September 2010).

Blair, T., speech delivered at the CBI National Conference, Birmingham, 11 November 1997, <http://www.number10.gov.uk/Page1072> (last accessed 26 March 2009).

Blair, T., speech delivered to the Christian Socialist Movement, London, 29 March 2001, <http://www.number10.gov.uk/Page3243> (last accessed 26 March 2009).

Blair, T., speech delivered at the Civil Service Conference, London, 13 October 1998, <http://www.number10.gov.uk/Page5283> (last accessed 26 March 2009).

Blair, T., speech delivered at the French National Assembly, Paris, 24 March 1998, <http://www.number10.gov.uk/Page1160> (last accessed 1 September 2010).

Blair, T., speech delivered at the Lord Mayor's Banquet, London, 14 November 2005, <http://www.number10.gov.uk/Page8524> (last accessed 1 September 2010).

Blair, T., speech delivered in Tokyo, 21 July 2003, <http://www.number10.gov.uk/Page4235> (last accessed 1 September 2010).

Blair, T., speech delivered on welfare reform, 10 June 2002, <http://www.number10.gov.uk/Page1716> (last accessed 25 January 2010).

Blair, T., speech on the economy delivered at Goldman Sachs, London, 22 March 2004, <http://www.number10.gov.uk/Page5555> (last accessed 1 September 2010).

Blair, T., *The Third Way: New Politics for the New Century* (London: Fabian Society, 1998).

Blears, H., 'Minister says govt backs UK pharma industry, highlights activities of PICTF', *ThePharmaLetter*, 22 April 2002, <http://www.thepharmaletter.com/file/46929/minister-says-govt-backs-uk-pharma-industry-highlights-activities-of-pictf.html> (last accessed 13 July 2010).

Blundell, R., H. Reed, J. Van Reenan and A. Shepherd, 'The impact of the New Deal for young people on the labour market: a four year assessment', in R. Dickens, R. Gregg and J. Wadsworth (eds), *The Labour Market under New Labour: The State of Working Britain* (Basingstoke: Palgrave, 2003), pp. 18–19.

Blunkett, D., 'Enabling Government: The Welfare State in the 21st Century' speech, London, 11 October 2000, <http://www.psi.org.uk/events/blunkett.pdf> (last accessed 11 September 2009).

Blunkett, D., 'No hiding place for fraudsters', *The Observer*, 14 January 2001, p. 31.

Boateng, P., 'Finance Bill: Tax Relief for Expenditure on Vaccine Research, etc.', *House of Commons Standing Committee F*, Session 2001–02, c. 217–18, 23 May 2002.

Bochel, H. and A. Defty, *Welfare Policy under New Labour: Views from Inside Westminster* (Bristol: Policy Press, 2007).

Bond, P., 'Global governance campaigning and MDGs: from top-down to bottom-up anti-poverty work', *Third World Quarterly*, 27(2), 2006, pp. 339–54.

Bono, speech delivered at the annual Labour Party conference, 29 September 2004, in Labour Party, *Verbatim Report of the 103rd Conference of the Labour Party*, Brighton, 26–30 September 2004 (London: Labour Party, 2004).

Bower, T., *Gordon Brown: Prime Minister* (London: Harper Perennial, 2007).

Brainard, L. and D. Chollet, *Global Development 2.0: Can Philanthropists, the Public, and the Poor Make Poverty History?* (Washington DC: The Brookings Institution, 2008).

Broadbent, J. and R. Laughlin, 'The role of PFI in the UK government's modernisation agenda', *Financial Accountability and Management*, 21(1), 2005, pp. 75–97.

Brown, G., *Beyond the Crash: Overcoming the First Crisis of Globalisation* (London: Simon & Schuster, 2011).

Brown, G., 'Budget Statement', *Official Report (Commons Hansard)*, vol. 346, c. 860–70, 21 March 2000.

Brown, G., 'Budget Statement', *Official Report (Commons Hansard)*, vol. 364, c. 299, 7 March 2001.

Brown, G., 'Budget Statement', *Official Report (Commons Hansard)*, vol. 383, c. 584–91, 17 April 2002.

Brown, G., 'The Central Economic Objectives of the New Government', 6 May 1997, <http://www.hm-treasury.gov.uk/statement_chx_060597. htm> (last accessed 2 April 2009).

Brown, G., 'A Comprehensive Plan for HIV/AIDS' speech, 12 January 2005, <http://www.hm-treasury.gov.uk/speech_chex_120105.htm> (last accessed 15 January 2010).

Brown, G., 'Comprehensive Spending Review', *Official Report (Commons Hansard)*, vol. 316, c. 193, 14 July 1998.

Brown, G., 'The conditions for high and stable growth and employment', *The Economic Journal*, 111(471), 2001, pp. 30–44.

Brown, G., 'A Culture of Peace' speech delivered at the UN General Assembly, New York, 13 November 2008, <http://www.un.org/ga/63/ meetings/pdf/ukE13.pdf> (last accessed 1 September 2010).

Brown, G., 'Debt 2000: The Mauritius Mandate' speech delivered at the Commonwealth Finance Ministers Meeting, 16 September 1997, <http://www.hm-treasury.gov.uk/speech_chex_160997.htm> (last accessed 2 April 2009).

Brown, G., 'Development Aid', *Official Report (Commons Hansard)*, vol. 398, c. 431, 23 January 2003.

Brown, G., 'Economy and Trade and Industry', *Official Report (Commons Hansard)*, vol. 394, c. 393, 18 November 2002.

Brown, G., 'Enterprise and Employment Opportunity for All' speech, London, 29 February 2000, <http://www.hm-treasury.gov.uk/speech_ chex_290200.htm> (last accessed 1 September 2010).

Brown, G., 'Exploiting the British Genius: The Key to Long Term Economic Success' speech delivered at the CBI, 20 May 1997, <http:// www.hm-treasury.gov.uk/speech_chex_200597.htm> (last accessed 2 April 2009).

Brown, G., 'Financial Statement', *Official Report (Commons Hansard)*, vol. 308, c. 311, 17 March 1998.

Brown, G., 'Financial Statement', *Official Report (Commons Hansard)*, vol. 327, c. 186, 9 March 1999.

Brown, G., 'Financial Statement', *Official Report (Commons Hansard)*, vol. 419, c. 330, 17 March 2004.

Brown, G., 'Financial Statement', *Official Report (Commons Hansard)*, vol. 432, c. 265, 16 March 2005.

Brown, G., 'Financing a World Fit for Children' speech delivered at the United Nations General Assembly Special Session on Children, New York, 10 May 2002, <http://www.hm-treasury.gov.uk/speech_ chex_100502.htm> (last accessed 14 January 2010).

Brown, G., The Gilbert Murray Memorial Lecture, delivered at Oxfam, Oxford, 11 January 2000, <http://www.hm-treasury.gov.uk/speech_chex_110100.htm> (last accessed 2 April 2009).

Brown, G., 'The Global Economy' Q&A session at the Brookings Institution, 9 February 2009, <http://www.fco.gov.uk/en/news/latest-news/?view=Speech&id=13475210> (last accessed 21 January 2010).

Brown, G., 'Globalisation' speech delivered at the Press Club, Washington DC, 17 December 2001, <http://www.hm-treasury.gov.uk/press_146_01.htm> (last accessed 31 August 2011).

Brown, G., 'International Debt Relief', *Official Report (Commons Hansard)*, vol. 400, c. 384, 27 February 2003.

Brown, G., 'International Development in 2005: The Challenge and the Opportunity' speech delivered at the National Gallery of Scotland, 6 January 2005, <http://www.hm-treasury.gov.uk/press_03_05.htm> (last accessed 18 January 2010).

Brown, G., 'International Finance', *Official Report (Commons Hansard)*, vol. 402, c. 435, 27 March 2003.

Brown, G., 'International Finance Facility', *Official Report (Commons Hansard)*, vol. 431, c. 1667, 10 March 2005.

Brown, G., 'International Monetary Fund', *Official Report (Commons Hansard)*, vol. 398, c. 421, 23 January 2003.

Brown, G., The James Meade Memorial Lecture, London, 8 May 2000, <http://www.hm-treasury.gov.uk/speech_chex_080500.htm> (last accessed 1 September 2010).

Brown, G., 'Making Globalisation Work for All: The Challenge of Delivering the Monterrey Consensus', London, 16 February 2004, <http://www.hm-treasury.gov.uk/speech_chex_160204.htm> (last accessed 3 April 2009).

Brown, G., 'New Global Structures for the New Global Age' speech, Ottawa, 30 September 1998, <http://www.hm-treasury.gov.uk/speech_chex_300998.htm> (last accessed 2 April 2009).

Brown, G., 'Poverty and Globalisation: Financing for Development' speech delivered at the Vatican, 9 July 2004, <http://www.hm-treasury.gov.uk/speech_chex_090704.htm> (last accessed 3 April 2009).

Brown, G., 'Pre-Budget Report', *Official Report (Commons Hansard)*, vol. 318, c. 683, 3 November 1998.

Brown, G., 'Pre-Budget Report', *Official Report (Commons Hansard)*, vol. 395, c. 326–40, 27 November 2002.

Brown, G., 'Pre-Budget Report', *Official Report (Commons Hansard)*, vol. 415, c. 1067–80, 10 December 2003.

Brown, G., 'Pre-Budget Report', *Official Report (Commons Hansard)*, vol. 454, c. 324, 6 December 2006.

Brown, G., 'Q. 254', Minutes of Evidence Taken before the International Development Select Committee, 7 April 1998, International Development – Third Report, Session 1997–98 (London: House of Commons, 1998).

Brown, G., 'Q. 99', in House of Commons Select Committee for International Development, 'Financing for Development: Finding the Money to Eliminate World Poverty', Fifth Report of Session 2001–02, Volume II: Oral and Written Evidence, HC 785-II, 2002.

Brown, G., 'Rediscovering Public Purpose in the Global Economy' speech delivered at Harvard University, 15 December 1998, <http://www.hm-treasury.gov.uk/speech_chex_151298.htm> (last accessed 2 April 2009).

Brown, G. 'The socialist challenge', in G. Brown (ed.), *The Red Paper on Scotland* (Edinburgh: EUSPB, 1975), pp. 7–21.

Brown, G., speech delivered at the annual British Chambers of Commerce conference, London, 31 March 2003, <http://www.hm-treasury.gov.uk/speech_chx_ 310303.htm> (last accessed 1 September 2010).

Brown, G., speech delivered at the annual CBI conference, Birmingham, 2 November 1998, <http://www.hm-treasury.gov.uk/speech_chex_021198.htm> (last accessed 1 September 2010).

Brown, G., speech delivered at the annual CBI conference, London, 26 November 2007, <http://www.number10.gov.uk/page13851> (last accessed 1 September 2010).

Brown, G., speech delivered at the annual CBI Scotland dinner, Glasgow, 5 September 2008, <http://www.number10.gov.uk/Page16751> (last accessed 1 September 2010).

Brown, G., speech delivered at the annual European Bank for Reconstruction and Development conference, London, 24 April 2001, <http://www.hm-treasury.gov.uk/speech_chex_240401.htm> (last accessed 2 April 2009).

Brown, G., speech delivered at the British-American Chamber of Commerce, New York, 22 February 2000, <http://www.hm-treasury.gov.uk/speech_chex_220200.htm> (last accessed 1 September 2010).

Brown, G., speech delivered to business leaders, London, 17 May 1995, <http://radio.bufvc.ac.uk/lbc/index.php/segment/0004200475015> (last accessed 2 February 2012).

Brown, G., speech delivered at the Federal Reserve, New York, 16 November 2001, <http://www.hm-treasury.gov.uk/press_126_01.htm> (last accessed 2 April 2009).

Brown, G., speech delivered at the 'Financing Sustainable Development, Poverty Reduction and the Private Sector' conference, Royal Institute of International Affairs, Chatham House, London, 22 January

2003, <http://www.hm-treasury.gov.uk/newsroom_and_speeches/press/2003/press_08_03.cfm> (last accessed 1 September 2011).

Brown, G., speech delivered at the Global Borrowers and Investors Forum, London, 17 June 2003, <http://www.hm-treasury.gov.uk/speech_chx_170603.htm> (last accessed 2 April 2009).

Brown, G., speech delivered at the International Action Against Child Poverty conference, London, 26 February 2001, <http://www.hm-treasury.gov.uk/press_19_01.htm> (last accessed 14 January 2010).

Brown, G., speech delivered at the Labour Party conference, Brighton, 2 October 1995, in Labour Party, *Verbatim Report of the 94th Conference of the Labour Party, Brighton, 2–6 October 1995* (London: Labour Party, 1995).

Brown, G., speech delivered at the Labour Party conference, Brighton, 2 October 2009, <http://www2.labour.org.uk/gordon-brown-speech-conference> (last accessed 20 July 2010).

Brown, G., speech delivered at the Lord Mayor's Banquet, London, 12 June 1997, <http://www.hm-treasury.gov.uk/speech_chex_120697.htm> (last accessed 2 April 2009).

Brown, G., speech delivered at the News International Conference, Sun Valley, Idaho, 17 July 1998, <http://www.hm-treasury.gov.uk/speech_chex_170798.htm> (last accessed 1 September 2010).

Brown, G., speech delivered at the Royal United Services Institute, London, 13 February 2006, <http://www.hm-treasury.gov.uk/speech_chex_130206.htm> (last accessed 1 September 2010).

Brown, G., speech delivered at the Smith Institute, London, 15 April 1999, <http://www.hm-treasury.gov.uk/speech_chex_150499.htm> (last accessed 1 September 2010).

Brown, G., speech delivered at the TUC Congress, Glasgow, 12 September 2000, <http://www.hm-treasury.gov.uk/speech_chex_120900.htm> (last accessed 1 September 2010).

Brown, G., 'Spending Review', *Official Report (Commons Hansard)*, vol. 389, c. 22–3, 15 July 2002.

Brown, G., 'State and market: towards a public interest test', *The Political Quarterly*, 74(3), 2003, pp. 266–84.

Brown, G., statement made at the International Monetary and Financial Committee, Washington DC, 12 April 2003, <http://www.hm-treasury.gov.uk/imfc_120403.htm> (last accessed 2 April 2009).

Brown, G., statement on the Pre-Budget Report, 8 November 2000, <http://www.hm-treasury.gov.uk/prebud_pbr00_speech.htm> (last accessed 14 January 2010).

Brown, G., 'Steering a Course for Stability' speech delivered at the Annual Meetings of the IMF and the World Bank, Washington DC, 5 October

1998, <http://www.hm-treasury.gov.uk/speech_chex_051098.htm> (last accessed 2 April 2009).

Brown, G., 'Third World Debt', *Official Report (Commons Hansard)*, vol. 308, c. 737, 12 March 1998.

Brown, G., 'Third World Poverty', *Official Report (Commons Hansard)*, vol. 425, c. 416, 14 October 2004.

Brown, G., 'World Debt', *Official Report (Commons Hansard)*, vol. 413, c. 409, 13 November 2003.

Brown, G., 'World Economic Situation and Prospects' speech delivered at the Commonwealth Finance Ministers Meeting, London, 25 September 2002, <http://www.hm-treasury.gov.uk/speech_chex_250902.htm> (last accessed 2 April 2009).

Brown, W., 'Debating the year of Africa', *Review of African Political Economy*, 34(111), 2007, pp. 11–27.

Browne, D., speech delivered at the British-American Business Council, Glasgow, 24 October 2005, <http://www.hm-treasury.gov.uk/speech_cst_241005.htm> (last accessed 1 September 2010).

Buckler, S. and D. Dolowitz, 'Can fair be efficient? New Labour, social liberalism and British economic policy', *New Political Economy*, 9(1), 2004, pp. 23–38.

Budd, A., 'Fiscal policy under Labour', *National Institute Economic Review*, 212(1), 2010, pp. 34–48.

Bullard, N., W. Bello and K. Mallhotra, 'Taming the Tigers: the IMF and the Asian crisis', *Third World Quarterly*, 19(3), 1998, pp. 505–56.

Burnell, P., 'Britain's new government, new White Paper, new aid?', *Third World Quarterly*, 19(4), 1998, pp. 787–802.

Burnham, P., 'New Labour and the politics of depoliticisation', *British Journal of Politics of International Relations*, 3(2), 2002, pp. 127–49.

Burnside, C. and D. Dollar, 'Aid spurs growth – in a sound policy environment', *Finance and Development*, 34(4), 1997, pp. 4–7.

Bush, G., 'Mr and Mrs Blair go to Washington', *The Independent*, 5 June 2005, <http://www.independent.co.uk/news/world/politics/mr-and-mrs-blair-go-to-washington-6144763.html> (last accessed 11 February 2012).

Byers, S., 'The Importance of the Knowledge Economy' speech delivered at the Knowledge 2000: Conference on the Knowledge Driven Economy, London, 7 March 2000, <http://www.dti.gov.uk/knowledge2000/byers.htm> (last accessed 21 January 2010).

Byers, S., 'Trade and Industry and Social Security', *Official Report (Commons Hansard)*, vol. 339, c. 242–3, 19 November 1999.

Cammack, P., 'Global governance, state agency and competitiveness: the political economy of the Commission for Africa', *British Journal of Politics and International Relations*, 8(3), 2006, pp. 331–50.

Cammack, P., 'The shape of capitalism to come', *Antipode*, 41(1), 2010, pp. 262–80.

Cerny, P., 'Paradoxes of the competition state: the dynamics of political globalization', *Government and Opposition*, 32(2), 1997, pp. 251–74.

Cerny, P. and M. Evans, 'Globalisation and public policy under New Labour', *Policy Studies*, 25(1), 2004, pp. 51–65.

Clark, T., 'New Labour's big idea: joined-up government', *Social Policy and Society*, 1(2), 2002, pp. 107–17.

Clarke, C., 'Identity Cards Bill', *Official Report (Commons Hansard)*, vol. 435, c. 1152, 28 June 2005.

Clift, B. and J. Tomlinson, 'Credible Keynesianism? New Labour macro-economic policy and the political economy of coarse tuning', *British Journal of Political Science*, 37(1), 2007, pp. 47–69.

Coates, D., *Prolonged Labour: The Slow Birth of New Labour Britain* (Basingstoke: Palgrave, 2005).

Coates, D. and C. Hay, 'The internal and external face of New Labour's political economy', *Government and Opposition*, 36(4), 2001, pp. 447–71.

Coffey, D. and C. Thornley, *Globalization and Varieties of Capitalism: New Labour, Economic Policy and the Abject State* (Basingstoke: Palgrave, 2009).

Commission for Africa, *Our Common Interest: An Argument* (London: Penguin Politics/Economics, 2005).

Cook, R., 'Britain in the World' speech delivered at the Royal Institute of International Affairs, Chatham House, London, 28 January 2000, in A. Chadwick and R. Heffernan (eds), *The New Labour Reader* (Cambridge: Polity, 2003), pp. 259–62.

Cox, R. W., 'Global *perestroika*', in R. W. Cox with T. J. Sinclair (eds), *Approaches to World Order* (Cambridge: Cambridge University Press, [1992] 1996), pp. 296–313.

Craig, D. and D. Porter, *Development beyond Neoliberalism? Governance, Poverty Reduction and Political Economy* (London: Routledge, 2006).

Crouch, C., 'The parabola of working-class politics', *The Political Quarterly*, 70(1), 1999, pp. 69–83.

Crouch, C., 'The terms of the neo-liberal consensus', *The Political Quarterly*, 68(4), 1997, pp. 352–60.

Curtis, M., 'Africa's false friends', *Socialist Review*, 297, June 2005.

Darling, A., 'Maintaining Stability in a Global Economy', the Mais Lecture, London, 29 October 2008, <http://www.hm-treasury.gov.uk/press_110_08.htm> (last accessed 1 September 2010).

Darling, A., 'Our Economic Approach' speech delivered at the Ernst and Young Network Dinner, London, 14 January 1998, <http://

www.hm-treasury.gov.uk/speech_cst_ 140198.htm> (last accessed 1 September 2010).

Darling, A., speech delivered at the CBI annual dinner, London, 20 May 2008, <http://www.hm-treasury.gov.uk/speech_chex_200508.htm> (last accessed 1 September 2010).

Darling, A., 'Welfare Reform' ministerial statement, *Official Report (Commons Hansard)*, vol. 318, c. 340, 28 October 1998.

Darnbrough, M., 'Q. 26', in House of Commons Select Committee for Health, *The Influence of the Pharmaceutical Industry*, Fourth Report of Session 2004–05, Volume II: Formal Minutes, Oral and Written Evidence, HC 42-II (incorporating HC 1030-i-iii), 2004.

Deakin, N. and R. Parry, *The Treasury and Social Policy: The Contest for Control of Welfare Strategy* (Basingstoke: Macmillan, 2000).

Denham, J., 'Welfare and Skills', *Official Report (Commons Hansard)*, vol. 468, c. 21, 26 November 2007.

Department of Health, 'Memorandum (P 11)', in House of Commons Select Committee for Health, *The Influence of the Pharmaceutical Industry*, Fourth Report of Session 2004–05, Volume II: Formal Minutes, Oral and Written Evidence, HC 42-II (incorporating HC 1030-i-iii), 2005.

Department of Health, 'Pharmaceutical Industry Competitiveness Task Force (PICTF)', n.d., <http://www.dh.gov.uk/ab/Archive/PICTF/index.htm> (last accessed 17 March 2012).

Department of Health (with the Association of the British Pharmaceutical Industry), *Pharmaceutical Industry: Competitiveness and Performance Indicators 2009* (London: Department of Health, 2009).

DFID, *Achieving Universal Access: The UK's Strategy for Halting and Reversing the Spread of HIV in the Developing World* (London: DFID, 2008).

DFID, *Business for Development: The UK Government Working with International Business to Achieve the Millennium Development Goals* (London: DFID, 2008).

DFID, *Eliminating World Poverty: Building Our Common Future*, White Paper on International Development, Cmnd. 7656 (London: TSO, 2009).

DFID, *Eliminating World Poverty: A Challenge for the 21st Century*, White Paper on International Development, Cmnd. 3789 (London: TSO, 1997).

DFID, *Eliminating World Poverty: Making Globalisation Work for the Poor*, White Paper on International Development, Cmnd. 5006 (London: TSO, 2000).

DFID, *Eliminating World Poverty: Making Governance Work for the Poor*, White Paper on International Development, Cmnd. 6876 (London: TSO, 2006).

DFID, *HIV and AIDS Treatment and Care Policy* (London: DFID, 2004).

DFID, 'IFFIm raises money for immunisation', 9 April 2008, <http://www.dfid.gov.uk/Media-Room/News-Stories/2008/IFFIm-raises-money-for-immunisation-/> (last accessed 25 January 2010).

DFID, *Increasing Access to Essential Medicines in the Developing World: UK Government Policy and Plans* (London: DFID, 2004).

DFID, *Increasing People's Access to Essential Medicines in Developing Countries: A Framework for Good Practice in the Pharmaceutical Industry* (London: DFID, 2005).

DFID, 'Industry Government Forum on Access to Medicines', 2009, <http://www.dfid.gov.uk/Global-Issues/Emerging-policy/IGFAM/> (last accessed 9 August 2011).

DFID, *Partnerships for Poverty Reduction: Rethinking Conditionality, a UK Policy Paper* (London: DFID, 2005).

DFID, *Statistics on International Development 2005/06–2009/10* (London: DFID and the Office of National Statistics, 2010).

DFID, *Taking Action: The UK's Strategy for Tackling HIV and AIDS in the Developing World* (London: DFID, 2004).

DFID with HM Treasury, *From Commitment to Action: Acting Now to Improve Living Standards, Health and Education for All* (London: HMSO, 2005).

DFID with HM Treasury and the Performance and Innovation Unit, *Forging a New Commitment: Tackling the Diseases of Poverty* (London: DFID, 2001).

Dixon, R. and P. D. Williams, 'Tough on debt, tough on the causes of debt? New Labour's Third Way foreign policy', *British Journal of Politics and International Relations*, 3(2), 2001, pp. 150–72.

Dow, J. C. R., *Major Recessions* (Oxford: Oxford University Press, 1998).

Driver, S., 'New Labour and social policy', in M. Beech and S. Lee (eds), *Ten Years of New Labour* (Basingstoke: Palgrave, 2008), pp. 50–67.

Driver, S., 'North Atlantic drift: welfare reform and the "Third Way" politics of New Labour and the New Democrats', in S. Hale, W. Leggett and L. Martell (eds), *The Third Way and Beyond: Criticisms, Futures, Alternatives* (Manchester: Manchester University Press, 2004), pp. 31–47.

Driver, S. and L. Martell, *Blair's Britain* (Cambridge: Polity, 2002).

Driver, S. and L. Martell, *New Labour*, 2nd edn (Cambridge: Polity, 2006).

Ellison, N. and S. Ellison, 'Creating "opportunity for all"? New Labour, new localism and the "'Opportunity Society'"', *Social Policy and Society*, 5(3), 2006, pp. 337–48.

Emmerson, C., C. Frayne and S. Love, *The Government's Fiscal Rules*, Briefing Note No. 16 (London: Institute for Fiscal Studies, 2002).

Fairclough, N., *New Labour, New Language?* (London: Routledge, 2000).

Falconer, P. K. and K. McLaughlin, 'Public-private partnerships and the "New Labour" government in Britain', in S. P. Osborne (ed.), *Public-Private Partnerships: Theory and Practice in International Perspective* (London: Routledge, 2000), pp. 120–33.

Fielding, S., *The Labour Party: Continuity and Change in the Making of 'New' Labour* (Basingstoke: Palgrave, 2003).

Fine, B., 'Neither the Washington Consensus nor the post-Washington Consensus', in B. Fine, C. Lapavitsas and J. Pincus (eds), *Development Policy in the Twenty-First Century: Beyond the Post-Washington Consensus* (London: Routledge, 2001), pp. 1–27.

Finlayson, A., 'Did Blair advance social democracy?', in S. Griffiths and K. Hickson (eds), *British Party Politics and Ideology after New Labour* (Basingstoke: Palgrave, 2010), pp. 11–17.

Finlayson, A., *Making Sense of New Labour* (London: Lawrence and Wishart, 2003).

Finlayson, A., 'New Labour: the case of the Child Trust Fund', *Public Administration*, 86(1), 2008, pp. 95–110.

Fischer, S., remarks made during a panel discussion concerning 'Macroeconomic Policies and Poverty Reduction', International Monetary Fund, Washington DC, 13 April 2001, <http://www.imf.org/external/np/tr/2001/tr010413.htm> (last accessed 11 December 2011).

Flinders, M. and J. Buller, 'Depoliticisation: principles, tactics and tools', *British Politics*, 1(3), 2006, pp. 293–318.

Foster, M., 'Developing Countries: Vaccination', *Official Report (Commons Hansard)*, vol. 499, c. 825W–826W, 12 November 2009.

Friedman, T., *The World Is Flat: The Globalized World in the Twenty-First Century* (London: Penguin, 2005).

G7, 'The Cologne Debt Initiative', *The Cologne Summit Communiqué*, 18–20 June 1999.

G8, *The Birmingham Summit Communiqué*, 15–17 May 1998.

G8, *The Gleneagles Communiqué*, 6–8 July 2005.

Galbraith, J. K., *The Affluent Society* (London: Penguin, [1958] 1999).

Gallagher, J., 'Healing the scar? Idealizing Britain in Africa, 1997–2007', *African Affairs*, 108(432), 2009, pp. 435–51.

Gamble, A. and G. Kelly, 'New Labour's economics', in S. Ludlam and M. J. Smith (eds), *New Labour in Government* (Basingstoke: Palgrave, 2001), pp. 167–83.

Gardner, K. and D. Lewis, 'Dominant paradigms overturned or "business as usual"? Development discourse and the White Paper on international development', *Critique of Anthropology*, 20(1), 2000, pp. 15–29.

Giddens, A., *Over to You, Mr Brown* (Cambridge: Polity, 2007).

Giddens, A., *The Third Way: The Renewal of Social Democracy* (Cambridge: Polity, 1998).

Giddens, A., *Where Now for New Labour?* (Cambridge: Polity, 2002).

Gill, S., *Power and Resistance in the New World Order* (Basingstoke: Palgrave, 2003).

Gill, S. and D. Law, 'Global hegemony and the structural power of capital', *International Studies Quarterly*, 33(4), 1989, pp. 475–99.

GlaxoSmithKline, *Global Public Policy Issues: Intellectual Property and Access to Medicines in Developing Countries*, a publication of Glaxo-SmithKline Government Affairs, Public Policy and Patient Advocacy (Brentford: GlaxoSmithKline, 2011).

GlaxoSmithKline, *GSK Annual Report 2009* (Brentford: GlaxoSmith-Kline, 2010).

GlaxoSmithKline, *Making a Difference Every Day* – Corporate Responsibility Report 2003 (Brentford: GlaxoSmithKline, 2004).

GlaxoSmithKline, *Our Responsibility* – Corporate Responsibility Report 2008 (Brentford: GlaxoSmithKline, 2008).

Glaze, S., 'The Gordon Brown problem: New Labour and the two "Adam Smiths"', *The Political Quarterly*, 79(3), 2008, pp. 377–87.

Glyn, A. and S. Wood, 'Economic policy under New Labour: how social democratic is the Blair government?', *The Political Quarterly*, 72(1), 2001, pp. 50–66.

Goes, E., 'The Third Way and the politics of community', in S. Hale, W. Leggett and L. Martell (eds), *The Third Way and Beyond: Criticisms, Futures, Alternatives* (Manchester: Manchester University Press, 2004), pp. 108–27.

Gondwe, G. E., 'The hazards of debt cancellation point to benefit in Africa finding its own sustainable growth path', *Financial Times*, 26 August 1998, <http://www.imf.org/external/np/vc/1998/082698.htm> (last accessed 6 July 2011).

Gornal, R., 'Q. 26', in House of Commons Select Committee for International Development, 'Department for International Development: Responding to HIV/AIDS', Fourteenth Report of Session 2004–05, HC 443 (incorporating HC 807-i, session 2003–04), 2004.

Gould, J., *The New Conditionality: The Politics of Poverty Reduction Strategies* (London: Zed Books, 2005).

Gould, P., *The Unfinished Revolution: How the Modernisers Saved the Labour Party* (London: Abacus, 1999).

Grieve Smith, J., *There Is a Better Way: A New Economic Agenda* (London: Anthem, 2001).

Hain, P., 'Business of the House', *Official Report (Commons Hansard)*, vol. 410, c. 481, 11 September 2003.

Hain, P., 'Next Steps to Full Employment', *Official Report (Commons Hansard)*, vol. 468, c. 6WS, 26 November 2007.

Hain, P., 'Social Summit: Geneva', *Official Report (Commons Hansard)*, vol. 353, c. 174WH, 11 July 2000.

Hall, S. and M. Jacques (eds), *New Times: The Changing Face of Politics in the 1990s* (London: Lawrence and Wishart in association with Marxism Today, 1989).

Harrison, G., 'The Africanization of poverty: a retrospective on "Make Poverty History"', *African Affairs*, 109(436), 2010, pp. 391–408.

Harvie, C., *Broonland: The Last Days of Gordon Brown* (London: Verso, 2010).

Hay, C., 'Credibility, competitiveness and the business cycle in "Third Way" political economy: a critical evaluation of economic policy in Britain since 1997', *New Political Economy*, 9(1), 2004, pp. 39–56.

Hay, C., 'Negotiating international constraints: the antinomies of credibility and competitiveness in the political economy of New Labour', *Competition and Change*, 5(3), 2001, pp. 269–89.

Hay, C., *The Political Economy of New Labour: Labouring under False Pretences?* (Manchester: Manchester University Press, 1999).

Hay, C. and B. Rosamond, 'Globalisation, European integration and the discursive construction of economic imperatives', *Journal of European Public Policy*, 9(2), 2002, pp. 147–67.

Hay, C. and M. Watson, 'Labour's economic policy: studiously courting competence', in G. R. Taylor (ed.), *The Impact of New Labour* (Basingstoke: Macmillan, 1999), pp. 149–61.

Healey, J., 'International Finance Facility', *Official Report (Commons Hansard)*, vol. 415, c. 1007W, 18 December 2003.

Healey, J., 'Overseas Aid', *Official Report (Commons Hansard)*, vol. 420, col. 869W, 27 April 2004.

Heffernan, R., *New Labour and Thatcherism: Political Change in Britain* (Basingstoke: Palgrave, 2001).

Heffernan, R., 'Perhaps, over to you, Mr Cameron . . .?', *Political Studies Review*, 6(3), 2008, pp. 285–96.

Hewitt, A. and T. Killick, 'The 1975 and 1997 White Papers compared: enriched vision, depleted policies?', *Journal of International Development*, 10, 1998, pp. 185–94.

Hewitt, P., 'World Bank', *Official Report (Commons Hansard)*, vol. 323, c. 195W, 13 January 1999.

Hills, J., *Thatcherism, New Labour and the Welfare State*, CASE Paper CASE/13, Centre for Analysis of Social Exclusion, London School of Economics, 1998.

HM Government, *Modernising Government*, White Paper prepared by the Cabinet Office, Cmnd. 4310 (London: TSO, 1999).

HM Government, *The UK's Contribution to Achieving the Millennium Development Goals* (London: HMSO, 2005).

HM Treasury, *Britain Meeting the Global Challenge: Enterprise, Fairness and Responsibility*, Pre-Budget Report, Cmnd. 6701 (London: TSO, 2005).

HM Treasury, *Building a Britain of Economic Strength and Social Justice*, Economic and Fiscal Strategy Report and Financial Statement and Budget Report, HC 500 (London: TSO, 2003).

HM Treasury, *Building Britain's Long-Term Future: Prosperity and Fairness for Families*, Economic and Fiscal Strategy Report and Financial Statement and Budget Report, HC 342 (London: TSO, 2007).

HM Treasury, *Building Long-Term Prosperity for All*, Pre-Budget Report, Cmnd. 4917 (London: TSO, 2000).

HM Treasury, *Building a Stronger, Fairer Britain in an Uncertain World*, Pre-Budget Report, Cmnd. 5318 (London: TSO, 2001).

HM Treasury, 'Call to action on global child poverty to meet 2015 development targets' press release, 26 February 2001, <http://www.hm-treasury.gov.uk/press_18_01.htm> (last accessed 14 January 2010).

HM Treasury, *The Code for Fiscal Stability* (London: HM Treasury, 1998).

HM Treasury, 'Employment opportunity for all – a new approach' press release, 27 November 1997, <http://www.hm-treasury.gov.uk/prebud_pbr97_presshmt8.htm> (last accessed 15 October 2009).

HM Treasury, *The International Finance Facility* (London: HMSO, 2002).

HM Treasury, *The International Finance Facility* (London: HM Treasury, 2004).

HM Treasury, *The International Finance Facility: A Technical Note* (London: HM Treasury, 2003).

HM Treasury, *Investing for Our Future: Fairness and Opportunity for Britain's Hard-Working Families*, Economic and Fiscal Strategy Report and Financial Statement and Budget Report, HC 372 (London: TSO, 2005).

HM Treasury, *Meeting the Aspirations of the British People*, Pre-Budget Report and Comprehensive Spending Review, Cmnd. 7227 (London: TSO, 2007).

HM Treasury, *Modern Public Services for Britain: Investing in Reform*, Comprehensive Spending Review: New Public Spending Plans 1999–2002, Cmnd. 4011 (London: TSO, 1998).

HM Treasury, *Opportunity for All: The Strength to Take the Long-Term Decisions for Britain*, Pre-Budget Report, Cmnd. 6408 (London: TSO, 2004).

HM Treasury, *Prudent for a Purpose: Building Opportunity and Security for All*, New Public Spending Plans for 2001–2004, Cmnd. 4807 (London: TSO, 2000a).

HM Treasury, *Prudent for a Purpose: Working for a Stronger and Fairer Britain*, Economic and Fiscal Strategy Report and Financial Statement and Budget Report, HC 346 (London: TSO, 2000b).

HM Treasury, *Saving and Assets for All: The Modernisation of Britain's Tax and Benefit System* (London: HMSO, 2001).

HM Treasury, *Steering a Steady Course: Delivering Stability, Enterprise and Fairness in an Uncertain World*, Pre-Budget Report, Cmnd. 5664 (London: TSO, 2002).

HM Treasury, *The Strength to Make Long-Term Decisions: Investing in an Enterprising, Fairer Britain*, Economic and Fiscal Strategy Report and Financial Statement and Budget Report, HC 592 (London: TSO, 2002).

Hodge, M., 'Chancellor and Minister for Children launch Child Trust Fund' press release, 10 January 2005, <http://www.hm-treasury.gov.uk/press_06_05.htm> (last accessed 1 September 2011).

Hoon, G., 'Foreign Affairs and Defence', *Official Report (Commons Hansard)*, vol. 370, c. 351, 22 June 2001.

House of Commons Select Health Committee, *The Influence of the Pharmaceutical Industry*, Fourth Report of Session 2004–05, HC 42-I (incorporating HC 1030-i-iii), 2005.

House of Commons Select Committee for International Development, *Financing for Development: Finding the Money to Eliminate World Poverty*, Fifth Report of Session 2001–02, Volume I, HC 785–I, 2002.

House of Commons Select Committee for International Development, *The Humanitarian Crisis in Southern Africa: Government Response to the Committee's Third Report of Session 2002–03*, Fourth Special Report of Session 2002–03, HC 690, 2003.

Hughes, C., *What Went Wrong, Gordon Brown? How the Dream Job Turned Sour* (London: Guardian Books, 2010).

Hutton, J., speech delivered at the CBI President's Dinner, London, 9 July 2007, <http://www.berr.gov.uk/aboutus/ministerialteam/Speeches/page40412.html> (last accessed 1 September 2009).

Hutton, J., 'Written Ministerial Statement', cited in N. Warner 'Employment, Social Policy, Health and Consumer Affairs Council', *Official Report (Lords Hansard)*, vol. 667, c. WS106, 20 December 2004.

Hutton, W., *The State to Come* (London: Vintage, 1997).

IDA, *IDA Eligibility, Terms and Graduation Policies* (Washington DC: IDA/World Bank Group, 2001).

IFFIm, 'Bond Issuances', <http://www.iff-immunisation.org/bond_issuances.html> (last accessed 3 March 2010).

IGFAM, *Summary Report of the Industry Government Forum on Access to Medicines* (London: DFID, 2009).

IMF, 'Code of Good Practices on Fiscal Transparency (2007)', <http://www.imf.org/external/np/pp/2007/eng/051507c.pdf> (last accessed 12 March 2012).

IMF, 'Communiqué of the Interim Committee of the Board of Governors of the International Monetary Fund' press release 97/44, 21 September 1997, <http://www.imf.org/external/np/sec/pr/1997/pr9744.htm> (last accessed 12 March 2012).

IMF, 'Debt Relief under the Heavily Indebted Poor Countries (HIPC) Initiative', IMF Factsheet (Washington DC: International Monetary Fund, 2011).

IMF, 'Financial System Soundness', IMF Factsheet, 23 March 2011, <http://www.imf.org/external/np/exr/facts/banking.htm> (last accessed 11 July 2011).

IMF, 'IMF Extended Credit Facility', 2011, <http://www.imf.org/external/np/exr/facts/ecf.htm> (last accessed 11 July 2011).

IMF, 'IMF launches revised transparency Code and Manual' press release 07/95, 15 May 2007, <http://www.imf.org/external/np/sec/pr/2007/pr0795.htm> (last accessed 12 March 2012).

IMF, 'Sound policies, support can help Africa ride crisis', *IMF Survey Magazine: Countries & Regions*, 20 February 2009.

IMF, 'Transforming the Enhanced Structural Adjustment Facility (ESAF) and the Debt Initiative for the Heavily Indebted Poor Countries (HIPCs)', 9 February 2000, <http://www.imf.org/external/np/esaf-hipc/1999/index.htm> (last accessed 20 July 2011).

IMFC, 'Communiqué of the International Monetary and Financial Committee of the Board of Governors of the International Monetary Fund', Minutes of Evidence Taken before the International Development Select Committee, 28 September 2002, International Development, Session 2002–03 (London: House of Commons, 2002).

Jessop, B., *State Theory: Putting Capitalist States in Their Place* (Cambridge: Polity, 1990).

Jubilee 2000 Coalition, 'Memorandum from Jubilee 2000 Coalition', Minutes of Evidence Taken before the International Development Select Committee, International Development – Third Report, Session 1997–98 (London: House of Commons, 1998).

Jubilee Debt Campaign, 'Heavily Indebted Poor Countries Initiative', 2006, <http://www.jubileedebtcampaign.org.uk/Heavily%20Indebted%20Poor%20Countries%20initiative+97.twl> (last accessed 20 July 2011).

Keegan, W., *The Prudence of Mr Gordon Brown* (London: John Wiley & Sons, 2004).

Keegan, W., *Saving the World? Gordon Brown Reconsidered* (London: Searching Finance, 2012).

Kennedy, J., 'International Finance Facility for Immunisation: Cost Effectiveness', *Official Report (Commons Hansard)*, vol. 472, c. 2185W–2186W, 3 March 2008.

Kenny, M. and M. J. Smith, '(Mis)understanding Blair', *The Political Quarterly*, 68(3), 1997, pp. 221–30.

Kettell, S., *Dirty Politics? New Labour, British Democracy and the Invasion of Iraq* (London: Zed Books, 2006).

King, D. and M. Wickham-Jones, 'Bridging the Atlantic: the Democratic (party) origins of Welfare-to-Work', in M. Powell (ed.), *New Labour, New Welfare State? The 'Third Way' in British Social Policy* (Bristol: Policy Press, 1999), pp. 257–80.

King, M., 'The Inflation Target 5 Years on' speech delivered at the London School of Economics, 29 October 1997, <http://www.bankofengland.co.uk/publications/speeches/1997/speech09.pdf> (last accessed 20 February 2012).

Köhler, H., 'Promoting Stability and Prosperity in a Globalized World' speech delivered at the IMF Council of the Americas, Washington DC, 7 May 2001, <http://www.imf.org/external/np/speeches/2001/050701.htm> (last accessed 11 July 2011).

Krueger, A. O., 'Pursuing the Achievable: Macroeconomic Stability and Sustainable Growth' speech delivered at the Economic Congress of Turkey, Izmir, 5 May 2004, <http://www.imf.org/external/np/speeches/2004/050504.htm> (last accessed 11 July 2011).

Krueger, A. O., 'Stability, Growth, and Prosperity: The Global Economy and the IMF' speech delivered at the Conférence de Montréal, Montreal, 7 June 2006, <http://www.imf.org/external/np/speeches/2006/060706.htm> (last accessed 11 July 2011).

Krugman, P., 'Dutch tulips and emerging markets: another bubble bursts', *Foreign Affairs*, 74(4), 1995, pp. 28–44.

Labour Party, *Britain: Forward Not Back*, Labour Party Manifesto for the 2005 General Election (London: Labour Party, 2005).

Labour Party, *Meet the Challenge, Make the Change: A New Agenda for Britain, Final Report of Labour's Policy Review for the 1990s* (London: Labour Party, 1989).

Labour Party, *Modern Britain in a Modern World: For the Good of All* (London: Labour Party, 1987).

Labour Party, *New Labour: Because Britain Deserves Better*, Labour Party Manifesto for the 1997 General Election (London: Labour Party, 1997).

Labour Party, 'Renewing the NHS: Labour's agenda for a healthier Britain', *International Journal of Health Services*, 26(2), 1996, pp. 269–308.

Labour Party, *A Socialist Foreign Policy*, a Labour Party Discussion Document (London: Labour Party, 1981).

Lee, S., *Best for Britain? The Politics and Legacy of Gordon Brown* (Oxford: Oneworld, 2007).

Lee, S., *Boom and Bust: The Politics and Legacy of Gordon Brown* (Oxford: Oneworld, 2009).

Lee, S., 'The British model of political economy', in M. Beech and S. Lee, *Ten Years of New Labour* (Basingstoke: Palgrave, 2008), pp. 17–34.

Lee, S., 'Gordon Brown and the "British Way"', *The Political Quarterly*, 77(3), 2006, pp. 369–78.

Lewis, I., 'HIV/AIDS', *Official Report (Commons Hansard)*, vol. 490, c. 289, 25 March 2009.

Lewis, I., 'International Finance Facility for Immunisation', *Official Report (Commons Hansard)*, vol. 434, c. 194W–195W, 26 May 2005.

Lewis, I., 'The Treasury and the City' speech delivered to the Association of Private Client Investment Managers and Stockbrokers, London, 17 October 2005, <http://www.hm-treasury.gov.uk/speech_est_171005.htm> (last accessed 1 September 2010).

Leys, C., *Market Driven Politics: Neoliberal Democracy and the Public Interest* (London: Verso, 2003).

Liddell, H., 'Debt Relief', *Official Report (Commons Hansard)*, vol. 314, c. 1160, 25 June 1998.

Liddell, H., 'Heavily Indebted Countries', *Official Report (Commons Hansard)*, vol. 307, c. 970–1, 3 March 1998.

Liddell, H., 'Mauritius Mandate', *Official Report (Commons Hansard)*, vol. 310, c. 963, 23 April 1998.

Lindblom, C. E., *Politics and Markets: The World's Political-Economic Systems* (New York: Basic Books, 1977).

Lister, R., 'To RIO via the Third Way: New Labour's "Welfare" reform', *Renewal*, 8(4), 2000, pp. 9–20.

Lockwood, M., 'Will a Marshall Plan for Africa make poverty history?', *Journal of International Development*, 17(6), 2005, pp. 775–89.

Lucas, I., 'International AIDS Day', *Official Report (Commons Hansard)*, vol. 440, c. 854, 7 December 2005.

McBride, D., *Power Trip: A Decade of Policy, Plots and Spin* (London: Biteback, 2014).

McIntosh, A., 'Globalisation', *Official Report (Lords Hansard)*, vol. 612, c. 785, 19 April 2000.

McKnight, A., 'Employment: tackling poverty through "work for those who can"', in J. Hills and K. Stewart (eds), *A More Equal Society? New Labour, Poverty, Inequality and Exclusion* (Bristol: Policy Press, 2005), pp. 23–46.

Macpherson, N., 'The Treasury: Rising to the Challenges of the Global Economy' speech delivered to the Association of Corporate Treasurers, London, 8 November 2005, <http://www.hm-treasury.gov.uk/speech_pst_081105.htm> (last accessed 1 September 2010).

McSmith, A., *Faces of Labour: The Inside Story* (London: Verso, 1997).

Make Poverty History, 'What Do We Want?', 2007, <http://www.makepovertyhistory.org/whatwewant/index.shtml> (last accessed 29 July 2011).

Malik, S., 'Developing Countries: Health Services', *Official Report (Commons Hansard)*, vol. 468, c. 1457W, 6 December 2007.

Mandelson, P., 'Post Office', *Official Report (Commons Hansard)*, vol. 322, c. 21, 7 December 1998.

Mandelson, P., speech delivered at the annual conference of the CBI, 2 November 1998, <http://www.berr.gov.uk/ministers/archived/mandelson021198.html> (last accessed 26 March 2009).

Manning, R., 'Development', in A. Seldon (ed.), *Blair's Britain 1997–2007* (Cambridge: Cambridge University Press, 2007), pp. 551–71.

Merron, G., 'International Finance Facility for Immunisation Bonds', *Official Report (Commons Hansard)*, vol. 478, c. 761W, 1 July 2008.

Morrissey, O., 'Aid and international development', in M. Flinders, A. Gamble, C. Hay and M. Kenny (eds), *The Oxford Handbook of British Politics* (Oxford: Oxford University Press, 2009), pp. 699–717.

Morrissey, O., 'British aid policy in the "Short–Blair" years', in P. Hoebink and O. Stokke (eds), *Perspectives on European Development Co-operation* (London: Routledge, 2005), pp. 161–83.

Mosley, P., 'Making globalisation work for the poor?', *New Political Economy*, 6(3), 2001, pp. 391–7.

National Institute of Clinical Excellence, 'Memorandum (P 32)', in House of Commons Select Committee for Health, *The Influence of the Pharmaceutical Industry*, Fourth Report of Session 2004–05, Volume II: Formal Minutes, Oral and Written Evidence, HC 42-II (incorporating HC 1030-i-iii), 2005.

Number 10, 'Her Majesty's Government' press release, 29 June 2007, <http://number10.gov.uk/page12240> (last accessed 26 March 2009).

O'Brien, M., 'Globalisation', *Official Report (Commons Hansard)*, vol. 418, c. 651W, 1 March 2004.

OECD, 'DAC1 Official and Private Flows', 2011, <http://stats.oecd.org/Index.aspx?DatasetCode=TABLE1> (last accessed 23 August 2011).

Öniş, Z. and F. Şenses, 'Rethinking the emerging post-Washington Consensus', *Development and Change*, 36(2), 2005, pp. 263–90.

Osler, D., *Labour Party PLC: New Labour as a Party of Business* (London: Mainstream, 2002).

Oxfam, *Debt Relief and Poverty Reduction: Strengthening the Linkage*, Oxfam Briefing Paper (Oxford: Oxfam UK, 1998).

Panitch, L. and C. Leys, *The End of Parliamentary Socialism: From New Left to New Labour*, 2nd edn (London: Verso, 2001).

Payne, A. 'Blair, Brown and the Gleneagles agenda: making poverty history, or confronting the global politics of unequal development?', *International Affairs*, 82(5), 2006, pp. 917–35.

Peston, R., *Brown's Britain* (London: Short Books, 2005).

Pettifor A., *Debt, the Most Potent Form of Slavery* (London: Debt Crisis Network, 1996).

PICTF, *Pharmaceutical Industry Competitiveness Task Force: Final Report* (London: PICTF, 2001).

Plant, R., 'Political thought: socialism in a cold climate', in A. Seldon and K. Hickson (eds), *New Labour, Old Labour: The Wilson and Callaghan Governments, 1974–79* (London: Routledge, 2004), pp. 18–33.

Porteous, T., 'British government policy in sub-Saharan Africa under New Labour', *International Affairs*, 81(2), 2005, pp. 281–97.

Prabhakar, R., 'What is the future for asset-based welfare?', *Public Policy Research*, 16(1), 2009, pp. 51–6.

Pym, H. and N. Kochan, *Gordon Brown: The First Year in Power* (London: Bloomsbury, 1998).

Rawnsley, A., *The End of the Party: The Rise and Fall of New Labour* (London: Penguin, 2010).

Rawnsley, A., *Servants of the People: The Inside Story of New Labour* (London: Penguin, 2001).

Richards, S., *Whatever It Takes: The Real Story of Gordon Brown and New Labour* (London: Fourth Estate, 2010).

Routledge, P., *Gordon Brown: The Biography* (London: Simon & Schuster, 1998).

Ruane, S. (2007) 'Acts of distrust? Support workers' experiences in PFI hospital schemes', in G. Mooney and A. Law (eds), *New Labour/Hard Labour? Restructuring and Resistance Inside the Welfare Industry* (Bristol: Policy Press, 2007), pp. 75–92.

Sachs, J., 'The IMF and Asian Flu', *American Prospect*, March–April 1998, pp. 16–21.

Sawyer, M., 'Fiscal policy under New Labour', *Cambridge Journal of Economics*, 31(6), 2007, pp. 885–99.

Seldon, A., *Blair* (London: Free Press, 2005).

Seldon, A. and G. Lodge, *Brown at 10* (London: Biteback, 2011).

Shaw, *Losing Labour's Soul? New Labour and the Blair Government 1997–2007* (London: Routledge, 2007).

Sherraden, M., *Assets and the Poor: A New American Welfare Policy* (New York: M. E. Sharpe, 1992).

Short, C., 'Can Africa Halve Poverty by 2015? The Challenge to the New Partnership for African Development', Johannesburg, 4 April 2002, <http://www.dfid.gov.uk/News/Speeches/files/sp4april02.html> (last accessed 1 September 2010).

Short, C., 'Central America (Hurricane Mitch)', *Official Report (Commons Hansard)*, vol. 319, c. 28–9, 9 November 1998.

Short, C., 'Debt Reduction', *Official Report (Commons Hansard)*, vol. 313, c. 356–8, 3 June 1998.

Short, C., 'Debt Relief', *Official Report (Commons Hansard)*, vol. 317, c. 357, 29 July 1998.

Short, C., 'Debt Relief', *Official Report (Commons Hansard)*, vol. 355, c. 204, 25 October 2000.

Short, C., 'Disease Prevention', *Official Report (Commons Hansard)*, vol. 381, c. 279–80, 6 March 2002.

Short, C., 'Global Free Trade', *Official Report (Commons Hansard)*, vol. 300, c. 890, 12 November 1997.

Short, C., 'Globalisation White Paper', *Official Report (Commons Hansard)*, vol. 360, c. 1068, 10 January 2001.

Short, C., 'Good Governance', *Official Report (Commons Hansard)*, vol. 396, c. 903W, 19 December 2002.

Short, C., 'Heavily Indebted Poor Countries Initiative', *Official Report (Commons Hansard)*, vol. 311, c. 312, 29 April 1998.

Short, C., 'HIV/AIDS', *Official Report (Commons Hansard)*, vol. 367, c. 289–91, 25 April 2001.

Short, C., 'HIV/AIDS Drugs (Africa)', *Official Report (Commons Hansard)*, vol. 361, c. 414W, 22 January 2001.

Short, C., *An Honourable Deception? New Labour, Iraq, and the Misuse of Power* (London: Simon & Schuster, 2005).

Short, C., 'International Development', *Official Report (Commons Hansard)*, vol. 297, c. 125, 1 July 1997.

Short, C., 'International Monetary Fund–World Bank Meeting', *Official Report (Commons Hansard)*, vol. 311, c. 319, 29 April 1998.

Short, C., 'Medicines (Access)', *Official Report (Commons Hansard)*, vol. 363, c. 528W, 26 February 2001.

Short, C., 'Medicines (Patents and Pricing)', *Official Report (Commons Hansard)*, vol. 373, c. 264, 19 July 2001.

Short, C., 'Q. 168', in House of Commons Select Committee for International Development, *The Humanitarian Crisis in Southern Africa*, Third Report of Session 2002–03, Volume I, HC 116–I (incorporating 1271-I, session 2001–02), 2003.

Short, C., *UK Working Group on Increasing Access to Essential Medicines in the Developing World: Policy Recommendations and Strategy* (London: DFID, 2002).

Short, C., 'World Trade Organization', *Official Report (Commons Hansard)*, vol. 340, c. 1088, 9 December 1999.

Smith, A., *The Wealth of Nations*, Books I–III (London: Penguin, [1776] 1999).

Smith, M. J., *The Core Executive in Britain* (Basingstoke: Macmillan, 1999).

Smith, M. J., 'Tony Blair: the first prime minister of the global era', *British Politics*, 2(3), 2007, pp. 420–7.

Soederberg, S., *The Politics of the New Financial Aid Architecture: Reimposing Neoliberal Domination in the Global South* (London: Zed Books, 2004).

South Centre, 'Foot-dragging on foreign debt', *South Bulletin*, 10, 15 April 2001, pp. 8–11.

Stiglitz, J., *Globalization and Its Discontents* (London: Penguin, 2002).

Taylor, I., '"Advice is judged by results, not by intentions": why Gordon Brown is wrong about Africa', *International Affairs*, 81(2), 2005, pp. 299–310.

Tebbit, N., Speech delivered at the Conservative Party conference, Blackpool Winter Gardens, 15 October 1981.

Thain, C. and M. Wright, *The Treasury and Whitehall: The Planning and Control of Public Expenditure, 1976–1993* (London: Clarendon Press, 1995).

Third World Network, 'Patent Rights vs. Patient Rights', 2000, <http://www.twnside.org.sg/title/twr120e.htm> (last accessed 11 August 2011).

Thirkell-White, B., *The IMF and the Politics of Financial Globalization: From the Asian Crisis to a New Financial Architecture* (Basingstoke: Palgrave, 2005).

Thirkell-White, B., 'The international financial architecture and the limits to neoliberal hegemony', *New Political Economy*, 12(1), 2007, pp. 19–41.

Thomas, G., 'Action on the Three Major Communicable Diseases', *House of Commons European Standing Committee B*, session 2002–03, c. 3, 16 July 2003.

Thomas, G., 'Developing World', *Official Report (Commons Hansard)*, vol. 437, c. 1285W, 21 October 2005.

Thomas, G., *EU Contribution to Achieving the UN Millennium Development Goals*, European Standing Committee, session 2005–06, c. 12, 3 November 2005.

Thomas, G., 'HIV/AIDS (Developing World)', *Official Report (Commons Hansard)*, vol. 424, c. 1530, 16 September 2004.

Thomas, G., 'HIV Treatment', *Official Report (Commons Hansard)*, vol. 430, c. 793W, 1 February 2005.

Thompson, N., *Political Economy and the Labour Party: The Economics of Democratic Socialism, 1884–2005*, 2nd edn (London: Routledge, 2006).

Timms, S., 'International Finance Facility', *Official Report (Commons Hansard)*, vol. 428, c. 443W, 7 December 2004.

Timms, S., 'Millennium Development Goals', *Official Report (Commons Hansard)*, vol. 429, c. 444W, 11 January 2005.

Timms, S., speech delivered at the South East England Development Agency Regional Employment Skills Summit, Gatwick Sofitel, 8 July 2008, <http://www.dwp.gov.uk/newsroom/ministers-speeches/2008/08-07-08.shtml> (last accessed 8 April 2010).

UNAIDS, *2004 Report on the Global AIDS Epidemic* (Geneva: UNAIDS, 2004).

UNDP, *Beyond the Midpoint: Achieving the Millennium Development Goals* (New York: UNDP, 2010).

UNDP, *Human Development Report 1990* (New York: UNDP, 1990).

Vadera, S., 'Q. 182', in House of Commons Select Committee for International Development, *DFID and the World Bank*, Sixth Report of Session 2007–08, Volume II: Oral and Written Evidence, HC 67-II, ev. 49, 10 January 2008.

van Heerde, J. and D. Hudson, '"The righteous considereth the cause of the poor"? Public attitudes towards poverty in developing countries', *Political Studies*, 58(3), 2010, pp. 389–409.

Wade, R., 'A new global financial architecture?', *New Left Review*, 46, July–August 2007, pp. 113–29.

Ware, Z., 'Reassessing Labour's relationship with sub-Saharan Africa', *The Round Table: The Commonwealth Journal of International Affairs*, 95(383), 2006, pp. 141–52.

Watson, M., 'Constituting monetary conservatives via the "savings habit": New Labour and the British housing market bubble', *Comparative European Politics*, 6(3), 2008, pp. 285–304.

Watson, M., 'Gordon Brown's misplaced Smithian appeal: the eclipse of sympathy in changing British welfare norms', *Journal of Social Policy*, 38(2), 2009, pp. 195–210.

Watson, M., 'Planning for a future of asset-based welfare? New Labour, financialized economic agency and the housing market', *Planning, Practice and Research*, 24(1), 2009, pp. 41–56.

Watson, M., 'The split personality of prudence in the unfolding political economy of New Labour', *The Political Quarterly*, 79(4), 2008, pp. 578–89.

Watson, M. and C. Hay, 'The discourse of globalisation and the logic of no alternative: rendering the contingent necessary in the political economy of New Labour', *Policy and Politics*, 31(3), 2003, pp. 289–305.

Webster, A. 'New Labour, new aid? A quantitative examination of the Department for International Development', *International Public Policy Review*, 4(1), 2008, pp. 4–28.

White, H., 'British aid and the White Paper on international development: dressing a wolf in sheep's clothing in the emperor's new clothes?', *Journal of International Development*, 10(2), 1998, pp. 151–66.

Wickham-Jones, M., 'Anticipating social democracy, pre-empting anticipations: economic policymaking in the British Labour Party, 1987–1992', *Politics and Society*, 23(4), 1995, pp. 465–94.

Wicks, M., 'Department of Trade and Industry', *Official Report (Commons Hansard)*, vol. 461, c. 366, 6 June 2007.

Wicks, M., 'Steel Industry', *Official Report (Commons Hansard)*, vol. 458, c. 933, 22 March 2007.

Williams, P. D., 'Blair's Commission for Africa: problems and prospects for UK policy', *The Political Quarterly*, 76(4), 2005, pp. 529–34.

Williams, P. D., *British Foreign Policy under New Labour, 1997–2005* (Basingstoke: Palgrave, 2005).

Williams, P. D., 'Who's making UK foreign policy?', *International Affairs*, 80(5), 2004, pp. 909–29.

Williamson, J., 'Democracy and the "Washington Consensus"', *World Development*, 21(8), 1993, pp. 1329–36.

Williamson, J., 'What Washington means by policy reform', in J. Williamson (ed.), *Latin American Readjustment: How Much Has Happened* (Washington DC: Institute for International Economics, [1989] 1990), pp. 7–24.

Wolfensohn, J., 'The Challenges of Globalisation: The Role of the World Bank' speech, Public Discussion Forum, Berlin, 2 April 2001, <http://go.worldbank.org/0RRABM8ZT0> (last accessed 31 August 2011).

Wolfensohn, J., remarks made at the Multilateral Development Banks Meeting on the HIPC Initiative, Washington DC, 4 April 2000, <http://go.worldbank.org/B8J2TWKD20> (last accessed 11 July 2011).

Wood, A., 'Making globalization work for the poor: the 2000 White Paper reconsidered', *Journal of International Development*, 16(7), 2004, pp. 933–7.

World Bank Group, 'Corporate Responsibility Program: International Finance Facility for Immunisation (IFFIm)', 2010, <http://go.worldbank.org/A6ND9OLM80> (last accessed 23 March 2010).

World Bank Group, *Economic Growth in the 1990s: Learning from a Decade of Reform* (Washington DC: World Bank Group, 2005).

World Bank Group, *The State in a Changing World: World Development Report 1997* (New York: Oxford University Press, 1997).

World Health Organization, *WHO Medicines Strategy: Countries at the Core 2004–2007* (Geneva: WHO, 2004).

World Health Organization, *The World Medicines Situation* (Geneva: WHO, 2004).

World Vision, 'Debt Cancellation', 2006, <http://www.worldvision.org.uk/server. php?show=nav.2571> (last accessed 20 July 2011).

Young, R., 'New Labour and international development', in D. Coates and P. Lawler (eds), *New Labour in Power* (Manchester: Manchester University Press, 2000), pp. 254–67.

Index

Printed and bound by PG in the USA

USA2019PGIL